Into the Mountains Dark

A WWII Odyssey from Harvard Crimson
to Infantry Blue

Franklin L. Gurley

THE ABERJONA PRESS
BEDFORD, PA

This book is dedicated to my wife, Elizabeth Ryan Gurley, and to my parents, George B. and Catherine V. Moran Gurley.

It is also dedicated to those American soldiers who, as boys, ventured into dark mountains, forests, deserts, jungles, beaches, and hedgerows . . . and came out men.

Finally, it is dedicated to those who suffered disabilities and to the widows and orphans of those who never returned.

Technical Editor: Keith E. Bonn
Production: Patricia K. Bonn
Maps: Aegis Consulting Group, Inc.
Printer: Mercersburg Printing

The Aberjona Press is an imprint of Aegis Consulting Group, Inc.,
    Bedford, Pennsylvania 15522
© 2000 Franklin L. Gurley
Printed in the United States of America
08 07 06 05 04 03 02 01 00   5 4 3 2 1

ISBN: 0-9666389-4-8

Contents

Editor's Note

The author compiled this book directly from his own journal, kept during combat in World War II and updated daily. Nothing has been added, deleted, or altered from the author's original, wartime record of his experiences, except some insights into activities of key personnel at some higher headquarters in the 100th Infantry Division. These were gained from anecdotes related directly by the persons involved to the author in his capacity as an official historian of the 100th Infantry Division Association. Such episodes are clearly identifiable as such in the text. Otherwise, every incident and quotation in this book is recounted exactly as observed by the author, and have been verified with other soldiers who were there. In this way, *Into the Mountains Dark* is much more than a retrospective narrative solo, but rather a battle hymn from a contemporary chorus that includes some voices not heard since 1944.

A very few names have been changed to protect the privacy of some of the characters in this book, but no characters have been synthesized or conjured. Everyone in this book existed, and their actions and words are purely non-fictional.

Army regulations forbade the maintenance of such diaries by combat troops, as they could provide valuable tactical information to the enemy if captured. Nevertheless, the author's comrades actively collaborated in the creation of Private Gurley's opus, and his chain of command tacitly looked the other way as he penned their unit's very unofficial history. Their collective decision to "bend the rules" may have had negative consequences if these papers had fallen into enemy hands, but they didn't. Writing and preserving this journal to sustain precise knowledge of the horror, the anger, the valor, and the comradeship that were the realities of the author's wartime existence was a risk that only now is paying off. Instead of enlightening some *Wehrmacht* intelligence officer, it is informing generations that have not known wars that require the kind of sacrifice that the characters of this book knew too well. It is fitting that this book, an account of the author's soldierly journey to manhood, is thus the product of the kind of courage, resourcefulness, and daring that were so manifest across the Army that won America's last decisive victory against a first-class foe.

Chapter One
St. Botolph's Town in the War
(1939–1943)[1]

On 1 September 1939, the day Germany invaded Poland, my father drove us out to our new home in Newton Highlands, a suburb southwest of Boston. The house was a small, white, Dutch colonial with red shutters. Soon a big "Mayflower" truck appeared, loaded with the family furniture trucked up from Philadelphia. The crew of four all seemed over sixty and endowed with generous Irish brogues.

"Those Europeans will be begging us to come over and save them just like last time!" one of them exclaimed between chaws of tobacco, leaning against the back of the truck to avoid overexertion.

"You'd think *they* were going over to save the Poles," Mother whispered behind her hand. It was obvious that these old Boston Irishmen were no more likely to become involved in a new war than my brother, George, fifteen years old, or I, thirteen. Years later, I would realize that the old Irishmen had a much clearer view of the situation than we did.

I think it was my Dad who said that if a new war repeated the four-year cycles of the First World War and the American Civil War, I would just about be graduating from high school when it was over. As it turned out, however, Hitler would keep the new war going for six years, far longer than the other two. My brother and I would be in it after all.

Before moving to Boston, we had lived in Upper Darby, Pennsylvania, a suburb of Philadelphia. Entry age for the Boy Scouts of America (BSA) was twelve, and by the time I left for Boston in 1939 at thirteen, I was a Star Scout and a patrol leader. I had also just completed the basic requirements for Life Scout (one rank below Eagle Scout), including the most difficult one, which was passing ten specified merit badge tests.

If I achieved this modest success in the Scouts, such was far from the case in school track. Many of my best friends at Upper Darby Junior High were on the track team, and I strove mightily to earn a place among

---

[1]"Boston" is a contraction of St. Botolph's Town, Boston's original seventeenth-century name.

them in the official track squad photograph. Track tryouts were held at the start of the 1939 spring season, and throughout the 440-yard race, I found myself boxed in with several other runners in the second row of straining aspirants. I failed to power my way into the front row despite two or three feeble tries. Throughout the race, I had to absorb a constant spray of wet cinders churned up by the flying spikes of those in the first row. Thus did my Upper Darby track career begin and end on the same day.

On 2 September, the day after the war began, I entered John Wingate Weeks Junior High School in Newton Center. A few days later, I attended a meeting of the local Boy Scout troop in Newton Center. To my horror, I found that the Newton kids my age were still Tenderfeet or Second Class Scouts. They looked at my rank and ten merit badges and stared, as though I had just landed from Mars. I never went back to another meeting, and my Boy Scout career was over.

The following spring of 1940, Hitler invaded Norway, France, and the Low Countries. As portable radios brought us the bad news from abroad, I was playing third base for the Newton Center Bobcats in back of the junior high school. In the ninth inning, the batter lofted a tremendously high pop fly to my side of the diamond. I circled around drunkenly under the tiny white disk that floated high in a sunny sky obscured by dust clouds and spring mist. By an almost superhuman effort, I managed to be in the right place as the ball came plummeting down out of the sun, mist, and dust. Miraculously, the ball smacked squarely into my waiting glove, but suddenly it bounced out again and fell to the ground. Two runners scored on my gaffe and our team lost the game.

"Who discovered Old Butterfingers?" a bystander snickered. I felt a sudden kinship with the French government as their Maginot Line crumbled and Paris was threatened by Hitler's *Blitzkrieg*.

On 22 June 1941, Hitler's armies invaded Russia, marking the third straight summer the dictator had shocked the world. My brother, George, and I spent the summer caddying at a golf course in the Adirondack Mountains in upper New York State. Each day we followed the news avidly and rooted for the "Rooskies" to stop the Nazi hordes. We also rooted for Joe DiMaggio in his quest to break the major league consecutive games hitting record, which he did in late summer, by hitting in his fifty-sixth straight game.

That fall of 1941, in accordance with school procedures, each junior was required to sign up for an extracurricular activity. Deciding to try out for the school newspaper, *The Newtonite*, I attended a meeting with fifteen or twenty other would-be journalists. A whiffle-haircut senior came over to where I was standing and introduced himself as David Robinson, sports editor of the paper. "Would you like to work on the sports page?" he asked.

"I sure would," I replied. I was a Boston Red Sox fan and also attended Boston College's football games about a mile from where we lived in Newton.

"Why don't you try doing a sports column about whatever you like and submit it to me next week?" he asked.

"I'll try," I said gratefully.

The following Saturday afternoon, I scaled the outer fence at Boston College Field to avoid paying admission and wrote an article about BC's opening day win against the St. Anselm's Hawks. I wrote,

"BC coach Denny Myers employed the services of every available player, but even with such frequent substitution, the scorekeeper was constantly tacking sixes and sevens to the aggregate BC score. As Coach Myers looked up into the stands in the final period and carefully scrutinized the youngsters sitting there, it occurred to this observer that perhaps he was devising a scheme to keep the score from mounting any higher."

I felt certain David Robinson would not run the article. To my astonishment, he gave me a byline and printed every word under a glaring black heading "Gridiron Glances."

I was now a *Newtonite* sports columnist. As I wrote each week about the muscle-bound set, classmate Richard Polonsky addressed the problems of the "real world" on the editorial page,

"The battles of France and Britain have taught us that defensive warfare is no longer a defense against aggression. Therefore our Allies must be supplied with *all* necessaries for an offensive so that the enemies of democracy will be destroyed. America must not remain passive while the bloody 'Waves of the Future' thunder menacingly."

America's wake-up call came on 7 December 1941, at Pearl Harbor. The following day, there was an animated discussion of the situation in Public Speaking class, presided over by our teacher, Miss Helen B. Lee. Miss Lee was known as the "Green Hornet" because of her predilection for green capes, scarves, stoles, dresses, suits, sweaters, and skirts. The consensus of the debate was that our nation had suffered one of the greatest humiliations in our history. There was also a sentiment within the class that the shock, suffering, and losses at Pearl Harbor might turn out to be a good thing for the nation in the long run. Might it not clear the air after the nation's long malaise where we had watched friendly nations being toppled one after another while our Congress declared we were not involved and refused to lift a finger to help?

Dick Polonsky put it this way in an editorial,

" 'Defense' before Pearl Harbor meant stupid, cowardly isolationism parading under the banner of Americanism. We allowed men and women of other nations to fight and die while we gathered in the harvest of profit gained by selling to them the weapons for our own preservation. Now that we are in it, let us have war factories, war stamps, and war bonds, not for 'defense' but for victory!"

General MacArthur's forces were forced back into a defensive perimeter on the Bataan Peninsula. The Japanese were approaching the gates of Singapore after a rapid five-hundred-mile advance. Five Newton seniors joined the colors despite pleas by school officials to continue with their education. *The Newtonite* reported,

"Newton school officers have endeavored to impress upon the boys that they would be of much greater value to the country if they completed their high school education before enlisting. Those who remain in school until April 1 will receive their diplomas."

On our family's Sunday drives through Boston's North and South Shore communities, blue stars were appearing with increasing regularity in living room windows. "Oh, I see that Junior is in the service!" my brother, George, snorted when we passed a window with a new blue star.

"What a hero!" I chimed in. George and I both considered the war to be someone else's problem. When Mrs. Emmanuelson across the street said to Mother, "I suppose your boys will be going soon," Mother made no reply, but wondered why her neighbor didn't stop talking rubbish and tend to her own affairs.

By the summer of 1942, our armed forces were rebounding from the losses of the first six months. The battles of Midway and Guadalcanal were the turning points. As the Marines and Army fought it out on Guadalcanal, enlistments by juniors and seniors at the high school increased precipitously. Again the school authorities appealed for calm,

"Those who have planned to attend college are urged to do so. These requests are made not only by school officials, but by the Army, Navy, and Draft Board as well. Their fear is that they will be faced with a shortage of skilled technicians and officer material. Modern war, they say, depends greatly upon men who have studied mathematics, science, mechanics, and modern languages. Only by training the talents of the country's young men in school can we expect to win."
(*The Newtonite*)

I seemed to regard my own role as some kind of sixteen-year-old "war historian" rather than that of potential participant. For example, I hailed in my sports column all the national sports heroes who were putting down their catcher's mitts and picking up rifles to defend the rest of us,

> "This is the last time for at least the duration of the war that such Diamond greats as Ted Williams, Ted Lyons, Petey Reiser, and Enos Slaughter will be seen on a baseball field. The boundaries of their realms of action one year from today will not be any ivy-covered four-hundred-foot sign in dead center field, but the very limits of the globe itself. The 1-2-3 punch in the Red Sox batting order—Ted Williams, Johnny Pesky, and Dom DiMaggio—will soon be the U.S. Navy's 1-2-3 punch against the aggressor."

A visitor to the high school that fall was U.S. Navy Lieutenant Hugh Van Roosen, class of 1938, who was home on a week's furlough from submarine duty in the Pacific. Van Roosen was the youngest graduate in the modern history of the U.S. Naval Academy. He was with English Department head Floyd Rinker one Saturday afternoon, driving past Harvard Stadium where Dartmouth and Harvard were playing. They heard the distant cheering and saw flashes of colorful clothing in the tall grandstand.

"Floyd," Van Roosen told Rinker, "the world has become too serious a place for football as usual. We're up against deadly enemies and our people are still sleeping like a bunch of beautiful dreamers."

"I know," Floyd Rinker said.

In November 1942, American troops invaded North Africa. A few weeks later, *The Newtonite* reported that First Lieutenant George Duane, Newton 1936 and Harvard 1940, had died in the landings. Forty Newton High men had died in the First World War, and George Duane now headed the list for the Second. The bronze plaque to the First Forty in front of the school read, "In Memory of the boys of the Newton High School who gave their lives in the World War that Justice, Freedom, and Righteousness might be exalted among the nations of the earth."

After the North Africa invasion, student enlistments jumped within the Class of 1943. The school authorities and editors of *The Newtonite* combined their talents in a hard-hitting editorial, urging the boys to keep their powder dry and suggesting they would be "damn stupid" to rush off to be privates when they could go much higher by waiting,

> "Young men of seventeen, eighteen, and nineteen today are debating whether to serve their country by enlisting immediately or by training themselves first in high school or college. Don't get too excited

by the newspaper stories on the need for eighteen- or nineteen-year olds. Sure, we need them; young men are more active and faster— frequently more rugged than older men.

"You can and should try to soak up the most education you can. This is not for the purpose of showing off your 'culture', but because it will pay you the biggest dividends in the Army. You have probably seen in the papers that this is a specialists' war; that the individual soldier has to be expert in a lot of things that the old-time soldiers never heard of. There is nothing wrong with being a private, but it is damn stupid to be a private if you are competent to hold a higher rank. Not only stupid from your point of view, but also from the Government's."

Soon came an announcement that highly qualified high school students would be able to choose between Army and Navy college programs which they would enter following graduation from high school and which would ultimately lead to officers' commissions. On a Saturday morning in April 1943, several hundred of us spent our day off at the high school taking a special examination sponsored by the Army A-12 and the Navy V-12 Programs.

The exam was identical for both branches of service, but we were to specify before taking the exam which branch of service we wished to be considered for in the event we achieved a passing score. Did I want to serve in the Army or the Navy? And what about my friends? Most of them said they had opted for the Navy. "What about you?" they asked. "I picked the Army," I said. I don't remember if anyone asked why I had selected the Army, but I think it was because of the Army's *solidity*, its having its feet planted firmly in the earth. The Navy, by contrast, sort of floated around the world without any fixed point of reference. Another factor, which I would never have admitted to anyone, was my fear that I would look ridiculous in one of those blue and white "monkey suits" which sailors wore.

I passed the exam and was told that I would be called to duty at some point following high school graduation, which would occur in late June 1943.

Chapter Two
"Annapolis on the Charles": Harvard in Summer 1943

The Army's call-up was set for fall 1943, which permitted us A-12 candidates to pursue one summer semester in college before the call-up. In peacetime, most of us would have taken the summer off between high school and college, but this was not peacetime. We all felt we must make every minute count.

I was admitted to Harvard College, probably because all the "brains" had gone off to war, thereby lowering admission standards for clucks like me. With most of Harvard's normal student body off to war, Harvard Yard and the student dormitories had been taken over in large part by Armed Forces college programs, especially the Navy's. Skimpy sailor suits scurried in all directions through the Yard, so that Harvard Square looked like a bustling seaport during fleet shore leave. The college newspaper, *The Harvard Crimson*, called Cambridge "Annapolis on the Charles."

A few days after the start of classes in early July 1943, the U.S. Navy and Allied fleets landed a large invasion force on the southern coast of Sicily. Our Harvard "sailors" seemed to have an extra spring in their steps as we all read the stories about the invasion in the Boston papers.

Freshmen were required to participate two afternoons per week in some organized sports activity. To select our sport, we took a physical exam at the Dillon Field House near Harvard Stadium. As I stepped off the scale, a smallish white-haired gentleman with ruddy cheeks and old-fashioned glasses came over to me.

"Say, fellow, the test shows you have a nice slow runner's pulse," he said. "How would you like to run track and cross-country? My name is Jaakko Mikkola. I am coach."

"Well, sure," I stammered, pleased and surprised at the interest being shown by this quaint-looking gentleman. But I wondered what he would say if I told him I had failed to make the track teams both at Upper Darby Junior High and at Newton High School. I decided to keep my mouth shut.

"Come out at three o'clock sharp tomorrow afternoon," the coach said. "Yes, sir," I replied.

After a week's training, Jaakko Mikkola said to me, "You have the natural ability to put your name up there with the Harvard record holders on the wall of Dillon Field House. With a bit more age, experience, and physical filling out, you should do 1:55 or 1:54 in the half-mile and 4:20 in the mile." I was flabbergasted.

In 1920 and 1924, Jaakko had coached the Finnish Olympic Team. In 1924, Paavo Nurmi had set new Olympic 1500- and 5000-meter records at the Paris Games under Jaakko's tutelage. Jaakko had a colorful way of talking which made him sound like an unlettered immigrant. In fact, it was said, he was as familiar with the nuances of the English language as many an English major.

In late July, *The Harvard Crimson* carried the announcement several of us had been waiting for under the headline, "ARMY TO TRAIN MEN UNDER 18 FOR WAR DUTY,"

"A new Army Specialized Training Reserve Program (ASTRP), which will enable youths under draft age to obtain college training almost in a civilian status at government expense has been announced by the War Department. Accredited trainees will be sent to specially designated Army colleges. The Army will provide tuition, housing, food, medical services, textbooks, and transportation to the school. Distinctive from other service training programs, the men will not be in uniform and slight discipline is expected."

The description of the new Army program made it sound almost like a country club. There was nothing more to do but wait for the convocation. It was not always easy to concentrate on studies in this climate, but we did our best. If we passed, we would be assured places at Harvard when the war was over and hordes of knowledge-hungry ex-GIs would be fighting to be admitted. Every member of my class soon had to face the world of the unknown that lay just beyond our eighteenth birthdays. There was a war on and we could not escape it, so we might as well go out and meet it half way. I wanted to go out and catch up with the war and get on with whatever my own small role in it might turn out to be.

On 30 August 1943, four years almost to the day after Hitler invaded Poland, I was sworn into the Army Reserve. An Army major with gray hair and blue eyes administered the oath to a small group of us. The major said we would be notified later about the university to which we would be sent and the date our courses would begin. He explained that after one semester of college study, we would be sent to Army Basic Training for three or four months, after which we would return to college for several more semesters.

Leaving the Induction Center, I hitched a ride back to Cambridge over Cottage Farm Bridge. Brimming over with pride and patriotism, I confided to the motorist who picked me up that I had "just enlisted in the U.S. Army."

"Oh, the war is so terrible!" he replied in a tone tinged with hysteria. "It's all such a senseless waste of life. Oh, it's such a slaughter!" He continued in that vein throughout the ride, as though I weren't even there. The slim white spire of Memorial Church came into view over Harvard Yard, looking like Don Quixote riding on his trusty Rosinante. Other Harvard towers seemed to be moving in tandem with the lofty Don, as though he were riding off to war at the head of a file of knights.

I thanked my loony companion for the ride as I got out at Harvard Square. His outburst had shaken me because it was the first time I had ever heard anyone criticize the war effort that way. Worse, he had chosen the precise hour of my enlistment to challenge everything I was about to do.

In early September, Winston Churchill made a surprise secret visit to Harvard, where President James B. Conant awarded him an honorary doctorate in laws. Thanking President Conant, the Prime Minister approached the podium on the steps of Memorial Church. "The war has not yet reached its climax," Winston Churchill said in his famous rumble. He paused a moment to look around at his audience, in which Navy uniforms were predominant. "I earnestly trust that when you find yourselves alongside our sailors in 1943 and 1944," he continued, "you will feel that we are your working brothers in arms."

From his talk about "sailors," Churchill had apparently correctly sized up his Harvard audience as being predominantly Navy. Churchill went on to propose a common citizenship for Britons and Americans, which drew applause from a surprised audience. The overall atmosphere was warm and fraternal, and when Winnie finished and raised his hand in the familiar "V," there was a roar of applause as though Navy had just scored a touchdown against West Point.

Two days after Churchill's visit, on 8 September 1943, the Allies announced the surrender of the Italian Government. In the early hours of 9 September, American and British troops waded ashore from landing craft onto the Italian plain between Salerno and the ruins of ancient Paestum where a Greek temple still stood. Churchill's Cambridge prediction of our "sailors working together" had apparently already been fulfilled.

To help defray tuition expenses, I landed a part-time sportswriting job at Boston's prestigious *Sunday Herald*. On the strength of my *Newtonite* football articles, I was hired as a "telephone man." Each Saturday afternoon and evening until the Sunday paper was put to bed, I spent several hours in a little booth taking incoming telephone calls from "stringers" who called in the results and highlights of high school football games across the Commonwealth of Massachusetts. After jotting down the stringers' reports, I then pounded out twenty or twenty-five very short articles which were submitted to Ed Costello, the deputy sports editor.

Finally, my Army travel orders arrived. I was to report to Ohio University in Athens, Ohio, on 7 October. Harvard announced that we would receive full credit for the semester without having to take final examinations. This came as a relief, since I did not see how I could pass calculus, about which I still understood nothing.

The cross-country team's first meet of the season would be held on Saturday, 2 October against MIT (Massachusetts Institute of Technology). Jaakko Mikkola called me into his office.

"I suppose you will be packing for the Army that weekend," Jaakko said.

"It's no problem if you want me to run," I said. "The meet is Saturday and I don't leave for Ohio until next Wednesday."

"I tell you the problem," Jaakko said. "At seventeen, you're a bit young to go up against MIT seniors. But one of our top men will be ineligible to run." He was referring to Duncan Blanchard.

"What happened?" I asked.

"He's in that darned Navy college program," Jaakko said. "One of the boys in his dormitory shot their officer with a water pistol, so the whole dormitory has been confined to quarters for the weekend."

"Okay, I'll run," I said.

"Good boy," Jaakko said. "I hoped you'd want to."

Before the start of the race, Coach Mikkola gave the team a pep-talk at the Dillon Field House.

"Here's our strategy," Jaakko said, "Bill Crowley and Mark Tuttle will go out fast at the gun and drive the MIT men to their knees. We got to kill them off right at the start."

Someone gasped involuntarily at the coach's lethal language. Jaakko looked around at his team.

"This is not a Boston tea party," he said. "Those MIT guys are well trained and their coach will cook up some clever strategy, too. We have to outsmart them."

The race was over the 3.7-mile course which I knew well from training. When the starter's gun went off, Crowley and Tuttle sprang out ahead of the pack in accordance with Coach Mikkola's instructions. Several members of the MIT squad spurted out after them like a pack of racing dogs chasing two mechanical rabbits. I wanted desperately to keep up with the parade, but my knees seemed made of rubber. There had been a recent thunderstorm and gobs of mud were being tossed back on me by dozens of spiked shoes churning along the soggy path ahead. The entire MIT team was already ahead of me. I felt ashamed and wanted to quit but knew I must keep going.

After about a mile, I finally overtook three Harvard teammates and an MIT runner. Passing them, I drew up behind two more MIT runners. Just then I caught a glimpse of the main pack about seventy-five yards ahead. A cluster of ten tightly-packed runners were making the little loop where the path turned back toward the starting point two miles away. Rounding the loop, they looked like a convoy of fast ships in a favorable wind.

Suddenly, I no longer felt panicky and was beginning to find a second wind. Half a mile into the return leg of the race, I overtook a Harvard man and two MIT runners. Another half mile and I spotted my teammate, Mark Tuttle, ahead. In front of Mark were five tightly packed red-and-white MIT jerseys, spurting along like a covey of fighter planes. The other Harvard front-runner, Bill Crowley, must be somewhere out ahead beyond my line of vision. Jaakko Mikkola's warlike strategy had not worked. Instead of becoming disorganized when Crowley and Tuttle had tried to kill them off at the start of the race, the top five MIT runners had stuck together and controlled their pace with the slide-rule precision for which MIT was justly famous. Now there was only one Harvard man ahead, Bill Crowley, and they were in the process of running up a lopsided score.

As I came abreast of Mark Tuttle, who was hobbling along with a pulled tendon, he glanced over and said, "Go after them, Red." I followed his advice and soon drew even with the last man of the MIT quintet. He looked depressed at seeing the color of my uniform. One after another, he and three MIT teammates faded behind my spikes. MIT's front runner, however, had moved about twenty yards out ahead of the others and was trying to catch Harvard's front runner, Bill Crowley. I had to eliminate that twenty-yard deficit in the two hundred yards that remained to be run. I swung my arms frantically and pumped my knees high as the finish line grew larger. The crowd soon cheered as Harvard's Bill Crowley crossed the finish line. I skirted a large puddle left by the thunderstorm and finally drew even with the MIT runner fifteen yards from the finish line. I spurted past him and finished with a lead of three or four yards. I could hear Jaakko Mikkola shout "Nice going!" just before I collapsed.

Crowley's winning time of 19:28 was followed by my 19:37 and the MIT man's 19:38. Harvard took first and second places, but MIT's closely-packed fivesome had scored just enough points to win the meet by a close

25–30 score (cross-country was the only sport at Harvard where the low scorer was the winner). I was sick for nearly an hour after the race, and when I finally reached the locker room, the other runners had long since left. *The Harvard Crimson* loyally blamed the loss on "bad weather, bad breaks, and on one man's ineligibility due to causes beyond his control."

I walked across the Lars Andersen Bridge, past Eliot and Kirkland Houses, to Harvard Square. I was suffering from some sort of exhaustion and could not hold my head up, but knew that sooner or later I should return to normal. After a quick supper at Bickford's cafeteria, I took the MTA to Boston and my job at the *Sunday Herald*. No one seemed to notice my drooping head as I ducked into a telephone booth and begun taking down the stringers' football and cross-country reports as they called in.

By 11:30 P.M., I had typed up fifteen or sixteen short articles for Ed Costello's consideration. To my surprise, he accepted all of them without changes. For the first time in my life, I had written about sports and had been an active participant in a sports event on the same day.

The following week, *The Crimson* looked ahead to the next Harvard cross-country meet on Saturday, 9 October, "Fred Gurley will be the main loss of the track men when they go to the Triangular Meet against Dartmouth and Tufts in Medford next weekend." My name wasn't Fred, but I guessed I knew who they meant.

Chapter Three
The Glory That Was Athens:
ASTP at Ohio University

Athens, Ohio, had a population of 7,000 who lived on all sides of Ohio University's dignified green college campus. Most of the male students had gone off to war, leaving the female campus population in a receptive mood toward the 583 Army "scholars" who had invaded the place by the autumn of 1943. Five hundred of the Army scholars had come to Athens from Army bases across the country, while the other eighty-three came directly from civilian life.

We were briefed at the University auditorium by Lieutenant Colonel John E. Brannan, head of the Army Program at O.U. and a dark bear of a man. Colonel Brannan said that, as seventeen-year-old members of the Enlisted Reserve Corps, we eighty-three new arrivals were only "Cadets" and "not even Privates." He then tempered that bad news with the surprise announcement that we would be issued ROTC uniforms with blue lapels. A satisfied sigh went up as the boys contemplated the glamour of a uniform in aid of our future pursuit of the O.U. co-eds. Our five hundred "Regular Army" competitors not only wore good looking uniforms but had an age advantage of one to four years over us "Cadets."

Colonel Brannan explained that the three-month semester would extend to the last day of 1943. After a short furlough, we would be inducted into the Regular Army and would go through three months of basic training somewhere in the South. After that, it would be back to college again, probably to Ohio U.

"Some of our critics call the ASTP the 'All Safe Till Peace' boys," Colonel Brannan went on. (It actually stood for "Army Specialized Training Program.") "But I'd like to know where else in the Army—or in civilian life for that matter—you are required to spend eleven long hours per day in tough intellectual and physical effort. On a straight time basis, that's nearly time-and-a-half. If it were up to me, I'd say ASTP stands for "All Studying Together Proudly." The Colonel blushed a bit as his audience of seventeen-year-olds applauded his last remark.

He then wound up the orientation with, "Please study hard and make yourselves a credit to the Army and the war effort!"

I reflected that by year's end I would have studied non-stop at three leading schools in 1943—Newton High, Harvard, and now Ohio U. If an educated soldiery was the key to defeating Hitler's designs—as all three institutions and Colonel Brannan claimed it was—we were in the process of becoming a clear threat to the Axis powers. I had complete confidence in our educators' position on the issue, since if they didn't know the answers to such weighty questions, then who did?

The next day, I wrote to my folks, giving our reactions to the university co-eds and the girls' reactions to our band of New England scholars,

> *The OU girls ("Oh You Kids!") are uniformly good-looking and built sort of stocky and husky (the latter attribute must come from the corn). Our New England guys who don't appreciate these local farmers call 'em "Just Plain Corn-Fed Hicks." The OU girls think all the New Englanders are anemic.*

I was on telephone duty that Saturday in the lobby of Palmer House. This enabled me to become familiar with the names of many of my classmates as their girlfriends and relatives called in. Some spoke with Kentucky or Southern Ohio drawls, others with "Down Maine" or Boston accents. Of the forty-five boys in Palmer Hall, twenty-four were from the Northeast and twenty-one from Kentucky and Ohio. The Easterners were housed on the ground floor, with the Kentucky-Ohio boys occupying the floor above. That Saturday evening, a lot of happy shouting was heard coming from upstairs, which the Easterners on the ground floor claimed was caused by Kentucky moonshine.

In addition to the forty-five Reservist students in Palmer Hall, there were another thirty-eight at Sprague Hall, making a total of eighty-three. Our little force of seventeen-year-olds was not impressive when compared to the five hundred older ASTP students who had already been through basic training before being assigned to Ohio U.

Our Army curriculum was called Basic Engineering-1 and consisted of Chemistry, Math, History, Geography, English, and Public Speaking. The quality of the teaching varied from professor to professor, but the majority seemed to know their stuff. My personal favorite was Professor Kirby, an unquestioned expert on local Ohio and American history. As I described him in a letter to my folks,

> *Our history teacher is a character. He told us we were the best class he ever had (because he tells us the answers on the tests). He wants us all to come back after the war and study history with him. He knows*

*more about the subject than any 10 other teachers. He can quote any-
thing that's ever been written, knows the Constitution by heart, etc.*

Professor Kirby made us relive the dramatic epic of the pioneers as they
tamed the wilderness and built the greatest nation in the world's history.
We were now the earthly Utopia and the envy of other nations. England,
France, and Spain had played important roles in our colonial history, and
other waves of immigrants had come to our shores from Germany,
Scandinavia, Ireland, Italy, and Eastern Europe. America's prologue was
now over, her structure complete. We were an independent and completely self-sufficient people. The vicissitudes and suffering of the Old World
might still be happening elsewhere, but America had left the age of kingly
quarrels, wars, and darkness far behind us.

The only thing I found confusing about Professor Kirby's version of
American history (which I had been taught in high school as well) was how
the two World Wars tied into the overall thesis that America's destiny was
totally independent of the fate of other nations. If that were really so, why
were we rushing off twice in twenty-five years to rescue Europe? I wondered: is our national destiny really unrelated to that of other nations, or
are there some sort of links that bind us all together after all?

No doubt as part of the pageant of history, Professor Kirby seemed fas-
cinated by the generations of attractive fresh-skinned coeds who passed
through his classroom portals year after year. According to one story, he
was an avid connoisseur of co-eds' legs, to a point where the wider a girl's
thighs happened to be ajar in class, the higher the final grade was likely to
be at the end of the course. In addition to Kirby's continuing research into
the Constitution of our nation and of the O.U. co-eds, he was also passion-
ate about golf. On the seventh hole of the local Athens course, which had
an elevated green beyond an imposing water barrier, a prankster friend
once placed Kirby's golf ball in the hole for a hole-in-one. Kirby was ecsta-
tic and treated everyone in the clubhouse to a highball that evening.

Another fascinating character among the faculty members was our
physical training instructor, Thor Olsen. Thor, from Sweden, had been
world champion in free-style wrestling and had worked for a carnival
along with his wife, Ollie, daughter, Thora, and son, Hjalmar. His tanned,
incredibly muscular body made him resemble a Scandinavian folk god or
an aging Charles Atlas. He told us in his Swedish accent, "What is life? Life
is a little love and a little adventure." I filed his remark away and brought
it out every now and then like an old piece of jewelry to reflect upon.

The Harvard Crimson's prediction that we would be subjected to little
or no discipline in the Army Program turned out to be no more accurate
than their statement that we wouldn't wear uniforms. We were marched

around the parade ground by the hour and chewed out for the slightest misstep, or so it seemed to us. As I described it in a letter to my folks,

> *The trouble with this life is that you don't, and better not, think. We're just machines, like Hitler's youth. It seems that I'm too tall to march right. My feet are always in step, but sometimes my body can't quite keep up, so they think I'm out of step. I think the Army was made for 5'9" people. The "shorts" and the "longs" must have been behind the door when the regulations were passed out.*

After a month, cadet officers were appointed, and Walter Ackerman from Dorchester, Massachusetts, was named our cadet Company Commander. Section and squad leaders were also appointed and given sergeants' stripes to sew on their uniform sleeves, signifying their cadet rank. I failed to qualify for any kind of rank, but couldn't resist twitting Mother about something she had said about Ackerman, our new leader,

> *Remember, you wrote that Ackerman sounded like a "good American name to associate with"? Well, he is a very good guy, with a very thick Palestinian accent. He's just been promoted to company commander and wears three silver bars on each shoulder.*

Not everyone, however, shared my enthusiasm about Walt Ackerman's appointment. Dirk Hammond and his roommate, Razor Bill Barnes, both from a large southern New England city, were heard muttering in the ranks the first morning Walt Ackerman stood out front of the company wearing his silver bars.

"All right, you guys, pipe down," Walt Ackerman said in his husky Palestine accent. Dirk and Razor Bill complied, but their behavior had been noticed. Razor Bill had acquired his nickname from the time he had waved his straight razor at one of the smaller Jewish boys in the common washroom at Palmer Hall.

Friday evening, 26 November (my eighteenth birthday), we heard that all the Army officers assigned to our Company except Captain Keufer would be transferred out at the end of the month (Captain Keufer was said to be too fat to move so he was staying). The report touched off a rash of rumors that the ASTP was about to be abolished. It also led to a night of imbibing and merriment on the part of the Kentucky-Ohio contingent up on the second floor of Palmer Hall.

Saturday morning, I slept late. When I finally awoke, the odor of southeastern Ohio's bituminous coal in the raw November air was more oppressive than usual. My roommate, a Vermont boy named Don Squires, was reading the Columbus, Ohio, newspaper which was full of stories about the day's upcoming Army-Navy and Notre Dame-USC games. In smaller print were reports on the U.S. Fifth Army's slow progress up the boot of Italy.

Not thinking about anything in particular, I opened the door to the hallway. There weren't any sounds in the corridor, which seemed odd for a Saturday morning. But I could feel (or imagined I felt) some sort of tension in the air. I closed the door again.

"Is something wrong?" I asked my roomie, Don Squires, who was frowning at the newspaper.

"Trouble," he said in that laconic way of Vermonters.

"What kind of trouble?" I asked.

"Jewish trouble."

"What's the problem?" I asked, remembering how quiet the corridor was.

"Dirk Hammond and his roomie, Razor Bill Barnes, are still pissed off about Walt Ackerman's appointment as company commander. Razor Bill has been running around in the washroom waving his straight razor at Les Rosenberg, little Davey Progosin, and the kid they call 'Five O'clock Shadow' because he always seems to need a shave."

"Aren't all of those guys from Providence?" I asked.

"Dirk Hammond and Razor Bill are, and so are Les Rosenberg and Five O'clock Shadow," Squires said. "Davey Progosin, I believe, is from Boston."

"I wonder if the Providence guys knew each other before they came out here," I said.

"Don't know," Don Squires said. "Dirk and Razor Bill say the Jewish boys will all have to move out of Palmer Hall. Jack Robottom is talking with Dirk and Razor Bill now."

I couldn't believe what I was hearing. Dirk Hammond had always impressed me as a sober, well-mannered individual. Razor Bill, on the other hand, struck me as a weird type, with his broad shoulders, big hands, long cheekbones, and strange facial expression. He had the build and the manner of a large red-cheeked butcher in an over-priced meat market.

There was a knock on the door. Without waiting, Jack Robottom entered, eyes sparkling behind his glasses.

"What's the latest?" Don Squires asked.

"Dirk and Razor Bill have limited their demand to the nine Jewish boys here on the ground floor," Jack Robottom said. "They want the thirteen other Gentiles to state their positions, so they'll know how much support they can count on. The nine they're after are Walt Ackerman, Dave Progosin, Les Rosenberg, Frank Housman, Duffy Marks, Murray Swartz, Eddie Weisberg, Wiz Wicentowsky, and Five O'clock Shadow."

"But where do they expect them to go?" I asked.

"They say they can request other accommodations," Jack Robottom replied. "Dirk and Razor Bill feel their chances of getting away with this are improved by the fact that our officers are leaving and the whole ASTP may be on shaky ground."

"Umm," Don Squires said non-committally. "Have you polled the others yet?"

"Yes. In addition to us three there are Don Baker, John Beebe, Phil Dodge, Don Garfield, Hank Girard, John Grady, Pete Lord, Francis Merrigan, Frank Murphy, and Red Whelan. I can't tell you how they voted without breaching my oath as intermediary."

"Did you actually take an oath?" I asked.

"Not really," Jack Robottom said, eyes twinkling. "I use the term broadly." Robottom seemed to be carrying out his mission in an unflappable manner.

"How do you two fellows stand?" Jack Robottom asked.

Don Squires frowned. "Dirk and Razor Bill will get no support from me."

"What about you, Red?" Jack Robottom asked, turning to me.

"Of course I don't support them," I said. I felt depressed and my head hurt. I was by nature an optimist, and did not like to concede that there were any really bad people in the world, except perhaps a few like Hitler who had brought us this war.

"Okay, that makes it a unanimous vote of 13 to 0 against Dirk's and Razor Bill's position." Jack Robottom said. "I'll go give them the news." He opened the door quietly and slipped out into the still silent corridor. A few moments later he was back.

"They say they're going to continue their action to expel the Jews anyway," Jack Robottom said. He blinked at Don Squires through his glasses. "Don, you have a certain amount of moral authority here in scholastic matters, and have probably even helped those two thickheads with their homework."

"That's right," Squire said, grinning.

"Why don't you and Red Gurley review the situation with Wiz Wicentowsky and Eddie Weisberg and then go talk directly to Dirk and Razor Bill?" Robottom said.

"Okay," Squires said.

"Count me in," I said.

We stepped into the corridor. Don Squires knocked on the Wiz-Weisberg door directly across the corridor. Jack Robottom returned to his own room.

"Who's there?" Wiz Wicentowsky's voice asked when we knocked.

"Its me and Red Gurley," Don Squires said.

"What's new?" Wiz asked, his usual broad smile missing for once. "I understand they insist that we move out." Eddie Weisberg was seated in a chair, looking out the window. He looked tense and unhappy.

"We're going to have a face-to-face with Dirk and Razor Bill," Don Squires said.

"And you want our ideas, right?" Wiz said.

Eddie Weisberg got up from his chair and turned to Don Squires. "I know what I'd say," Eddie said.

"Good," Squires said.

"We're all supposed to be fighting against anti-Semitism," Eddie Weisberg said. "But Dirk and Razor Bill are behaving like the enemy."

Wiz's features brightened. "You could also point out the strong odds of their getting thrown out of the Program if they don't cut out this nonsense."

Squires said, "Maybe they feel they have little to lose because of the rumors that soon there may be no more ASTP to get thrown out of. Any more ideas? Okay, thanks, guys."

We walked down the silent corridor and knocked on Dirk's door. Dirk opened. From his serious, well-mannered appearance he seemed the type of young man who would end up as a successful doctor, judge, or business man. Behind him, Razor Bill was seated in an overstuffed chair.

"Hi, guys." Razor Bill said. "I understand you're not with us. Why the hell not?"

"Let's put the question the other way," Squires said. "What kind of doodle bug has bitten you guys?"

"We've had enough of being so closely associated with those people," Dirk Hammond said quietly. "There are nine of them on this floor alone, and another one upstairs, Chuck Schwartz from Cleveland. Down in Sprague Hall are Norman Redlich and that big Shapiro fellow who plays in the band. That makes at least a dozen of them out of eighty-three. Do you follow me?"

"You're talking like a lunatic, Dirk," Don Squires said.

"The last straw was when the authorities appointed Walt Ackerman to be cadet company commander," Dirk continued. "It shows a wanton lack of sensitivity to traditional American values."

"Traditional American values?" I questioned. "Walt is an American citizen and lives in Dorchester, Massachusetts. He was at Boston University before the Army invited him to join the ASTP. What's un-American about his values?"

"He came from Palestine before Dorchester," Dirk said.

"Everybody came from somewhere except Indians," Don Squires said.

"Let's cut this short," Dirk said. "The Jewish boys must request quarters outside Palmer Hall where they can be together and do whatever they like."

"They have already refused and the rest of us support them," Don Squires said.

"Then we'll take it up with the authorities," Dirk said.

"And Colonel Brannan, the bull moose, will put your asses in a sling," Don Squires said.

"It's a question of principle," Dirk said.

"Whose principle, Joseph Goebbels'?"

"Aw, bullshit," Razor Bill said.

"Let me handle it, Bill," Dirk Hammond said soothingly. "This has nothing to do with the Nazis. Our position is one hundred percent American and would be exactly the same if Dr. Goebbels had never been born."

"You guys are fossils," Don Squires said.

"Dirk Hammond turned to me. "How about it, Red? Aren't you a good old Yankee from New England?"

"I'm from New England, Dirk," I said. "but I never met anybody like you two before." Dirk's question had touched off an irrational vein of anger somewhere inside me.

"You're barking up the wrong tree," I said. "We're in this war to fight some nasty bastards, and we've got to avoid becoming like them in the process." Expressing myself, I felt less tense and depressed than when we had entered the room a few minutes before.

"Can't you try to see the problem from our standpoint?" Dirk asked.

"The Army has assigned us to live together in Palmer Hall," I replied. "If you don't accept it, you can ask Colonel Brannan to move you and Bill to other quarters. A month from now we'll all be in the real Army and you won't be asked who you'd like to have in your barrack. But if you decide to stay here in Palmer Hall, you'll have to stop threatening people with razors and making others feel unwelcome. My advice is for you to stop your action now."

"And if we don't?" Dirk asked.

"If you don't," I said, "there will be reprisals." It was a word that I had heard often in the news, usually in connection with German reprisals against resistance fighters in the occupied countries.

"Some what?" Dirk asked.

"Reprisals," I repeated. I didn't know what I had in mind, but had apparently stumbled upon a good word.

"What kind of reprisals?" Dirk asked.

"Wait and see," I said. I looked over at Don Squires who nodded solemnly.

Dirk and Razor Bill exchanged glances. There were several seconds of silence. Finally Dirk spoke. "Okay, Bill and I will talk it over some more and let you know our final decision."

Don Squires and I left the room. An hour passed. We went to lunch in the university cafeteria. Dirk Hammond and Razor Bill were nowhere to be seen. The afternoon passed quietly. The tension that had reigned in the corridor that morning seemed to have dissipated. The crisis was apparently over. The only after-trace was the word "reprisals" which floated around Palmer Hall for the next day or two.

A day or two later, one of the officers appeared at a company formation and announced several changes in our cadet officers and non-coms, based upon marks. Don Squires became a squad leader and cadet sergeant, and Walt Ackerman lost his three cadet captain's bars. Where Dirk Hammond and Razor Bill had failed to bring Ackerman down, he was "done in" by his own less-than-outstanding grades (ten days after that, I became a cadet staff sergeant and section leader, thus suggesting some sort of graft within the marking system).

As Christmas approached, Colonel Brannan summoned all the ASTP students to the Memorial Auditorium. The Colonel seemed troubled as he leaned over the lectern, looking like a grizzly bear called upon to deliver a sermon.

"You may have heard rumors to the effect that the Army College Program will be shut down," Colonel Brannan said. "I can assure you that there is no truth whatsoever to the rumors. Moreover, I can't imagine anything more likely to disrupt your study program and the war effort generally." The Colonel hadn't quite equated the rumors with enemy sabotage, but the suggestion was there.

"Next week you'll be subjected to the GI Government Exams," Colonel Brannan continued. "I can promise you that you'll need clear heads free from wild rumors to score well. The week after that, between Christmas and New Year's, you'll have another grind of the regular Ohio University exams. If you hope to succeed in your exams and take that important next step toward becoming officers, you've got to learn the difference between hard facts and loose rumors. Are there any questions?"

Memorial Auditorium was absolutely still. No one asked a question. "We're now going to show you a film about the Nazis' failed effort to knock Russia out of the war." Colonel Brannan said. "It's part of the 'Why We

Fight' series." He was applauded warmly as he withdrew from the lectern and the lights were dimmed. I loved every one of these Frank Capra films, which to my eighteen-year-old mind perfectly summed up why we were doing what we were doing.

December's final weeks flew by in a flurry of final exams. I had studied hard—much harder than at Newton High or Harvard—and felt that I would not be left behind in the grading. Suddenly it was New Year's Eve and the tests were over. We were standing on the railroad station platform, waiting for the train, delayed by a snowstorm over Indiana and Western Ohio. We waited for over an hour as thick snowflakes covered our trunks and overnight bags. I didn't know it then, but I had opened my last school textbook for nearly three years. By that time, the Axis leaders would be long dead if not yet close to being forgotten.

Chapter Four
The Fort Benning Blues

On the last day of my furlough, 16 January 1944, my parents and I had Sunday dinner at the Revolutionary Tavern on the road between Concord and the village of Ayer where the Fort Devens Reception Center was located. In Concord, we visited what Ralph Waldo Emerson had called the "rude bridge that arched the flood," where the fight for American independence had begun in 1775.

"You've got his chin," Mother said to me as she studied the Minuteman's statue beside the bridge.

"Oh, come on now, Mother," I said.

My parents explained that our ancestor, Phineas Gurley, had marched to the relief of Boston as part of a company of "Minutemen" (Militia) from Mansfield, Connecticut, in April 1775. Phineas' father had been a captain in the Minutemen. After the Revolution, Phineas moved with his wife and ten children to Potsdam, New York, where my dad was born nearly a century later.

"Remember," Pop told me as we gazed at the Minuteman's statue, "Try to get ahead [in the Army] and let me know if there's anything I can do to help."

"Thanks, Pop."

Driving home through Ayer we passed the main gate of Fort Devens. Soldiers in very long new overcoats, surrounded by shivering relatives, stood around in clusters in the frosty January air.

The next morning, 17 January 1944, I was back in Ayer again, being inducted into the Army and issued one of those big overcoats. Soon I was being interviewed by an Army psychiatrist. "Do you like girls?" he asked me. I thought he had a slightly peculiar expression on his face.

I wanted to answer, "Doctor, I could write you a book!" but I kept my mouth shut and simply answered, "Sure." He gave me another odd look and let me go.

The next day I was interviewed by a handsome Army Air Forces captain, who looked as though he had just stepped out of a recruiting poster.

"I've reviewed your record, Gurley," he said. "Is this 149 on the Army General Classification Test you took yesterday correct?"

"I hope it is!" I blurted out.

"A 110 score is required for officer candidates," he said. "Do you know what ASTP requires?"

"No, sir."

"120. So you did all right. And your Ohio U. record of five As and two Bs is also correct?"

"Yes, sir," I replied, more calmly. I was beginning to suspect he was simply making conversation to size me up.

"Gurley," the captain said, "how would you like to be a bomber pilot?"

A BOMBER PILOT? In its own way, this was even crazier that the psychiatrist's "Do you like girls?" Did this captain know I didn't even have a driver's license? Or that I had turned eighteen less than two months ago and hadn't even had a date with a member of the opposite sex until a year before? I tried to picture myself roaring through the sky at the controls of a B-17 while several older crew members with dependents wondered whether they'd ever see their loved ones again.

"Er, what would be involved, sir?" I said.

"You would go through Air Cadets first and later take pilot training," the captain replied.

There was another thing. The Army, when it had invited me to join its College Program, had made a good faith commitment to me. Shouldn't I, in fairness, "dance with the guy who brung me"?

The captain was waiting for an answer. He shuffled my file briefly.

"No thank you, sir," I said, reacting more from instinct than from a careful weighing of the pros and cons.

"Very well," the captain said with a friendly smile. "It was nice talking to you." I learned afterwards that the Air Force and paratroops were permitted to "solicit" new soldiers as they passed through the Induction Center. But they were not permitted to use sales talks or other forms of persuasion. This explained why the captain had simply accepted my "No, thank you" without trying to change my mind.

Three of our Ohio U. group—Garfield, Girard, and Grady—said "Yes" to the captain and switched from A-12 to the Air Cadet Program. The paratroop captain, who was also actively fishing for bait among the new inductees, had not had a single nibble, we were told.

The same day I turned down the Air Cadets, the *Boston Globe* predicted flatly that the A-12 program would be dissolved. I thanked my folks for sending me the clipping,

Jan. 20, 1944
So they're going to abolish ASTP. Maybe I oughta be a flyer if noth-
ing else turns up. Second Looie in 15 months. Yeah, I know, coffin in
16. But exciting.

After a week at Fort Devens, our little group of recent O.U. alumni left
Ayer, Massachusetts, by train. We slept in Pullman-style upper and lower
berths and I awoke as we were passing through Baltimore. In Washington,
we were given four hours of freedom between trains to see the sights. As
I described Washington to my folks,

Jan. 27, 1944.
We wore our Commando Helmets and pretty girls waved at us. We
found out why when a couple of fellows went into the Senate and heard
someone whisper confidentially, "Overseas Division." Our helmets
and lack of insignia made them think we were outbound for overseas.
What heroes!
At 2 P.M., we left the Capital and saw Virginia and North Carolina
in the afternoon. The next morning, we were in Atlanta for two hours.
From Atlanta to Columbus, all we could see were scrub pines and red
earth and tumbledown huts with Negroes living in them. What deso-
lation! I'll bet Russia in wartime looks better.
We entered Columbus, which looked awful, and then on to
Benning. We entered the gate and then went at least fifteen miles to our
present spot. They tell us we'll be here five months—two weeks for Basic
Training, thirteen weeks ASTP Basic, and seven weeks waiting for
reassignment to another college. But even the officers here don't accord
us much chance of getting back to school.

We were assigned to Company B, 4th ASTP Training Regiment, in the
section of the post called "Harmony Church."

Sergeant Jordan, whom we called "Big Joe" behind his back, bunked in
a private room in the corner of the barrack just beyond my cot. Big Joe
never smiled, although he was handsome, and it might have done him
some good. Instead, he spent his time criticizing whatever we did and generally trying to make us feel inferior and stupid. Big Joe may have been a
throwback to an earlier Army, though, judging from the high quality of
many of the officers. I told my folks,

Feb. 8, 1944
We just finished the second day of Basic. Only 89 more days to go—
cheer up. Our Lieutenant's name is Frisk and he's really "Frisky." His

big idea is getting the platoon to run as much as possible, which is O.K. with me. We went about a half-mile today and I finished one polite pace behind him. I'd pass him, only I don't know what the rank lower than Buck Private is.

All these officers seem to know their stuff and are jacks-of-all-trades. All the 2d Looies are better guys than the higher ranks because they're young, modern, and broad-minded.

Georgia's frequent rainshowers did little to dampen the spirits of our college crowd. As we marched we sang the "ASTP Song" to the tune of "My Bonny Lies Over the Ocean,"

Some Mothers have sons in the Army,
Some Mothers have sons on the sea,
Take down your service flag, Mother,
Your son's in the ASTP.
TS, TS, TS for the ASTP,
TS, TS, TS for the ASTP!

In the Personal Hygiene lecture, graphic charts and slides showed how syphilis developed within the body and what its devastating and debilitating effects could be. The charts alone were enough to put men off food for a full day afterwards. We were also warned to stay out of nearby Columbus, where even a simple restaurant meal would expose us to millions of deadly bacteria brought by our friendly waitress directly to our table from the contaminated ladies' washroom. They did not make the city of Columbus sound like Harvard Square or Athens, Ohio. We were barely through the sixth day of the thirteen-week cycle when rumors swept through the pines that our college program would soon be terminated. I told my folks,

Feb. 13, 1944
The ASTP seems—nay, is—on the rocks. They want us for Infantry. The only thing in sight is Aviation Cadet, and maybe that won't be available either. What do you think I ought to do, walk or fly? The Air Corps requires three letters of recommendation from persons other than parents, so will you get them if you think I ought to apply?
Love,
Franklin

Big Joe Jordan, our Sergeant, tried to paint the blackest possible picture of what awaited us if we were transferred to the regular infantry. Meanwhile, our dynamic platoon leader, Lieutenant Frisk, continued to double-time us through the Georgia mud, and the ASTP boys continued singing (to the tune of "Mademoiselle from Armentières"),

The WACs and WAVEs will win the war,
Parley vous,
The WACs and WAVEs will win the war,
Parley vous,
The WACs and WAVEs will win the war
So what the heck are we fighting for?
Hinkey dinkey parley vous.

They say this is a mechanized war,
Parley vous,
They say this is a mechanized war,
Parley vous,
They say this is a mechanized war,
So what the heck are we marching for?
Hinkey dinkey parley vous.

The ubiquitous rumors we had been hearing about the demise of ASTP suddenly took tangible form as the officers who served as our company and battalion commanders disappeared into thin air without even saying goodbye. I told my folks the news,

Feb. 29, 1944
The Battalion and company commanders have just been trans-ferred and the whole place seems to be folding up in gradual stages. Pst—don't look now, but I think your son is in the infantry for his whole life plus six months.

On March 26, we may be moved to an Infantry Replacement Training Center in another camp. In other words, when some line Infantry Division gets a few men knocked off, enter us. And the Air Corps is "frozen" to ASTP men. They got me cornered, Ma. Tell Pa to call Roosevelt.

An Infantry Replacement Training Center (or IRTC) provided sixteen weeks of intense combat training, following which the trainees were sent either to a division fighting overseas or to a stateside division getting ready to ship overseas.

One of my friends at Harvard sent me an article from *The Harvard Crimson* of 25 February 1944,

Harvard Loses 550 ASTP Men by New Ruling

Cambridge—550 of Harvard's 800 Army Specialized Training Program students will leave the University for parts unknown on April 1, pursuant to a new Army regulation to drop 110,000 men from ASTP units and transfer them to active duty.

The War Department ruling specified that only men taking advanced courses in medicine, dentistry, and engineering would be considered for future education.

The nation's university heads, who were not warned of the Army order until they saw it in the newspapers, met in Washington to urge a new policy on the War Department. A council of university presidents, including James B. Conant, '14, requested that the War Department attempt to make up the deficit by sending some 100,000 more seventeen-year-old volunteers to college this summer.

Some move such as the one taken Friday by the Army had been anticipated in college circles for more than three months.

Last summer, it had all seemed almost too good to be true, when that same *Crimson* had described how the Army would give us *free* college training with a *minimum* of military discipline, and we wouldn't even be required to wear *uniforms*. Now, barely half a year later, ASTP was a dead letter. The rug had been pulled out from under not only the ASTP students, but also Harvard President James B. Conant, who was obviously furious that he had not been "warned" that the ASTP boys would be leaving "for parts unknown" in the same way they used to shanghai young sailors to sail the seven seas.

On 5 March, I gave my folks our future itinerary despite censorship rules prohibiting such communications,

> *We leave Benning some time before March 26 and go to any one of 1,001 camps in the IRTC (Infantry Replacement Training Centers). Chances are we'll begin Basic over again (seventeen weeks) and then— guess what?*
>
> *Our Captain said every physically fit man in the company would be overseas within six months. The Air Corps is overcrowded, frozen, and the Infantry needs men (statistically speaking).*

When the captain said we would all be overseas within six months, he spoke sadly as though he feared we weren't really old enough for such a challenge and felt sorry for us. Personally, I felt a bit sorry for *him*, since I saw nothing to be depressed about. If our country really needed us overseas, that was quite flattering. Also, we would see strange new places and have experiences we couldn't even imagine now.

"What happened, sir?" one of the boys asked the captain. The college kids always wanted to know "why."

"Somebody up in the Pentagon forgot that the way wars are won is to send in the infantry and take the enemy's land from him," the captain replied. "Our people apparently figured that if our air force bombed the enemy's cities and our Navy successfully deposited our armies on enemy shores, the enemy would get the message and quit. They forgot that those operations are only a prelude to what war is really all about. Fort Benning is the home of the nation's Infantry School. We *know* how wars are won."

"Were our manpower needs underestimated, sir?" the same boy asked.

"Let's say we didn't expect as many casualties as we're taking in Italy," the captain replied. "Also, the draft boards can't find enough men to tote rifles. Americans all want to be chiefs and nobody wants to be an Indian. The best men have gone into the Army Air Forces, Navy, Engineers, Chemical Warfare, Ordnance, Artillery, you name it. The infantry served as a dumping ground for men lacking brains to get into one of the high technology branches of service. So, as a result, our present-day infantry is not only inferior to the other services from an IQ standpoint, but they are even *physically* inferior to the others."

Until now, our Basic Training cycle at Fort Benning had been a kind of "avocation"—useful but essentially unrelated to our future college work. Now suddenly, training for infantry combat had been converted from a hobby into a life-and-death vocational necessity for all of us. I didn't want to leave the comfortable "known world" of the ASTP, yet the mysterious attraction of the unknown was pulling at me with almost equal force. I could feel a strange tug of excitement and even romance at the thought of being needed by our country to fight on some foreign beachhead or battlefield.

The fifth and sixth weeks of our basic training cycle flew past as we sweated out our 6–19 March deadline for transfer to a "Repple-Depple" (as replacement centers were sometimes called).

Then, on Thursday, 23 March, our orders were changed. We were to leave within twenty-four hours for Fort Bragg, North Carolina, where we would join the 100th Infantry Division.

"The way I get it," the captain explained, "our Anzio Beachhead forces were at risk of getting shoved back into the sea. So they shipped several thousand riflemen from the 100th Division overseas to Italy as replacement soldiers for the Anzio divisions. You boys will refill the ranks of the 100th boys who have gone overseas. The 100th will presumably go overseas later like any other division presently in training."

"Do you know anything about the 100th, sir?" the boy asked.

"Only that it's a good solid division, commanded by a Virginian named Major General Withers A. Burress," the captain replied. "There's a big advantage to going overseas with a division instead of as a lonely replacement soldier," he added. "In a division you'll be with men you have shared training and drunk beer with."

The next evening the colors of the 4th ASTP Training Regiment were furled and cased at the conclusion of the Retreat ceremony.

"Tomorrow will be a sad day for all of us, men," some high-ranking officer we had never laid eyes on before told us. "But how I envy your unexcelled opportunity to join the 100th Division!"

Chapter Five
What Do We Do in the Infantry? We March!

Saturday, 25 March 1944. As our train convoy pulled off the main right-of-way into the Fort Bragg siding, we were surprised to be greeted by a brass band and a soldier wearing the two silver stars of a Major General. He was Withers A. "Pinky" Burress, Commanding General of the 100th Infantry Division. The General nodded and waved as the new arrivals dismounted from the troop train. He was a handsome individual of above average height, with wavy reddish-blond hair, large eyes and mouth, and tanned skin. He almost looked like a Hollywood conception of an American General.

On Sunday, twenty-five of us were assigned to Company A, 399th Infantry Regiment. I described the view to my folks,

"My window offers a perfect view of the airport, about a mile away over rather flat ground. We're slightly higher than the airstrip, so I can see everything. The planes taking off all fly low right over our barrack."

Many of the C-47 transport planes that took off from Pope Field and flew over our barrack had a pair of glider planes tethered behind them on long cables like braces of calves following their mammas. These were glider troop exercises of an airborne unit who was among our neighbors at Fort Bragg. Perhaps they were rehearsing for D-Day in France. Who could tell?

The 399th, of which I was now a part, was called the "Powderhorn" Regiment from the device on its heraldic shield. Coincidentally, the crest which surmounted the shield was the Minuteman with whom I was so familiar.[2] The official regimental motto, "I Am Ready," was also derived from the Revolutionary militiamen.

---

[2]The Lexington Minute Man, facing to the proper (right of the figure) surmounts the shields of all regiments and separate battalions of the Army Reserve.

Monday morning, our ASTP group in Company A, twenty-five strong, were called to a meeting with our new Commanding Officer, Captain Richard G. Young. The captain was a big man, well over six feet, with reddish-blond hair and a deliberate slow hip-swinging gait that resembled the shuffle of a large bear. He had a handsome boyish face like an Olympic swimmer.

"I took over this company last month just after the big POE [Port of Embarkation] shipment to Italy," the captain growled from the corner of his mouth. "I called the men who were left together and gave them my 'Famous Speech,' which I'm going to repeat for your benefit. I was put here by our Regimental CO, Colonel Tychsen, to prepare Company A for combat. It's my job to weed out the sick, the lame, and the lazy, because where we're going we don't need them. So if anyone in your ASTP group falls in one of those three categories, I want to be informed right away."

This was the toughest talk I had heard from any Army officer so far. Perhaps the captain sensed the boys' sobered reactions—similar to my own—because he suddenly grinned and changed his tone. "I'm pleased to have you college boys on our team," the captain continued, still speaking out of the corner of his mouth, which seemed to be his normal way of talking. He said he had been ROTC at the University of Connecticut and was commissioned immediately after graduation in June 1941. He was sent to Fort Benning, where then-Major General Omar Bradley was head of the Infantry School (Young even dated Bradley's daughter, Elizabeth). General Burress came in as Assistant Commandant while Lieutenant Dick Young was there. Once or twice he saw General George Patton "striding around with that cavalryman's walk of his."

From Benning, Captain Young was transferred to Camp Croft, South Carolina, where he served as an instructor in all basic infantry weapons—M-1 rifle, Browning Automatic Rifle (BAR), 60mm and 81mm mortars, and .30 and .50 caliber machineguns. On Louisiana Maneuvers, when they forgot to send his unit the anti-tank guns that were needed to stop enemy armor, Young rushed up hay-rakes as a substitute and was awarded a "win" by the umpires.

"Sometimes you have to improvise," he commented. From Croft, he returned to Benning for the Infantry Advanced Course, and then was promoted to captain and sent to the 100th Infantry Division. He was offered a transfer to the Rangers rather than the 100th but thanked them and said he preferred to stay with the Infantry. Captain Young added, "I don't know if any of you saw the film *The Big Parade* about the First War. I saw it when I was a kid and have been fired up about the Infantry ever since. I'm sure you will get fired up, too, before this thing is over."

Captain Young looked around the group. "Are there any questions you'd like to ask?"

"The Division newspaper said we are coming into the Division as 'fillers'," one boy said.

"That's just some bureaucrat's expression," Captain Young replied with a chuckle. "It doesn't mean you're part of a hotdog bun." The Captain looked over our group again, but seemed to be concentrating on the tops of our heads. "Most of you need a haircut," he said. "Doc Emmons, the Company Barber, will standardize you to look like the rest of us."

The next morning (Tuesday), we began our four-week ASTP training cycle under the tutelage of First Lieutenant Jack Harrell, a Texan. He explained that at the end of the cycle, we would be assigned to one of three rifle platoons or to the weapons platoon (which had the .30-caliber light machineguns and the 60mm mortars) and would be classified as riflemen, machinegunners, mortarmen, etc.

On Wednesday, 29 March, the Division received a visit from Lieutenant General Leslie B. McNair, Commanding General of the Army Ground Forces (AGF). He had come to Fort Bragg's Pike Field to pin the nation's first Expert Infantryman Badge (EIB) on an NCO from our company, Technical Sergeant Walter Bull. The Badge was a three-inch strip of sterling silver with a silver rifle mounted on an enameled infantry blue background.

If it seemed rather late in the war to be awarding the Army's "first" EIB, the time lag was explicable in terms of the fact that the Infantry had only now finally come into its own in early 1944. At Cassino, the Army Air Forces had recently demonstrated its inability to win even a small battle, not to mention an entire war. The only way Cassino would be taken would be by head-on assault by the Infantry. Similarly at Anzio, more infantry would have to be thrown in if the Allies ever hoped to reach Rome.

Coming up soon would be the D-Day invasion of France, where the Navy and Army Air Forces would make their contributions, but only the Infantry could root out the entrenched German defenders from their bunkers. On all those fronts and many others as well, hundreds of thousands of new infantrymen would have to be found and trained for the fighting in 1944. It was important to try to upgrade the Infantry's stature in the public mind, even to "glamorize" the foot soldier so that the American people would understand his dangerous but indispensable role in winning the war.

Parallel to the "Expert" badge was another new badge, the Combat Infantryman Badge (CIB), which would be granted exclusively to infantrymen who had actually performed infantry duties under fire. Both badges brought pay increases for the individual dogface who would earn them.

With the publicity aspects of the EIB in mind, beyond mere technical proficiency, the first man to earn the badge had to also appear to be an attractive human being as well.

Technical Sergeant Walter Bull probably had both positive and negative points in his career from a public relations standpoint. He was a solidly built individual who looked every inch a soldier. A chronic school truant in his teens, he had spent eighteen months in the Maryland School for Boys. Later he served in the Civilian Conservation Corps (CCC) and worked in a Pennsylvania steel mill before being drafted.

In the Army, he also earned the Soldier's Medal for rescuing several civilians from a burning train wreck outside Baltimore. After escaping from the wrecked train without mishap, Bull suddenly remembered a large whiskey inventory locked in one of the cars. Returning to the scene of the accident in hopes of liberating the booze, he stumbled over some trapped civilians and led them almost by accident, one might say, to safety as described in the Soldier's Medal citation.

It was bruited about that several others among the 120 finalists in the Expert Infantryman competition had scored more points than Sergeant Bull, but his soldierlike bearing and Soldier's Medal had seemingly tipped the scales in his favor.

I think we all felt a thrill as we watched General McNair pin the elongated blue and silver badge on Sergeant Bull's chest and heard the General's words over the loudspeaker system, "The Badge is intended to recognize the importance of highly proficient, tough, and aggressive infantry. To the Infantry belong the strong. The Infantry, above all others, must be able to take it. May we always remember that the infantryman has nothing in front of him but the enemy." I told my folks about our eminent visitor,

March 30, 1944

Three-Star General McNair, Chief of U.S. Army Ground Forces, was here yesterday. There was a Big Show. He awarded the first "Expert Infantryman" badges of the war to several men. The No. 1 soldier among four million was a Sergeant from my own little barrack, Sergeant Bull. He's a good guy and modest, but was blue when the plane carrying Life, Time, etc. photogs and interviewers got lost in the North Carolina rain and fog.

The *Boston Globe's* John Barry, who was not kept away by the rain or fog, reported on the ceremony and the requirements for earning the Expert Infantryman Badge,

To win this badge there are thirty tests, all physical. The hand-to-hand combat tests make snarling beasts of the boys, ruthless animals instructed to throw away every vestige of any code of sportsmanship they have ever learned at home, in school, or on the playing field.

Barry also explained how his Air Cadet son and we ASTPers had wound up in the Infantry,

The total number of youngsters in uniform taken from classrooms and sent to ground forces is in the neighborhood of 200,000. Many of these boys feel that the Army gave them a raw deal and broke its contract with them. But the fact seems to be that no man could have foreseen the manpower needs and the Army has to make readjustments when the demands of the moment arise.

My folks were, perhaps understandably, a bit upset at the sudden demise of the college program and our transfer to the 100th Infantry Division. Mother worried that my new companions might be "rowdies." At her suggestion, Pop had obtained a "To whom it may concern" letter from a neighbor across the street in Newton Center, who was a Regular Army Colonel. Colonel Moyle's letter attested to my Harvard and Ohio U. credentials and pointed out that I knew how to operate a typewriter. Pop apparently felt that if I had to be in a rifle company, I should at least try to put a bulky Underwood or Royal typewriter between me and the enemy.

April 4, 1944

In answer to your question, Mother, the 100th [Division] isn't a bit "rowdy." Everybody's swell. To answer Pop's questions, there are no transfers from Infantry any more, nor any from this Division as far as I know. . . . As for typing, I don't see where I could do that in the Company, and even at that, I think I'd rather be a rifleman than a "khaki-collar" worker. Not that I have a choice. I've taken pride in El Infantry, because although it is the dullest (to others) branch of the service, it is by far the manliest (paratroopers excepted).

A few days later it was announced that some of our group of ASTP emigrés from Fort Benning would be transferred again, some to a combat engineer unit at Camp Chaffee, Arkansas, and others to a field artillery battalion in Fort Riley, Kansas.

Everyone I talked to was relieved not to see his name appear on the shipment list. Each of us had the feeling that if our company CO really considered us worthless, he could simply have put our names on that shipping list. A month earlier at Benning, when we were told we would become infantry replacements, we all tried to figure out how to avoid the Infantry and get into some less lethal branch of service. Now, several of the guys were being told that they were out of the Infantry, but seemed stunned. The rest of us felt pride at having been kept on by the 100th.

The main order of business during April was the integration into the Division's bloodstream of the 3,000 or so college boys from Benning, as well as transferees from the Air Cadets and several other branches.

At month's end, we were classified and assigned on a permanent basis among the company's headquarters section, three rifle platoons, and the weapons platoon. I was assigned to the 1st Platoon as a rifleman. Three other ASTPers landed in my twelve-man squad—Bob Kyle from Medford, Oregon; Herb Rice from Peoria, Illinois; and Tom Case from San Francisco. Lieutenant Harrell was still our platoon leader.

Of the 1st Platoon's eight NCOs, some seemed to resent our presence and perhaps one or two even feared we would try to take their stripes away from them. My squad leader, Staff Sergeant Jim Gardner, told us frequently and pointedly that, "Youse boids ain't getting paid to think" (Gardner was from the Bronx). In a way, he was right, of course, since on the battlefield it would be crucial to follow almost any order unquestioningly rather than first engaging in a scholarly debate and weighing the pros and cons with an occasional "on the other hand" thrown in. But his remark was also ironic, since until the last day of 1943 at Ohio U. we were, in fact, "paid to think." But they were right and our status had changed from college thinkers to obedient executors of someone else's orders, however brilliant or stupid that someone might be.

Among the platoon's top three men, however, our reception was warmer. First Lieutenant Jack Harrell, our Platoon Leader, was a square-jawed Texan who manifested no job insecurity whatever and treated us exactly like everyone else. The Platoon Sergeant, Chuck Stanley, a taciturn West Virginian, didn't say much but we sensed that he was on our side. The same sympathy was evident on the part of the Platoon Guide, Sam D'Arpino. If Chuck Stanley rarely spoke, Sam D'Arpino was rarely at a loss for words. He never used two or three easy words when eight or nine jaw-breakers would serve just as well. As a matter of fact, he seemed to enjoy hearing the "Quiz Kids'" grammar and diction and having young people to debate with, in a branch of service not known for its intellectual content. I wrote to my folks,

> In the Infantry—we march! Seven miles Tuesday, six today, ten tomorrow, and fast marching all the way. They treat us as equals and not inferiors as in ASTP. I hope those guys who used to train us at Benning are in the front front-lines.

As we became better acquainted with the older men, we learned of their many frustrations during the eighteen months of training they had gone through. They had all been sent to the Division shortly after it was activated on 15 November 1942. General Burress' orders from General Marshall were to organize and train the Division and have it ready for combat in nine months to a year. Some 14,000 NCO cadre members and junior enlisted men poured into Fort Jackson, South Carolina, the Division's first home. Within the prescribed nine-to-twelve-month time frame decreed by General Marshall, General Burress had welded the new Division into a smoothly functioning unit ready for combat duty overseas.

However, General Marshall was not ready for them. When he had originally given Burress his orders, the cross-Channel invasion of France was targeted for the summer of 1943. Within that scenario, the 100th might have gone overseas in the summer or the fall of 1943 to reinforce the veteran divisions which would have by then established the beachhead in France. However, when the invasion was postponed to 1944, the Division was sent in November 1943 to Tennessee for winter maneuvers, more or less to keep busy and kill time while awaiting the order to pack for overseas.

The Division completed Tennessee Maneuvers in January 1944, and was sent to its new home at Fort Bragg, North Carolina. Then the roof fell in. Several thousand of the Division's best young officers, NCOs, and enlisted men, who had trained together for fourteen months in fair weather and foul, were plucked from the Division for immediate overseas shipment to join units that had suffered heavy casualties at Cassino and Anzio, or were in England preparing for the D-Day invasion. The soldiers who remained with the Division after all their close friends had shipped out were bitter. "This 4-F outfit will never go overseas," they said. "We're nothing but a training division, a glorified Repple Depple now."

The veterans said the Division "wasn't up to stuff militarily speaking." They hinted darkly that General Burress did not measure up to the Pentagon's prescribed standards of leadership for combat. One fellow said, "Who would you rather follow into combat, a man called 'Old Blood and Guts' or 'The Desert Fox' or some wavy-haired guy called 'Pinky'?"

But Pinky Burress had his defenders within the 100th's ranks, too. Some said he was highly regarded by General George C. Marshall. Others called him "the GI's General" and said it wasn't just an act or eyewash on Pinky's part either.

According to the scuttlebutt, the shock waves from the January exodus were so great that General Burress told his telephone operator to "get me General George Marshall in Washington."

"Sir?" the man asked, slow to realize that our General had the highest possible connections in the Army.

"You heard me," General Burress said.

General Marshall listened to what Burress had to say, and then offered to do two things. First, he would issue a notice to all officers and enlisted men of the Division, reasserting the fact that they had not been forgotten and would indeed be sent overseas as soon as possible. Second, he would do his best to assure that Burress received some first-rate "fillers" (that word again) for his decimated ranks, including men from the recently disbanded Army college program (including our group from Benning).

True to his word, General Marshall addressed a memo to every man in the Division.

17 February 1944

TO THE OFFICERS AND MEN OF THE 100TH DIVISION:
    Inspections indicate that the preparation of your division has been thorough and that you will soon be ready for combat, which means your transfer to an active theater
    I look to your division to give us powerful assistance in bringing this war to an early end.

George C. Marshall
Chief of Staff

"Haw haw!" one of the veterans said. "We'll transfer to an active theater as soon as we get a fresh shipment of WACs and double sleeping bags."

Withers Alexander Burress graduated from the Virginia Military Institute in 1914, at the age of twenty. On Burress' first day at VMI, an upperclassman entered his room to explain school procedures. Seeing that the fifteen-year-old Burress and his new roommate both had red hair, the upperclassman announced dryly that the other boy would uniformly be called "Red" and Burress would be called "Pinky." The nickname stuck and during the rest of his Army service, Burress would dutifully list it on official War Department forms under the category "Nicknames, Aliases, or Change of Names."

In August 1917, a bit over three years after graduating from the VMI, Burress was promoted to captain and sailed for France a month later. There he served as Assistant Regimental Operations Officer in the 2d Division's 23d Infantry Regiment through five campaigns—Château-Thierry, Aisne-Marne, Troyen, Pont-à-Mousson, and St. Mihiel.

After the war, Burress was appointed an instructor at Fort Benning's Infantry School, a prestigious assignment indeed in those days. While there he met Virginia Collier Chappell, the daughter of the Columbus mayor, Lucius Henry Chappell. They married in 1922, and moved to Lexington, VA, where the VMI had appointed him Assistant Professor of Military Science.

After two years at the VMI, Burress returned to Fort Benning. There his performance caught the eye of the Infantry School's Assistant Commandant, George C. Marshall. Marshall recommended him to the VMI for the No. 2 position as Commandant of Cadets.

To General Lejeune, the Superintendant at the VMI from 1929–1937 (and Commanding General of the 2d Division during WWI, when young Captain Burress served in his division), Marshall wrote,

> The detail as Commandant at VMI is naturally regarded as one of the most desirable in the country. Burress (now at the Command School at Leavenworth) I consider one of the finest young men in the Army. Splendid head, energetic, vision, student, ambitious, exceptional rider, shot and athlete. Stood splendidly in school here. . . . Among the young men of the Army you cannot do better than Burress. He has developed amazingly.

Two years later Lejeune reported to Marshall that Major Burress "has been very successful as a leader of young men."

A few days after Germany's invasion of France in 1940, Burress was ordered to report for duty in Washington. There Marshall (who had by this time become Chief of Staff of the Army) proceeded to groom him for command responsibility. After a year and a half with the Army Staff in Washington, Marshall sent Burress to Fort Benning as Assistant Commandant of the Infantry School under Omar Bradley. In 1942, Marshall put through two quick promotions for Burress, to brigadier general and major general. Then he assigned Burress the task of organizing the 100th Infantry Division.

One Saturday night, our sergeants were all off in Fayetteville, drinking at the Town Pump[3] or pursuing women up one side of Hay Street and down the other. The Marquis de Lafayette, for whom the two-horse town was named, would doubtlessly have been surprised to see so many Americans still in uniform a century and a half after he thought he had helped them to throw off the foreign sovereign's yoke.

Private First Class (Pfc.) Carlos Daledovich, the eldest of our platoon's ten-man college group, was the proud holder of a North Carolina liquor license which was only granted to twenty-one year olds. Several of the

---

[3]The Town Pump was an institution on the three blocks or so of Hay Street between the railroad station and the Prince Charles Hotel which constituted the honky-tonk sector of the town. The owners of the Town Pump continued to serve the military trade until the edifice burned down in the mid-1970s; Hay Street continued to be a mecca for soldiers seeking cheap beer, cheap women, and cheap thrills well into the 1990s, when it became a subject of large-scale urban renewal.

Quiz Kids commissioned Carlos Daledovich to go to town and procure a supply of rum. Meanwhile the others acquired a store of Coca-Cola and empty pickle jars from the PX and mess hall. Soon rum-and-cokes were being mixed in the pickle jars and someone broke into "I used to work in Chicago." A few hours later, after midnight, the sergeants began returning from their Fayetteville pursuits. As they entered the barrack they were offered a pickle jar filled with rum and Coke mixed to suit their individual taste. By two in the morning the place was a madhouse of shrieking humanity leaping and racing across the beds from one end of the barrack to the other. There was loud singing, laughing, and throwing up according to each man's taste and state of health. Next morning the barrack was very quiet as the men "slept it off."

"Did you hear what Sergeant Jim Gardner said last night before he passed out?" my friend Robert "Scotty" Kyle asked me. "He said, 'Youse brainy boids is no different from us normal joiks!'" Kyle laughed and slapped his knee with satisfaction. The Saturday night rum-and-Coke party marked a significant dissipation of the NCOs' mistrust of us. No longer did they seem fearful that the Quiz Kids would pull out a slide rule and demonstrate with a few deft calculations that the noncoms were certifiable imbeciles who should be replaced promptly by younger blood.

Most of us Quiz Kids were little-versed in the art of dealing with women. A public-spirited older man stepped forward to provide us with necessary counsel and advice. He was Pfc. Thomas "Rip" Farish, a massive New Yorker with a pre-Neanderthal jaw and eternal good humor. Rip Farish's sex lectures (or "sextures" for short) were presented in a shady spot outside our barrack with the aid of a flip-chart, pointer, and colored crayon— like Field Marshall Montgomery explaining the battle of El Alamein or Frank Leahy girding the Notre Dame eleven for the big game. We learned that the expression a "nice clean girl" had nothing to do with a girl's moral principles or even whether her dresses were freshly starched or her shampoo faultlessly fresh. No, a nice clean girl was simply someone not infected with a communicable venereal disease. Like a commando squad being prepared for landing on an enemy shore by the black of night, Rip Farish painstakingly briefed us on where the strong and weak points of the female anatomy were located, and how best to infiltrate and make surprise contact or even penetrations of various types.

The 399th was called "The Singing Regiment," and we did our best to maintain the tradition. To the tune of "Stars and Stripes Forever," we sang,

> Be kind to our fair-feathered friends,
> For a duck may be somebody's mother.
> She lives in the dark in the swamp

Where it's very very domp.
You may think this is the end of our song,
Well it is!

The feeling shared by most GIs—that World War I had been a futile affair that had settled nothing—found overtones in our World War II version of "Over There,"

Over there! Over there!
Send the word, send the word
Over there.
We'll be over,
We're coming over,
And we won't be back !

Chapter Six
If You Don't Like It Here,
Go Join the Paratroopers

A Regimental Review was to be held on Saturday afternoon, 6 May. The three line battalions of the 399th would execute various marching maneuvers before parading past the reviewing stand to give the salute and be rated on their performance. Our Acting 1st Battalion Commander, Major Bernard V. Lentz, Jr., assembled the Battalion two hours before parade time to rehearse the various marching steps and mass movements. "Barney" Lentz frowned frequently as the rehearsal began, as though determined to carry off the top rating of the day.

I was in Company A's front rank in accordance with the Army rule of arraying units from tallest to shortest, from front to back. My first-rank vantage point allowed me to see what was going on, but also permitted Major Lentz to see me better than if I had been buried back in the ranks somewhere. Barney Lentz stroked his chin very deliberately, his right hip stuck out and the top button of his shirt firmly buttoned (no one else in the Battalion had his shirt buttoned that way). Then the major launched into a hippy sort of swinging that looked like an unusually burly high-fashion model sashaying down a runway, with a canteen slapping like a pendulum against his oddly outthrust right hip.

According to battalion scuttlebutt, Barney Lentz was an "Army brat" by heredity and a Philadelphia tax lawyer by profession. Back in the 1920s, his father, Colonel Bernard V. Lentz, had been Professor of Military Science at the University of Minnesota. His Assistant Professor at the time was Captain Andrew Christian Tychsen, now Colonel Tychsen, our Regimental Commander.[4] Time passed, World War II broke out, and Colonel Lentz's son, Barney, was commissioned and later promoted to First Lieutenant. Colonel Lentz asked his old friend (now Colonel) Chris Tychsen to have Barney transferred to the 399th Infantry Regiment. "Put him in any job you wish," Barney's dad asked, "but keep him under your

[4]Tychsen was called "Chris" by some friends and family members, and "Andy" by others.

direct orders." Since his transfer to the 399th, Barney had been promoted first to captain and later to major. At the moment he was Acting Battalion Commander. Shortly before our arrival at Bragg, Major Felix Tharpe, the Battalion CO, had been transferred to the 398th to make room for a West Point lieutenant colonel who was rumored to be on his way to Bragg from another post. During the *interregnum*, Major Lentz seemed to be enjoying the power and prestige of being Acting Battalion CO.

Major Lentz proceeded to put the Battalion through its paces under the hot Carolina May sun. We seemed to be performing well as we marched in unison like some kind of heavily-armed centipede. There was an occasional snicker from the ranks when Major Lentz's strut became even more exaggerated than usual, or when he paused, hand on outthrust right hip, to study the Battalion as though he were back in his Philadelphia law office looking for typographical errors in a complicated contract.

"Barney could set a potted geranium on that hip and it wouldn't fall off," I heard someone say under his breath.

"All he needs is a parasol," someone else said.

"How does he get away with it?"

"He don't have to care about how *he* looks 'cause he's one of Andy's boys."

"At ease!" Captain Young growled out of the corner of his mouth. The murmuring ceased.

Then I heard Major Lentz's voice across the hard-packed sandy field. "The third man from the right in the front rank, fall out and return to barracks." I had an uneasy feeling that I might be the one he was referring to, but what had I done that was out of order? I had kept in step (I hoped), and hadn't snickered, wisecracked, or otherwise subscribed to the prevalent notion that someone who walked like that must be queer. I didn't want to believe what I had just heard, and made no move to comply with the order.

"You heard what he said," Lieutenant Harrell told me with his Texas twang. Out of the formation I stepped, like a leper, and slunk back to the Company A area. To avoid a parade was the ambition of many marchers, but to be excluded from one by someone's order was something else again.

Afterwards Sam D'Arpino, our highly professional Platoon Guide, explained charitably that I had only *appeared* to be out of step because of my long legs. Captain Young told me afterwards, "Forget what happened, I know you can march." Expelled from the parade and returning in a state of humiliation to the barracks, I longed to get to combat, if only to see how Barney Lentz would react to unrehearsed challenges far from parade grounds, pivoting mass formations, and the Regiment's compulsory reading pamphlet, *Cadence Marching*, authored in the 1920s by Lentz *père* and Tychsen when they were both teaching at the University of Minnesota.

Later in May, we spent three days and nights out on a field problem designed to teach us to survive out in nature. We wore green fatigue uniforms and steel helmets, and carried field packs and M-1 rifles. In our packs we carried a blanket, shelter half, raincoat, underwear, socks, soap, towel, and shaving equipment.

These field problems really weren't too bad and got us out of the rut of barracks life for a few days. We left the cantonment area early Monday evening and ran into a heavy downpour just as it was getting dark. Although most of us were soaking wet, by 0100, we had gone seventeen miles from the division area. Told to bed down where we were, we slept on the ground like dead men until 0800. The cooks brought up a mess truck, set up beside a little creek, and fed us quickly; then we were off again.

We marched cross-country through dense undergrowth which frequently had to be cut with knives and bayonets. We successfully "captured" our objective (a deserted tree-covered ridge) and continued our advance toward a point on the map where we would "secure our rations." We soon came to a small river that appeared to be two or three feet deep. The stream's embankment was covered by thick vines with small thorns all over them like rose bushes. Cutting and hacking our way through the vines and the thorns, we finally reached the stream.

"Scouts and assistant BAR gunners deploy and search for some sort of fording opportunity," Sergeant Sam D'Arpino, called out in his usual complicated syntax.

"In English, that means find a bridge!" Pfc. Leonard Hershberg said. Hershberg was Sergeant Amoroso's BAR man, assisted by a Chicago Swede named Bob Hogberg. Hogberg, called "Hoggie" because of his gargantuan appetite, joined the other assistant gunners and scouts in the search for a fording site. Suddenly Hoggie slipped on some damp grass and fell into the river. He emerged shaking himself like a dog.

When no "fording opportunity" could be found, we were told to strip down to our underwear and carry our M-1 rifles and other equipment over our heads. The water felt very good after the long hot march.

Just then our new Battalion CO, West Point graduate Lieutenant Colonel Elery M. Zehner, appeared. Our new CO had a massive head and pointed nose and carried a walking stick. It wasn't immediately clear how much of Hogberg's misadventure he had witnessed.

"Why don't you use that little suspension bridge about two hundred yards upstream?" Colonel Zehner asked our Platoon Sergeant, Technical Sergeant Chuck Stanley.

"Just what Pvt. Hogberg was looking for, sir," Sergeant Stanley replied, saluting smartly.

"Saluting in proximity to potential enemy forces is to be avoided, Sergeant," Colonel Zehner said.

"Sorry," Sergeant Stanley said.

"Who's your Platoon Leader?" Colonel Zehner asked.

"Lieutenant Harrell isn't with us," Sergeant Stanley replied.

Before leaving us, the Colonel managed to find a ripe Florida orange in my pack, which doubled Sergeant Stanley's discomfiture (not to mention my own due to the proscription against carrying extra food).

Shortly before noon Sergeant Amoroso's squad again ran into bad luck. Pfc. Leonard Hershberg had developed a small, but painful, bruise on his right hip from carrying the BAR for a day and a half. To alleviate the pain and to avoid burdening his assistant, Hoggie Hogberg, with the weapon, Hersh had moved his canteen several inches back from its standard position on his ammunition belt toward the buttocks and had hooked the BAR sling around the canteen. In its new position the BAR no longer grated against his hip.

Suddenly Major Lentz stepped out from behind a tree, like a character in a Shakespeare fantasy.

"Sergeant Stanley," the Major said, "who is this soldier with his BAR sling draped over his canteen?"

Hershberg halted and stood to attention, saying nothing. Sergeant Stanley and Major Lentz looked over the offending equipment carefully.

"Sir, Pfc. Hershberg has a bruise on his hip," Sergeant Stanley said.

"If your unit should fall into an enemy ambush," Major Lentz said, "will this man tell the enemy he'll need a little more time because his weapon is tangled up with his canteen and is reposing on his rear end?"

"No, sir." Sergeant Stanley replied.

"Carry on, Sergeant," Major Lentz told Sergeant Stanley, fading back into the trees to await new victims.

By late afternoon, we had covered over ten miles and seemed to have crossed every swamp in North Carolina. When we reached the point on the map where, according to Platoon Guide D'Arpino's compass, we were to pick up our rations, we found nothing but bare ground. Although local farmers were to be considered as "enemy" forces under the rules of the field problem, our men quickly breached the directive. Hoggie Hogberg began discussions with a farmer's wife while the non-coms stood listening as though Hoggie were the platoon sergeant and the non-coms were the privates. Soon our thirty-man platoon had consumed over one hundred eggs, compliments of the farmer's wife. After sundown, when the Army rations finally arrived, the farmer's wife combined the rations with her own staples and served a home-cooked meal assisted by her teenage daughter.

Thus ended in harmony a day that had involved a certain amount of stress. Guards were posted as the platoon bedded down in the orchard near the farm.

Next morning, as we saddled up for the long march back to Fort Bragg, Sergeant Stanley inspected the platoon carefully to make sure our uniforms and equipment were worn in accordance with regulations.

We stopped before noon near a strawberry patch. Hoggie went off and quickly procured a supply of fresh milk from another "enemy" farmer. Soon everyone in the platoon was enjoying a messkit full of strawberries and milk.

In mid-afternoon, our column passed Major Lentz who this time was not hiding behind a tree but stood in plain view beside a dirt road. With him was Captain Park L. "Cross Country" Brown, Battalion Operations and Training Officer (S-3) and former Big Six half-mile champion at Northwestern University.

"Sergeant Stanley," Major Lentz called. "Who is that little man over there?"

"Little man?" Sergeant Stanley asked, looking in the direction indicated by the Major. "Why, it looks like Private Paul Kuhla from the company kitchen, sir."

"You act surprised to see him, sergeant," the major said.

"I'm more than surprised," Sergeant Stanley said. "I'm flabbergasted."

"Did you notice that his sleeves are rolled up at least half a roll above the wrist?" Major Lentz asked. "And why is he wearing *two* canteens?"

"Sir, Paul Kuhla isn't even in my platoon," Stanley replied. "I inspected the platoon before we started after lunch and every man's uniform was strictly S.O.P. I swear Kuhla wasn't in the column when we started."

"Then he infiltrated you!" Major Lentz said triumphantly. "It offers an interesting lesson in never taking for granted the men who happen to be marching in your column. Could they not be enemy if not checked constantly?"

"I guess so, sir," Stanley replied, nonplussed.

Major Lentz and Captain Brown moved back from the road to a cleared area where maps were set up on makeshift tables. That appeared to be the Battalion's Command Post for the field exercise.

Later, as we approached the cantonment area, we could make out the figure of a sturdy officer of medium height standing on a knoll. It was our Regimental Commander, Colonel Tychsen, chomping furiously on a big cigar. We were all feeling a palpable *esprit de corps* after surviving together in the wilds for three days.

"Captain Young?" Colonel Tychsen called.

"Sir?" Captain Young replied. The Captain seemed to be expecting some sort of compliment at the smart way we were swinging along in cadence.

"Can't you maintain that five-yard marching interval better than you're doing?" Colonel Tychsen asked dryly.

"Yessir," the Captain said, throwing a salute in the Colonel's direction. Those who knew our tough oversized captain could tell he was angry. Captain Young had been in this game before Pearl Harbor and knew we were remarkably fresh for an outfit that had been staggering through swamps under a hot sun for days.

If Pinky Burress was the undisputed leader of the Division, Colonel Andy Tychsen and the other two Regimental Commanders wielded tremendous potential power to shape their respective 3,600-man fighting teams in their own image. Colonel Tychsen had several nicknames, not all complimentary, including "Old Spit and Polish" and "the Chicken Colonel." In 1914, when he was almost twenty-one, he dropped out of the University of Minnesota and requested parental permission to join the 1st Minnesota Infantry, a National Guard Regiment. His father, Andreas Christian Tychsen, a Protestant minister, refused to give his consent, but Tychsen's mother came to the rescue and signed the necessary papers.

In the 1st Minnesota, Tychsen rose quickly through the ranks from private to first sergeant. After America entered the Great War in 1917, he was sent to Officer Candidate School. By scoring in the top ten percentiles, he received a direct commission to captain, thereby skipping his lieutenancy entirely. He went overseas with the 88th Division and commanded a company of machinegunners in the Vosges Mountains sector of the Western Front near Belfort just before the Armistice.

After the war he returned to the University of Minnesota, as Assistant Professor of Military Science under Professor Colonel Bernard V. Lentz, father of our Barney Lentz. Colonel Lentz took a fatherly interest in Tychsen and made him co-author of a tome on which Tychsen had helped with the research. The book, *Cadence Marching*, was still on sale at our Regimental PX twenty years after its initial publication. Regimental officers understood that demonstrating a detailed knowledge of its contents might be advantageous in some ways.

Tychsen later served as a staff officer under then-Lieutenant Colonel George Catlett Marshall at Fort Snelling, an Army installation near Minneapolis. Tychsen remembered Marshall as a "stern but diligent" officer. Colonel Marshall was already at work behind his desk by 0800 each morning when he called Captain Tychsen in for discussions. At some point, he would interrupt their discussion with a curt "Excuse me," and turn on a small radio on his desk. This put him in touch with an airplane circling overhead where it oversaw the movements of the troops under his command. Tychsen was greatly impressed by Marshall's pragmatic use of the technology of his time in his work. Marshall struck Tychsen as being austere, "extremely suspicious of his peers," and a difficult person with whom to deal.[5]

After Pearl Harbor, Tychsen requested combat duty and was transferred in late 1942 to the newly organized 100th Division to command the 399th Infantry Regiment.

"The Regiment had a very handsome coat of arms," Tychsen noted in his memoirs, "consisting of a gold powderhorn on a chain against a blue background. I grew to be very proud of that insignia. We were known at once as the Powderhorn Regiment."[6]

For the next fourteen months after the 100th's activation on 15 November 1942, Colonel Tychsen worked his heart out building what he considered a magnificent 3,600-man fighting force, only to lose everything at the stroke of some bureaucrat's pen up in the Pentagon. As he later recounted it in his memoirs,

> From Tennessee Maneuvers we then trucked in a long convoy to Fort Bragg, North Carolina. There we settled down and tried to digest the awful fact that we were to lose almost our entire strength, which was to be transferred to other divisions scheduled for early deployment overseas. We were then reduced to about one-tenth of our command, leaving only a cadre.
>
> This situation was soon repaired, however, when we received some 3,000 new men from various elements such as the Air Cadet Program, returnees from overseas, and especially ASTP men. The Army Specialized Training Program was sponsored by the wife of the President to save the lives of those who were highly gifted with brains [sic]. Needless to say, when those men found themselves in a fighting outfit, they tried their best to get out of it. But somehow they soon learned to appreciate the honor, and as everybody knows, developed into the finest set of combat men that ever fought under Uncle Sam. We are all immensely proud of their conduct, and it was wonderful what they accomplished. We regretfully lost some of them in combat and will always be inordinately proud of their strong devotion and patriotism.[7]

[5]Tychsen interview with the author, 10 September 1982.

[6]Tychsen memoirs, US Army Military History Institute (USAMHI), Carlisle Barracks, PA.

[7]Ibid.

Meanwhile, Colonel Tychsen's old boss and benefactor, and father of Barney Lentz, Jr., Colonel Bernard V. Lentz, Sr., had neither "died nor faded away," but was presently Commanding Officer at Fort Schuyler, New York, and the seniormost Colonel in the entire U.S. Army.

One of the 399th officers, who hailed from New York City, reported that the old Colonel was an "even bigger ball-breaker than the son." Colonel Lentz *père* had hung a prominent sign over the entrance to Fort Schuyler's main building with the injunction, "Turn off the gas and turn on the work!" The old boy reportedly came south occasionally to watch his son, Barney, put our battalion through its "cadence marching" paces.

Although Barney Lentz was unimpressed by my efforts to march in step with the others, Platoon Guide Sam D'Arpino thought I at least showed spirit. After the field problem, he wrote in the regimental newspaper, *The Powderhorn* (for which he was Company A's correspondent),

Pvt. Red Gurley is a rather big fellow and woe-betide the Jerry he comes in contact with. After hearing so much about the importance of being aggressive, he proceeded on a field problem. Going into the assault phase, he attacked and jabbed a simulated dummy stuffed solidly with sand. After withdrawing his rifle from the dummy's entrails, he suddenly realized he had no bayonet attached. I concluded, however, that the bayonet would not have been necessary at all, to take care of the Jerry, that is.

Before daylight on 6 June 1944, we were awakened by distant sirens, whistles, and church bells. Radios were turned on and we heard General Eisenhower saying that the Allies had put men ashore in Normandy a few hours earlier and that the invasion was so far a success. General Burress and his staff participated in a D-Day prayer session at the Division Chapel. On D-Day Plus 2, the German high command identified one of the Allied invasion units as the U.S. 100th Division. The Germans had apparently confused us with the 101st Airborne Division because of the closeness of the numbers and the fact that the 101st had also trained at Fort Bragg before shipping overseas.

This reopened the old discussion of when (if ever) our Division would go overseas. While nobody I knew was shedding tears over the fact that we had not been present for the "grand opening" of the European "Theater" on 6 June on those fire-swept Normandy beaches, we were nevertheless an infantry division. Our basic mission was to go where the enemy was and fight him. But would we go, and when?

A certain tension was sensed to be building up between Colonel Tychsen and the men of the Regiment as the end of June approached. The root of the problem seemed to be that while the fighting in Normandy continued unabated, there was still no hint that the 100th might ever go over to join the fighting. Tempers grew short and the Colonel's spit and polish ways were resented even more than usual. Finally, Colonel Tychsen passed the word that the men were free to join the airborne forces if they were so impatient to see the face of war. Notices to this effect were posted on company bulletin boards and airborne recruiters, seeking to make up the heavy D-Day losses of the 82d and 101st Airborne Divisions, were allowed to post their own notices. Colonel Tychsen's action was interpreted by some as an effort to "call" what he apparently considered a collective bluff on the men's part.

At that point, 1 July, I departed for Boston on what the Army euphemistically called an "overseas" furlough, even though none of us saw any prospect at that moment of going overseas. When I returned to Fort Bragg on 15 July, the Regimental area was in a near state of bedlam. As I wrote to my folks,

> *Captain Young is standing on a burning deck. Our Platoon Leader Lieutenant Harrell, Platoon Sergeant Chuck Stanley and ten other men from the platoon joined the paratroopers while I was home on furlough. I may join too, but then again, I might not. I'm still thinking.*

Ernie Emmons, our barber, solicited me to join the parachutists, but I put him off while I reflected more about the matter. Wasn't six feet the limit to be eligible? If so, I was three inches over the limit. Hundreds of men from the Regiment signed up with the paratroop recruiters. General Burress called to ask Colonel Tychsen "what in hell is going on" down in the 399th Infantry. Red-faced, Colonel Tychsen almost had to resort to getting down on his knees (like his father, the Protestant minister) to dissuade the men from carrying out their threat.

As it worked out, a relatively small number still insisted on leaving after he apologized for questioning their genuine desire to see combat. In my platoon, Captain Young persuaded Chuck Stanley to withdraw his application, and Stanley persuaded the other ten volunteers to do the same. Lieutenant Jack Harrell, the Texan, however, was adamant. He wanted to fight in this war and strongly doubted he would ever see action if he remained with the 100th. When I returned from furlough he was already gone for good. I regretted that I never had a chance to say goodbye to him, because he had always been such a straight-shooter with everyone.

Chapter Seven

We Are Tested for the Expert Infantryman Badge

On Wednesday, 19 July, my third day back on the job, our battalion put on a simulated combat show for a group of southern cotton growers. I was to play the role of a German soldier in the final feature event, where I would attack Platoon Sergeant Ralph Harrington of the 3d Platoon with a trench knife. Sergeant Harrington, like his 2d Platoon counterpart Technical Sergeant Walter Bull, boasted one of the most beautiful physiques in the entire battalion (Chuck Stanley of our 1st Platoon was Harrington's and Bull's counterpart platoon sergeant); Harrington had broad, sloping shoulders, a narrow waist, and piston-like legs. I described the scene to my folks,

> Our company put on a show for the cotton bigwigs of the south (about sixty of them). The loudspeaker slung the bull about how rugged we were and then with about eight men in each event, we ran the Expert Infantry tests one after another—pushups, three hundred yard run, seventy-five-yard pick-a-back, burpees, zig-zag creep-crawl course.
>   Then came the tumblers and the hand-to-hand combateers, the disarming of the bayonet, and last on the program was the knife-wielding Gurley getting thrown on his head and eating a seven-course sawdust meal not including dessert (also sawdust).

The Captain really pulled the wool over the cottongrowers' eyes. They left thinking we were supermen. Wotta farce. All during the parade ground exhibition, there were other companies in all directions doing calisthenics, games, or running and making noise in general. The idea of the Army is to fool the guy immediately over you, and for, consequently, F. D. R. to fool E. D. R.

First Lieutenant Raymond "Mamma" Landis, Captain Young's executive officer, was temporarily in charge of our platoon while we awaited a new officer to succeed the departed Lieutenant Harrell. As part of the classification of each man to a specific job within each squad, Lieutenant Landis proposed that I become second assistant to BAR man Robert E.

Jones, whose first assistant was Doc Emmons, the Company Barber. It was natural for Lieutenant Landis to think of me, since it took a big man to carry the twenty-one-pound weapon and its heavy load of ammunition magazines, each containing twenty .30-06 rounds. The role of the two assistant BAR men was to carry ammo and be ready to take over if something happened to Robert E. Jones.

To me the BAR was anathema for several reasons, starting with my extreme technical and mechanical ineptitude. If I couldn't hit the target with my 9.5-pound M-1 rifle, how could I expect to control a twenty-one-pound monster like the BAR? Also, I was a runner by temperament and wanted to travel as light as possible. I wished to be responsible only for my own fate and not be weighed down by a lot of metal as part of somebody else's vulnerable, slow-moving "team." Hoggie Hogberg, first assistant to BAR man Lennie Hershberg in Sergeant Amoroso's squad, described the BAR man's role in a letter to his folks,

> *The BAR man is the one whom the enemy gets first if they can, as it lays down such a heavy and deadly volume of fire. I carry my own M-1 ammunition for my gun and about 500 rounds of ammunition for the BAR. So my equipment weighs about 150 pounds, with pack and everything else included.*

"I don't want to be a BAR assistant, sir," I told Lieutenant Landis frankly.

"Why not?"

"Because I'm a poor shot."

"What did you score on the M-1?"

"146, sir."

"Not too high. Did you ever fire the BAR for score?"

"No, sir."

"All right, how would you like to be Second Scout behind Herb Rice instead?"

"That sounds better for me and for the squad, sir," I replied.

"Okay," Lieutenant Landis said. Turning to Scotty Kyle, he said, "Kyle, you're now second assistant BAR man to Bob Jones and Doc Emmons."

"No, sir!" Kyle flared. "I know less than nothing about that damn oversized weapon!"

"I'm sorry, but you can't choose," Lieutenant Landis said.

"But Red Gurley just talked you out of it!" Kyle sputtered.

"True, but he took the Second Scout's slot instead. Would you be interested in the scout opening?"

Scotty Kyle didn't reply to the lieutenant's question, but stood glaring at him as though hoping he would reconsider. Even I could see the humor of

Scotty Kyle as a rifle scout, bobbing up and down with that bouncy walk of his as he advanced through the Siegfried Line, peering through those goggles of his as he sought out enemy targets.

"All right, then, that's final," Lieutenant Landis said. "Gurley is Second Scout and Bob Kyle is ammo bearer on the BAR."

In mid-August a number of promotions were announced. Four of the ten ASTP boys in our platoon were promoted to Private First Class—including Herb Rice and Bob Kyle in my squad (and excluding Tom Case and me). Sergeant Gardner had opposed Kyle's promotion, but was told that he had no say in the matter since Kyle was classified as jeep driver. Scotty Kyle had signed up for the jeep drivers' school to get out of marching, but a second unexpected benefit accrued as his driver's license turned out to be a ticket to promotion to Private First Class. My brother, George, had just earned a commission in the Army Air Force at Yale University without even cutting down on his number of dates per week, it seemed, while I couldn't win the measly single chevron of a Pfc. The Army had lured me into enlisting by dangling offers of free college training and a future officer's commission. But once they had me, even a $4.80 per month boost to Pfc. seemed beyond their scope. As I told my folks,

> *A lot of ASTPs were made Pfc. Not me. In our platoon four out of 10 got a stripe. No use griping, it doesn't get you anywhere.*
>
> *The Pfcs walk in the clouds. A star on their shoulders couldn't make them happier. Kyle, a S.N.A.F.U who got his because he's a spare jeep driver, smokes cigars, threatens to beat up everybody (he couldn't beat his way out of a paper bag with a flame-thrower) and acts like he's on a perpetual drunk. High morale.*

I didn't know if it was a consolation prize or a coincidence when Sergeants Stanley and D'Arpino told me to take the platoon through close-order drill for a few minutes the day after the promotions were announced. As I told my folks,

> *Last Monday, I got to drill the platoon for about five minutes. They're used to one command every half-minute or so. So I gave 'em one every two seconds and really had a couple of our slower-witted Sergeants on their ears. They said very good work, but I should growl instead of using a high-pitched voice.*

Our turn came to go through the famous Night Infiltration Course we had heard so much about. A violent thunderstorm came up as we were preparing to leave the barracks at 2000 hours. The rain let up some after a while and we were able to start out, but lightning flashes continued throughout the night. The purpose of the Infiltration Course was to accustom infantrymen to the sights and sounds of combat, including barbed wire, live overhead machine-gun fire, and the simulated exploding of land mines. The Infiltration Course might be dry or muddy depending on the weather, but on this particular night, it was very muddy. To negotiate the Infiltration Course, one had to creep and crawl for nearly one hundred yards, passing under several strands of barbed wire while three machine guns fired live rounds overhead, half ball ammo and half tracers.

The guns fired intermittently for a while and then they all fired at once, creating enough noise to give strong men heart failure. The tracer rounds resembled fireworks as they crisscrossed a few feet over our heads in the darkness. To pass under the barbed wire obstacles, we had to roll over on our backs and wallow along inch by inch in the red-clay mud like hogs on a farm. After I had gotten through the barbed wire, a dynamite charge exploded three or four feet ahead. The concussion heaped more of Carolina's red-clay all over me and I couldn't hear anything for two or three minutes afterwards. The lightning flashes lit up the Infiltration Course like distant artillery. The whole scene seemed right out of the Battle of Verdun in the First World War. We had heard stories about low machine-gun fire or ricocheting bullets accidentally killing or wounding men as they crawled with heavy back packs and other gear beneath the barbed wire strands. However, there were no casualties in Company A that night, nor as far as I knew anywhere else in the Battalion.

Finally, on 19 August, seventy-four days after D-Day in Normandy, the glacier of our Division's long immobility began to melt and crack. Signs began appearing that we were perhaps not fated to spend the rest of the war among Fort Bragg's scrub pines after all.

Sunday, August 20
We got no Sunday off this week. They got us up at 5:30 this AM for an inspection on the paradeground of all our belongings. There is, as zey zay, zomting in der vind. All formal training in Fort Bragg for the Division ends next Saturday the 26th. After that, who knows? Overseas perhaps?

During the following week, the most persistent rumor among several dozen that swept through the divisional barracks was that the Division would "go POE" (move to a Port of Embarkation) in the final ten days of September.

Saturday, 26 August we wound up our formal Fort Bragg training program with another parade ground demonstration for visiting VIPs. This time Technical Sergeant Ralph Harrington of the 3d Platoon was cast in my old role as the Nazi stormtrooper with knife, while Technical Sergeant Walter Bull played Harrington's former role as the man who takes the knife away from the German after tripping him in the sawdust pit. However, when the dust had cleared and the VIPs began applauding, there was the Nazi "enemy," Sergeant Harrington, still on his feet clenching his knife while Walter Bull lay sprawled in the dust where Harrington's foot had sent him. Sergeant Harrington had not followed the script, but had "slung the Bull" (literally speaking). The holder of the nation's first Expert Infantryman Badge had been humiliated before a crowd of visiting VIPs. I caught a glimpse of Sergeant Chuck Stanley shaking his head in disapproval of Harrington's action. I wondered how this doublecross would play out between the two men when and if our company reached combat.

On Tuesday, 29 August, General Burress addressed the entire Division on a large drill field. He said the Division had received its orders and would be leaving Bragg before long.

"Ah heard some fellows complainin' we been trainin' too long here at Fort Bragg," General Burress said, exaggerating his own Virginia accent a bit in an apparent gesture of folksiness. "But Ah'll tell you this, when you're gonna take on Jack Dempsey, the Big Champ, you need all the trainin' you kin git!" Wild applause followed.

He added that Lieutenant General Ben Lear, the late Lieutenant General Leslie McNair's successor as chief of the Army Ground Forces, would inspect the Division during the next few days.

General McNair, who had pinned the first Expert's badge on Sergeant Bull in March, had been killed in Normandy in July by our own bombers in a tragic mixup. Two weeks later, his only son, Colonel McNair, was killed in action on the same front.

At the conclusion of General Burress' speech, we all stood and saluted as the Division Band played "The Star-Spangled Banner."

No one seemed more pleased and relieved than General Burress over the fact that we had finally received our marching orders. A few days earlier he had received a pathetic letter from a GI wife, who said her husband's "overseas furlough" to New York City had been a disaster,

All his unkind friends kept asking him why he had been in training with the 100th for nearly two years and why he was still a Private and still in the States. When he got back to Fort Bragg after furlough, he

was so depressed he went AWOL and of course got caught and is now languishing in the Stockade. Dear General Burress, can't you please get him out of that Stockade and take him overseas before he and the rest of us go completely crazy?

                Sincerely,
                Emma Frantz[8]

Emma's plea was acted upon; her husband deployed overseas with the Division.

———————

That afternoon we rehearsed a coordinated infantry-armor attack. Our line of riflemen moved forward on foot, then clambered onto the tanks for a rapid forward deployment of about three hundred yards. We leaped to the ground, fixed bayonets, and launched an infantry assault across a low draw against the "enemy's" front-line positions. Behind us the tanks, which stood on a small rise in the ground, fired blank rounds in "support" of the attack.

General Burress worked closely with the War Department in preparing every detail of General Ben "Yoo-hoo" Lear's visit. For example, one of the War Department's many suggestions about General Lear's personal preferences was to "give him plenty of coffee and butter his toast light to medium."[9] On 31 August 1944, General Lear's plane touched down precisely on time. General Burress hurried forward to salute and shake hands with the Division's eminent guest. He then handed General Lear a copy of what he thought was the official program of the visit. The General, upon opening it, looked perplexed as he began reading about his coffee, toast, and other personal preferences. After that, nothing seemed to go right for General Burress during the two day visit.

Captain Young nearly panicked when he received word that General Lear's party would visit our company. Captain Young was very much afraid that General Lear would discover Company A's large stock of unauthorized, non-standard equipment of the kind every company seemed to accumulate. A second dangerous liability was Private Paul Kuhla of the company mess section, who seemed incapable of keeping his uniform on straight, especially when "Brass Hats" came around inspecting. In a flash

---

[8]Staff Sergeant Frederick F. Lyons papers, USAMHI (Lyons served as General Burress' personal secretary through the war. His papers are voluminous and an excellent source.)

[9]Former Captain Richard G. Young, interview with the author, 11 September 1982.

of invention, Captain Young thought he had the solution. All unauthorized equipment was piled into a two-wheeled push-cart (which was also non-standard equipment) and was hidden in the woods, with Paul Kuhla guarding it. The scheme worked brilliantly—General Lear never discovered the forest hideout.[10]

General Lear was not known for making effusive reports to General Marshall after inspections of this type. Usually his report consisted of one word, either "satisfactory" or "unsatisfactory." However, he gave General Burress no advance indication as to which opinion he would give Marshall about our Division.[11] One rumor said that General Marshall had to talk General Lear out of giving Burress' division an "unsatisfactory" rating.

"Oh, I know Pinky Burress and he's a top notch general," Marshall was reported to have told Lear, thus ending the discussion of our Division's readiness for overseas action.[12]

Soon the newspapers were full of photos of the liberation of Paris and stories about General Patton's Third Army's advance toward the German border. General George C. Marshall, was quoted in the press as predicting the possible end of the war in Europe by Christmas. A day or two after the press reports appeared, the men of our Regiment were convoked by Colonel Tychsen. From where I stood listening in the ranks, I sensed that Colonel Tychsen was upset about something.

"There are those who would tell you to relax, that the war in Europe is all over but the shouting," Colonel Tychsen said. "But I'm here to tell you we'll need less shouting and more *shooting* if we hope to win. I can promise you that this Regiment will see plenty of combat before it's finally over, 'over there'."

"Ever since they stole most of our men last winter," Colonel Tychsen continued, "I have heard doubting Thomases who said this Regiment would never go overseas. Do you remember those prophets of gloom and doom?"

"YEAH!" the men roared.

"Well, they were wrong, weren't they?" Colonel Tychsen asked, his voice rising.

"YEAH!" the men of the Regiment shouted back at their leader. "YEAH!"

"Now the doubting Thomases are saying there won't be any war left when we get there. They say we'll be Army of Occupation wearing fancy MP uniforms with white helmet liners, white nightsticks, and white leggins. Have any of you heard those rumors?"

[10]Ibid.
[11]Ibid.
[12]Ibid.

"YEAH!" the men roared. "YEAH!"

"Do you believe that?" the Colonel asked.

"NO!" the men shouted. "NO!"

"I was over there in the First War," Colonel Tychsen went on. "I know the Germans. They won't quit until they absolutely have to."

The Regiment broke into applause, punctuated by loud cheering.

"Historians say you can't really understand anything about war until you have fought the Germans," Colonel Tychsen continued.

"YEAH!" the men answered, taking his word for it.

"I can't think of a worse way to spoil men's motivation to fight than to tell them the war will end before they get there," Colonel Tychsen said. "What do you think?"

The men cheered again. "Let's go!" several voices cried.

"To conclude," Colonel Tychsen said, "the Regiment is superbly trained to fight and that's exactly what we're going to do—and soon!"

The men cheered again. Staccato applause rattled like automatic weapons fire in the warm September air. Colonel Tychsen peered down at his Regiment's officer corps standing in the front ranks, and they peered back up at him on his wooden platform. On the Colonel's face seemed to be a question, "Do you believe what I just said?" On his officers' faces a question seemed to be chiseled, "Whom should we believe, General Marshall or *you*?"

Who was right, General Marshall or Colonel Tychsen? According to the scuttlebutt, Colonel Tychsen considered General Marshall's remark about the war ending by Christmas the worst blunder by any general on either side during the war to date. One thing you could say for Andrew Christian Tychsen—he wasn't afraid to get up on his hind legs and sound off, no matter who got hurt or how high their rank. He could be tough not only on his subordinates but also on his superiors, no matter how exalted their station.

We finally received our new platoon leader, Second Lieutenant Bob Mueller. He had obtained a commission on the strength of two or three years of ROTC at the University of Washington, and did not have to go through the crucible of Officer Candidate School. At twenty-one, he was younger than most of the non-coms and older than most of the ASTP group. Sergeant Real Parenteau, Assistant Squad Leader under Jim Gardner, whose Guadalcanal experience with the Americal Division had given him a real or imagined ability to judge leaders and men, did not seem too impressed by our new leader. Parenteau referred to him behind his back as "Junior." However, Sergeants Chuck Stanley and Sam D'Arpino, our two top non-coms, seemed to accept his authority without question.

Just as they had welcomed us Quiz Kids as potential platoon assets six months earlier, they seemed to regard Lieutenant Mueller's college education as a source of potential benefits to the platoon. Part of Lieutenant Mueller's problem, perhaps, was the simple fact that his predecessor, First Lieutenant Jack Harrell, was an extremely difficult act to follow.

We were told that every man in the Division would be required to take the Expert Infantryman Badge test before leaving Fort Bragg. Time was set aside every day to train and practice the thirty events that made up the agenda for the tests. Among the subjects on which we would be tested were pushups, night land navigation, scouting and patrolling, and even the three-hundred-yard shuttle run. In the latter event, the runner turned around at the halfway point and rushed back to the starting line. Because I had been a Harvard runner, Sergeant Bull used me to demonstrate to the rest of the company how the race should be paced to reach the finish line within the required fifty-two seconds. I reported to my folks,

> *Monday we practiced the physical requirements for the Expert Infantryman test. I (ahem) was called upon by Sergeant Bull (No. 1 expert infantryman) to run the 300 for exhibition purposes to show the correct plan of running it in less than fifty-two seconds. I had a great loaf in forty-seven seconds, which was slow but that was the idea. I didn't even breathe through my mouth as runners generally do. I was just showing off. So about two minutes later the still-fresh (I thought) me had to run the 300 again in one of the heats. I was pooped all the way and barely made it in forty-six seconds.*

The non-com who devoted the greatest time and effort to teaching Company A's men how to pass the various "Expert" tests was Staff Sergeant Clarence "Pop" Sutton, a squad leader in the 3d Platoon. If the rest of us hoped to have any success at all in the tests, we knew it would be because of "Pop" Sutton's training during the preceding weeks. Like a good teacher, the baldish Sutton had infinite patience even with the least gifted among us as we went over and over the test requirements.

The Expert Infantryman Badge tests were administered on 18 and 19 September to all those able-bodied men in the Division who had not already been tested. We received the following outline of the two-day program,

Tues. A.M.	Military Courtesy
	Physical Fitness
	Field Sanitation
Tues. P.M.	First Aid
	Camouflage & Individual Protection

Tues. Night	Night Compass Course
Weds. A.M.	Bayonet Course
	Grenade Course
Weds. P.M.	Scouting & Patrolling (including Day Compass Course)
	Field Proficiency

For me, the first Physical Fitness event, the thirty-four-pushup require-
ment, looked to be one of the most difficult But after practicing every
morning and night for weeks, I managed to produce thirty-seven pushups
on the test. Next came the three-hundred-yard run, which I negotiated in
thirty-nine seconds, well below the permissible fifty-two-second maximum. There followed the seventy-five-yard pick-a-back carry, Burpees, and
the zig-zag creep-and-crawl course.

The most difficult part of the second day's test was "scouting and
patrolling" involving movement through hostile territory. When cardboard
targets popped up unexpectedly on hills to the left or right, you had to hit
the ground, fire (with live ammo) until the targets were pulled, and then
leap to your feet and continue the advance. I blasted away with my M-1
rifle and was gratified to see the targets pulled promptly by the men concealed in deep holes. I noticed that one target was pulled almost as soon
as I started firing, and wondered if the pit men were exercising greater
leniency than they had on the rifle range where I had barely passed muster.

On Monday, 25 September, the Division's last day at Bragg, the Expert
Infantryman Badge was awarded to those of us who had come through the
tests successfully. I was among the roughly twenty-five percent of the candidates to receive the badge in our regiment. Bob Kyle had passed every
test except scouting and patrolling where perspiration had caused his
glasses to fog up and spoil his aim. Pfc. David Goland of the 4th Platoon
flunked the same test by demonstrating "too much aggressivity with his
pistol" as he fired at those same targets with a .45 Colt automatic. When I
remembered the apparently lenient attitude of the target-pullers as I
passed through their territory and potted away at their targets, I appreciated how lucky I had been to squeak through the combat course while
good men like Kyle and Goland were coming to grief.

That same day, Captain Young told Sergeant Stanley that the Signal
Corps needed a man with high IQ for immediate transfer. Sergeant Stanley
proposed the transfer to my friend, Private Ed Cook, a slender youngster
from Sedalia, Missouri, who was Lieutenant Mueller's runner and radio
man.

"No, thank you," Ed Cook replied. "I want to stay with the outfit."
Sergeant Stanley next tried Pfc. Bob Kyle, who responded with a similar

turndown. Sergeant Stanley reported back to Captain Young that there were no takers in the 1st Platoon for the proposed transfer to a safe job.

"I have another request here," Captain Young told Sergeant Stanley. "OCS wants to know whether I will release our Private Robert Hogberg to them. But tell Hogberg it's no dice. Where we're going, we'll need every man big enough to lug that BAR."

"Yessir," Sergeant Stanley said.

That evening I stood outside the barrack watching the sunset's rays glint against the sterling silver trim on the little blue badge worn above my left breast pocket. The summer heat was gone and the weather was perfect now.

Six months ago to the day, on 25 March, we had arrived at Fort Bragg from Fort Benning. Our captain at Benning had predicted that in six months every able-bodied man among us would be overseas. We seemed to be running pretty close to the captain's schedule.

I felt sentimental watching the sun go down, knowing that tomorrow we would leave that place forever. I had liked Fort Bragg and the 100th Infantry Division from the very first day. I had never felt as proud about anything that ever happened to me as I did about being allowed to wear that little blue Expert Infantryman Badge. I could understand the fierce pride men like Pinky Burress, Chris Tychsen, and Dick Young felt for the Infantry. A last ray of sun struck the badge, making it glow in the twilight of our last Carolina sunset.

Chapter Eight
New York Port of Embarkation

The Division Band serenaded our departure from Fort Bragg with the strains of Sousa's "The Stars and Stripes Forever." We marched proudly to the train despite the burden of seventy-pound packs surmounted by horse-shoe-shaped blanket rolls. In the train, every man had a reserved seat with his name on it. Our journey would be under secure conditions and we were told to keep our weapons away from the train windows where they could be seen. It was Tuesday, 26 September 1944.

Late that evening, we reached Camp Kilmer, New Jersey, our transitory home. Camp Kilmer was a troop staging area for overseas shipment, so we were expecting to live in pup tents. To our surprise we found double-deck-er barracks much like the ones we had left behind at Fort Bragg. The main difference was that these barracks wore multiple hues of camouflage paint as a precaution against air raids.

The Division's Advance Party had arrived at Camp Kilmer before us. Tonight they were rumored to be aboard a troopship over in New York harbor, ready to sail at midnight for England as an advance contingent of the Division. England was the usual staging area for transshipping troops over to France. Later that night, as we were getting ready to hit the sack, two command cars were seen leaving the Division area. Word flashed around like summer heat lightning that the officers in the command cars, headed by General Burress' Assistant Division Commander, Brigadier General Maurice G. "Bill" Miller, were bound for La Guardia Airport. The new rumor was that the move to England had been suddenly superseded by Southern France as the Division's probable destination. The next morning, the England Advance Party was back in camp, looking tired and dejected. Their departure by ship had been canceled a few minutes before the mid-night sailing hour, and they were told to return to camp.

The reason for the sudden change of destination was that the French ports and dock facilities along the Channel coast had either been destroyed by the Germans or were still occupied by them. Lacking unloading facilities, Allied reinforcements were obliged to debark on the original Normandy invasion beaches, a long and cumbersome process. Meanwhile, the port of Marseilles on France's south coast had been cleared of Germans during the August invasion and its port facilities were now capable of debarking Allied troops. General Burress chose Bill Miller to lead the special mission because Miller, a West Point graduate, knew France already. In the First War, he had risen to battalion commander and had been wounded in action a month before the Armistice. General Miller's party flew from La Guardia Airport to Newfoundland, the Azores, Casablanca, Oran, Algiers, and finally Naples where they changed to a smaller British plane. From Naples up to Marseilles, they had to run the gauntlet of German air bases in northern Italy, but passed undetected. After a brief stop on the island of Corsica, they landed at Marseilles' Marignane Field after a thirty-four-hour air journey. From there, they were taken to Lyon where they met Generals Jake Devers, Sixth Army Group Commander, and Alexander Patch, Seventh Army Commander. The 100th Infantry Division, they were told, would be assigned to General Lucian Truscott's VI Corps. Truscott's Corps had spearheaded the bold landings on the French Riviera coast the previous month.

General Truscott's latest directive to the officers and men gave a somber picture of what lay ahead,

> Our task is not yet done. Hard fighting remains. The enemy, reorganized and reinforced, is on the border of his own country. Difficult and rugged terrain confronts us. Rain, cold, and snow will increase the difficulty of our operation. However, I face the future with complete confidence that, surmounting every obstacle and taking every objective in your accustomed manner, you will destroy the enemy before you, and will be a vital factor in the defeat of the enemies of our country.

After less than two days in France, General Miller's party was again airborne en route back to La Guardia and Camp Kilmer. Things were now set.

The Camp Kilmer cadres processed us with efficiency and respect. They seemed to be saying, "You are fighting men about to depart these shores to tangle with a dangerous enemy. It is our job to make your final days in the States as pleasant and memorable as possible." They said that a few weeks earlier they had been telling another outbound division (the 84th) that the war would end soon and they would pull Army of Occupation duty as MPs. To us their message had changed, "You might very well see combat."

In less than nine months in the Army, I had already gone through three distinct phases of a doughboy's evolution. At Fort Devens and Fort Benning, my buddies and I were often treated as a pack of hopelessly incompetent juveniles who were to be intimidated and humiliated by all possible means. At Fort Bragg, by contrast, we were treated as *men* for the first time, despite unsuccessful efforts by some of the non-coms to convince us that we were "not being paid to think." Now, at Camp Kilmer, we were being treated like some sort of privileged characters, for whom no courtesy or comfort was too great. Twelve-hour passes were granted liberally, and many of the guys who lived in the New York area were able to briefly visit home and loved ones a final time. I even got the opportunity to visit my old home town of Upper Darby, Pennsylvania, and visited with some old friends and acquaintances. As it turned out, it was a bittersweet trip; I learned that twin brothers who were schoolmates of mine had already been killed in action.

The interminable clothing inspections we had gone through in our final days at Fort Bragg were resumed the morning after our arrival at Kilmer. There were also lectures about the importance of safeguarding military information, particularly if we were taken prisoner and subjected to enemy interrogation.

"The Geneva Convention requires you to answer your captors' questions only to the extent of telling your name, rank, and serial number," the lecturing sergeant said. "But nothing else, such as the number of your division, the name of your company commander, or what you had for breakfast. All confidential military information must be denied to the enemy. Are there any questions?" There were only a few. My personal reaction to the lecture was one of indignation, since I could not conceive of myself as being so morally inferior as to fall into enemy hands. I assumed the others felt the same way.

The lecturing Sergeant went on to discuss the penalty under the Articles of War for desertion in the face of the enemy. "The penalty is death by firing squad," he said, enunciating each word clearly. "Are there any questions?" Everyone seemed to have understood.

There was no official discussion of the penalties for shooting superior officers or non-coms in combat, but there was considerable whispering about this possibility among the men. There was a sense within the ranks that a rapid settlement of accounts would be in order for any officer or non-com who didn't treat his men properly. If we had had to put up with the whims and antics of Major Lentz and dozens of other weird stuff in training, the same would not be true in combat where the offenders would be far from Washington's protective skirts.

"Wait till he gets overseas," the men said about their particular pet peeve among their superiors. "Either he shapes up or we ship him out."

We were told that the Germans might make a last desperate effort to win the war by unleashing poison gas similar to that used in the First War.

To guard against this risk we would be issued new lightweight gas masks and given careful instructions on their care and use.

In case our ship was torpedoed by a German submarine between New York and our still unknown destination, we were taught how to climb down a cargo net into a lifeboat and how to survive for several days on the open sea. Armed with rifles and packs, we clambered down a rope cargo net from the top of a high wall into a real lifeboat rocking on the real water of a cleverly designed "moat." Our Platoon Guide Sam D'Arpino got stuck on top of the wall and needed help in getting down. The same thing had happened at Fort Bragg when he tried to negotiate a wall barrier as part of the Expert Infantryman Badge tests.

Our final pre-overseas physical exam was conducted in a low building partitioned into an undressing room and an examination room. Several bored-looking medical officers sat waiting in the examination room as a Technician 5th Grade (T/5) medic stuck his head into the room where we were disrobing. "Take off everything but your shoes," he instructed us, "and don't forget to bring your cocks." After the laugh subsided he explained the procedure. We were to bend over and spread our gluteal cheeks in front of the examining officers, and then extend our tongues to be checked for nose and throat ailments.

"Don't the docs want us to squeeze our cocks for them, corporal?" someone asked. "You know, VD detection."

"Not today," the medic replied. "All problems not covered by the final exam should be referred either to your company medic or to the chaplain."

I was among the first to enter the examination room. The medical officers were seated on folding chairs behind card tables, as though waiting for a bridge or chess tournament to start. I bent over and conscientiously spread my cheeks as instructed.

"Straighten up, soldier!" the doctor snapped impatiently, as though I had somehow overdone the exercise. "Stick out your tongue quick and be on your way." Startled, I stuck my tongue out and in rapidly like a hissing snake and was on my way. Behind me I could see men bending over, spreading their cheeks, straightening up and sticking out their tongues in a single sweeping movement, like professional football players jogging, crouching, and jumping through a warmup drill.

"Hurry it up!" the T/5 urged. The men did their best to step up the pace, until they were literally *running* through the exam. Despite what appeared to be a doctors' conspiracy to certify everyone medically fit to face the foe, (whether they were or not), two men actually failed the exam. One stuck out his tongue and the doctor diagnosed a bad case of hemorrhoids. The other was disqualified when a fair-sized hole of undetermined origin was discovered in the back of his head. It seemed that the Army had never examined him from the rear before and the hole had passed unnoticed until he was on the verge of going overseas.[13] Captain Young explained the mail censorship procedures that would take effect immediately. "The outgoing mail will be censored by each platoon leader. On the battlefield your platoon may be isolated from the rest of the company for days at a time, so censorship at the platoon level will be the most efficient solution. Are there any questions?"

Real Parenteau, my Assistant Squad Leader, spoke up. "Sir, I got a problem." He did not elaborate, but his face was flushed and he looked angry.

"Okay, see me afterwards," Captain Young replied.

When they were alone, Captain Young asked Real Parenteau what the problem was. "I don't want Lieutenant Mueller reading my letters," Parenteau said.

"Er, why not?" the Captain asked. Captain Young was known to have a high opinion of Sergeant Parenteau, who had been in the service since 1940 and had seen combat on Guadalcanal.

"There's something about him," Real Parenteau said. "When I write to my girlfriend in Fayetteville and to my relatives down in Maine, I don't want him sticking his nose into my personal life."

"All right, Sergeant Parenteau, no problem," Captain Young said. "Would you object if I or my Exec Officer Ray Landis censor your letters?"

"No objection, sir," Real Parenteau said.

On Monday, October 2 at 0600, the Division was put on overseas alert. All passes and telephone calls were terminated. It felt as though we were all crew members of a gigantic submarine that was about to submerge beneath the sea. Then nothing happened until late Thursday afternoon, 5 October, when we were told to "saddle up." We marched to the train wearing our winter overcoats and carrying full combat equipment. After an hour on the train, we reached our destination, the Hudson River docks in Hoboken on the New Jersey side. We were told to drag our duffel bags about a quarter of a mile to the ferry slip. Since our back packs weighed seventy pounds and the average duffel bag topped one hundred pounds in weight, many of the boys were transporting weights well in excess of their own body weight. But as usually happened when the chips were down, a few grumbled but no one dropped out to my knowledge.

Along the route we passed Colonel Tychsen, who was not chomping on his long cigar but, for once, was smiling. It was obvious that he was proud of his Regiment today. Also, Hoboken had awakened old memories for him. He had been born there a short time after his parents came over from

[13]Bass, Michael A., *The Story of the Century*, 40.

Denmark. When he returned from France after the First World War, his troop ship had docked at Hoboken. Today it was Hoboken all over again, and again he was off to France. Another oddity was that Colonel Tychsen had gone over on the U.S. Army Transport (USAT) *Washington* (a confiscated German liner) in the First World War, and he had just learned today that he would be on the same ship again for this crossing.

We were all pooped by the time we reached the ferry. "Why was I so anxious to go overseas anyway?" Scotty Kyle asked, getting a laugh.

"Pinky Burress fiddled away until the candle was burned at both ends," someone said. "According to the rumor I heard, we are absolutely the last division to go overseas in the whole Army."

As was so often the case, the "last to go over" rumor was untrue. If we had had the full picture of the overseas deployment of the Army's infantry divisions, we would have been surprised. Among forty-seven divisions that were already participating or would soon become involved in the liberation of Europe, twenty-six had gone overseas before the 100th and twenty more would follow us. However, *all twenty-six* of the divisions which preceded the 100th overseas had been activated earlier than the 100th, in some cases (such as the Regular Army and National Guard divisions) several *years* earlier. Of the twenty divisions that would follow the 100th overseas, seven had been activated *before* the 100th, two others *the same day* we were activated, and only eleven after us. Thus, instead of being the Army's laughable laggards (as we had all assumed), the 100th had moved faster than most of the others through the training cycle to overseas.

The ferry ride to Manhattan took about thirty minutes. Beyond the silhouettes of a hundred helmets and clutched rifles, I saw thousands of squares of light from the windows of Manhattan's skyscrapers. The contrast between the tall modern buildings and the heavily armed soldiers on the ferry made me think of a tribe of Indians paddling across the Hudson in the darkness, ready to assault the original Dutch settlement with bows and arrows.

As we dragged our duffel bags off the ferry onto the slip, a small band greeted us with ragged peals of "Somebody Else Is Taking My Place."

"Speak for yourself, buddy," one of our group called back to the band. "Ain't nobody taking *my* place."

A long, steep, steel stairway led from the slip up to the pier where a troop transport waited in the darkness. After the long ascent, we dragged our duffel bags to the end of the pier and dumped them on the planking. Perspiration soon dried off and teeth began to chatter despite our heavy woolen overcoats. Red Cross girls in neatly tailored uniforms served hot coffee and doughnuts—the best things I had ever tasted.

As our names were called, we filed up the ship's gangplank, across the steel main deck, and down a steep stairway into the hold, which had been converted into troop sleeping quarters. Tiers of iron frames had been erected and four layers of canvas strips roped onto the frames. This filled the hold with an endless series of four-tier "bunk beds" from floor to ceiling, with narrow aisles between the tiers. I was lucky enough to draw a top bunk which allowed me to stare at the ceiling a few inches above my nose rather than at the bulge of someone else's buttocks as the other three men in my tier were fated to enjoy for the duration of the trip. The lights in the hold seemed to have been designed to illuminate Dante's Inferno on a dark night. So dim were they that I couldn't see my immediate neighbors' faces and in fact never learned who any of them were throughout the entire voyage.

Lieutenant Mueller, accompanied by Chuck Stanley and Sam D'Arpino, came down to call on his charges. Pfc. Lennie Hershberg, a New Yorker with an offbeat sense of humor, was entertaining us when Lieutenant Mueller arrived. "This boat is the U.S. Army Transport *McAndrews*," Lennie Hershberg said.

"It's a ship, not a boat," Lieutenant Mueller corrected him.

"Anyway, sir," Hershberg said, "this tub *was* a boat even though the Army may have converted it into a *ship*. Or to be more precise, it was a *banana* boat."

"Who told you *that*?" Lieutenant Mueller asked.

"My old man worked at Brooklyn Navy Yard and was assigned to work on this tub," Hershberg replied. "It's an old United Fruit Company banana boat."

"Your Dad actually worked on the *McAndrews*?" Lieutenant Mueller asked, wondering if Hershberg was just inventing a tale.

"Yes, sir," Hershberg said. "In fact, my Old Man helped build these four-layered bunk beds that everybody is griping about. He said if my outfit ended up on this tub, to tell you all he's sorry and was only following orders." Lieutenant Mueller joined in the laughter that followed.

"Where does your family live, Hershberg?" Lieutenant Mueller asked.

"601 West 184th Street," Hersh replied proudly. "It's the Washington Heights section of Manhattan."

"Did you get home on your twelve-hour pass?"

"I sure did, sir. The folks were having a visit from my Uncle Abe, who got gassed in the First World War. He later married a young floozie but let her keep her old boyfriend. He owns a bar in Pittsburgh. He told me about a hundred times to watch out for the German machine guns."

"Well, that sounds like good advice still." Lieutenant Mueller said. "Good to see you're all settling in, despite the somewhat cramped quarters. Carry on, men."

"Tench-*HUT*!" Pfc. Hershberg called out. We all stood as the young Lieutenant started up the steep stairway. Chuck Stanley winked at the boys before he and Sam D'Arpino followed.

Chapter Nine
Atlantic Crossing

When we awoke on Friday, 6 October 1944,we expected to be on the high seas. But the ship was motionless and we found ourselves still in port. Many of us went topside to have a last look at the New York skyline. After a while, an authoritative voice said over the loudspeaker, "Close all ports and hatches, fasten and secure. All troops return to your compartments," Disappointed, we descended to our quarters in the hold.

After the ship began to move, Scotty Kyle suggested we return topside. I reminded him that no one was allowed on deck.

"What are they worried about?" Scotty Kyle asked.

"My Old Man says there may be German agents with binoculars on the rooftops," Lennie Hershberg replied.

"Follow me, Red," Scotty Kyle said to me. He sprang toward the guard at the foot of the stairs and said Lieutenant Mueller had summoned the two of us topside for a special detail. The guard said nothing but let us pass. Once we reached the deck, we forgot about Lieutenant Mueller. Following Scotty Kyle's instructions, I knelt on the deck and began measuring metes and bounds with a tape measure which he took from his pocket. Scotty Kyle stood over me, hand on chin, issuing a constant stream of instructions, corrections and criticisms as I measured the imaginary distances. If asked what we were doing, we would say we were measuring off the platoon's future physical training and drill area on the deck. Scotty pasted a tiny white Band-Aid on the front of his helmet liner, which from a distance made him look like a reasonable facsimile of a first lieutenant. If confronted by an MP and charged with impersonating an officer (a serious offense), Scotty planned to eat the Band-Aid or throw it overboard as circumstances dictated. However, we were not challenged on the nearly deserted deck.

The ship moved slowly down the Hudson. Soon we were approaching the Statue of Liberty, which stood there (I imagined) like an infantry scout, hand raised high over her head in a "Follow Me" gesture. The tall green lady seemed to be leading the platoon of skyscrapers from lower Manhattan back to France where an Alsatian named Bartholdi had sculptured her in the first place. So great was her stature and beauty that for once in his life, Scotty Kyle was speechless as we watched her glide past. Our ship passed through the Verazzano Narrows and proceeded to its rendezvous point with ten other troop ships, a destroyer and four smaller destroyer escorts.

Our escort force, hulls streaked with camouflage paint, zig-zagged ahead of us and to our flanks, as a small blimp hovered overhead. In contrast to our escorts, the troop ships moved ahead slowly without evasive maneuvers.

When the troops were finally allowed to come up on deck, Scotty Kyle ripped the Band-Aid off his helmet. First to emerge from the galley-way was Pfc. Robert Escoube of Company C, who led the charge out of the hold like the New York Yankees leaving the dugout and spilling onto the playing field on Opening Day.

"How did you guys get up here before me?" Bob Escoube asked, wide-eyed.

"Special detail," Scotty Kyle replied grandly.

"I'll bet," Escoube said sourly. He made his way to the very prow of the ship and proceeded to strip off his fatigue shirt and undershirt. There he stood, chest bared to the wind.

"He can't wait to get there, can he?" I asked.

"It's jerks like him that give ASTP a bad name," Scotty Kyle said.

Only two meals were served daily, due to the logistical problems of feeding large numbers of troops in space designed for bananas rather than people. After sweating out a long line on deck, we descended steep ladder-like steps to the mess galley where food was pounded into our mess kits and our meal tickets punched as a necessary precaution against "chow hounds."

French and German classes were held on deck each morning for those who were interested. Those who went to German classes reminded us that a few words of that language (such as "Kommen Sie aus!") might come in handy in a tense combat situation. It was a hard argument to dispute, but I decided nevertheless to try to upgrade my pre-existing French rather than struggle from scratch with the arcane mysteries of the German language.

If I was happy to have drawn a top bunk, Scotty Kyle was equally pleased at drawing a bottom bunk. He described it to his folks back in Medford, Oregon,

I was lucky and got a lower bunk so I put my stuff under it (every morning I strain a ligament putting the stuff on my bunk for inspection). Within the spread of my arms are bunks for eleven men and all

their equipment. I sleep with my feet on my duffel bag, my head on my pack, my rifle as a pillow and my bayonet shoved up my back. We all walk with cricks in our backs. Yesterday, we had Southern Oregon Pears. Ah, brother, the fresh Bartlett taste reminded me of home. The dinners are ok but the breakfasts are terrible.

Lieutenant Ed Casazza, our Battalion Transportation Officer, appeared on deck one morning acting quite shaken up.

"What happened?" someone from our company asked.

"It's that Lieutenant Dave Ballie of yours," Casazza replied. "There are four of us sharing a cabin and all he talks about is how he's dying to kill Krauts. I won't shirk my duties in combat, but I'm not really looking forward to killing anybody, not even a rabbit."

Lieutenant Ballie, a cocky officer, was leader of the 3d Platoon for which Technical Sergeant Ralph Harrington served as platoon sergeant. Ballie came from Oahu, Hawaii, where he had worked on the family-owned sugar plantation before being drafted. I supposed Ballie might be riled up at the Axis powers because of what the Japs had done to Pearl Harbor. With fighting men like Lieutenant Ballie and Sergeants Harrington and Walter Bull on our side, we thought, the Germans would be in for some bad times when our outfit reached the front lines.

Gambling was forbidden, but the restriction failed to dampen the ardor of the true card players. They simply used matchsticks for currency and kept dollar bills hidden in their shoes or wool caps until the time came to settle up.

Church services were held near one card game and it was difficult to tell where the penitents ended and the poker players began in the crowded troop quarters where clusters of green bananas had hung on previous voyages.

"The Lord is my shepherd, I shall not want. . . ," the Chaplain intoned.

"Little Joe, come on boy!" one of the players cried.

"He maketh me to lie down in green pastures . . . ," the Chaplain continued.

"Come on, Poppa! Baby needs a new pair of shoes!"

Doc Emmons, the Company Barber and a member of our squad, set up his chair near the largest card game. His established tariff was twenty-five cents, but many of the boys tipped him two or even three dollars because they were big winners or simply found little else to spend their money on.

Although German subs hadn't laid a glove on us, disaster suddenly struck from a totally unexpected corner. On our sixth day out of port, we were hit by an eighty-five-mile-per-hour hurricane, described by one of the sailors as the worst storm he had seen in seventeen years at sea. All ports and hatches were sealed to prevent the angry water from pouring into the ship's innards. Deprived of fresh air, the troop quarters soon became stagnant and foul smelling. The few who were able to keep food down were conducted by interior passageways to the kitchen, where not even the most voracious chow-hounds were in evidence. Most of the men lay strapped down with ropes or belts to avoid being toppled from their bunks onto the steel floor by the ship's motion.

For the first twenty-four hours, the ship rocked groggily from side to side. Every few minutes some new sufferer joined the chorus of those heaving their guts. Men wept, groaned, and prayed loudly, without shame or embarrassment. The Convoy Captain had decided to maintain course and battle the mountainous seas. However, the first night our ship came within five degrees of capsizing, and a few hours later was almost rammed in the dark by the USAT *George Washington*, which outweighed our frail hulk 26,000 tons to 8,000. After those near calamities, the Captain changed strategy and the convoy began to run with the storm rather than fight it.

Although the Captain's new strategy eliminated the sideways rocking movement, new tensions arose as we felt the ship's prow lifting up, up, and up out of the water, with accompanying "cracking" sounds. Finally the prow came crashing back into the water and went down, down, and down beneath the surface with even worse "cracking" sounds than during the ascent. This rising and falling motion of the ship's prow repeated itself thousands of times as the terrified men strapped to their bunks listened to the cracking noises.

On the morning of the third day, the storm's force finally began to subside and the venturesome were permitted to go up on deck again. By afternoon, the sea had returned to normal. French and German classes resumed, and a movie was screened every night, including an old Glen Miller movie with that incredibly smooth music. Rip Farish, who had conducted the informal seminar on sexology for us ASTP neophytes back at Bragg, emceed a variety show on deck every evening with three singers, a small band, and other entertainers. Rip kept the Chaplain busy censoring his shows before they were staged.

We seemed to have wandered into southern waters because the breezes were mild and the starry heavens cloudless. Then one afternoon, excited voices were heard along the rail. Loud cheers went up as a low chain of pale purple peaks appeared far off to starboard. The distant land was Africa, and the way the men were whooping and clapping one another on the back, you would have thought we had discovered her. We were approximately seventy miles off Casablanca in French Morocco.

The convoy executed a slow half turn to the left and followed the coastline northward as our destroyer and destroyer escorts busily exchanged Morse signals with flashing lights. Later our destroyer screen began a right wheeling movement around a high headland and headed east toward the Straits of Gibraltar. We were passing the northwest corner of the ancient African continent. As we entered the Straits, the normally dispersed units of the convoy seemed to "inhale" toward the center. For the first time during the long voyage, our protective ships were clearly visible on the flanks, their paint-streaked hulls lightly furrowing the calm waters of the Straits. Without the gallant crews of those little ships, which had become as much part of our lives as guard dogs to a large flock of sheep, a wolf pack of U-boats might have put our ship on the bottom or left her burning hundreds of miles from the nearest land.

At twilight, schools of graceful porpoises made their appearance, as though wishing to share the honor of guiding our convoy through the Straits. In groups of five and ten, the porpoises burst up out of the water in silent, effortless arcs, reentering the deep with the same casual grace. Too soon, the ballet was over and the porpoises disappeared into their own mysterious element.

Soon we saw what looked like a large black velvet pincushion ahead, twinkling with tiny specks of light. It was the Rock of Gibraltar. As we passed directly south of the Rock, the Big Dipper loomed down like a giant steam shovel about to scoop up the historic boulder which had guarded the Old World's western portal for so many eons. Directly above the Rock, the North Star shone.

Before turning in, Scotty Kyle and I watched the dim outlines of the tiny destroyer escorts as they plunged ahead fearlessly into the black Mediterranean night.

Bing Crosby intoned "That Old Black Magic" for the two-dozenth time during the long voyage. Bing was followed by Harry James' "You Made Me Love You." Those tunes had been popular in 1942 when Scotty Kyle and I were in high school and other slightly older GIs were *here*, hitting the beach on North African shores. The songs now had a hauntingly forlorn note to them, as though recalling times and events already forgotten by most people.

Where were they now, the brave young men who had invaded North Africa in November 1942? Could they still hear those love songs, or were they dead or lying mutilated in hospitals? I wondered if their girls had waited for their return, as the Mills Brothers had asked them to do in the ballad "Till Then."

The sea was still and offered no answers.

Again Bing Crosby sang in the night,

Long ago and far away
I dreamed a dream one day,
And now that dream is here beside me;
Once the skies were overcast
But now at last
You're mine;
Chills run up and down my spine,
Aladdin's lamp was mine,
The dream I dreamed was not denied me;
Just one look and then I knew
That all I longed for long ago was you.

All the next day our convoy cruised along in the protective lee of the African coast. The city of Algiers could be seen off to the right. After dark the canopy of stars suddenly swung around the ship's rigging to starboard. We knew we were finally heading north toward the French coast. But the following morning we saw no trace of land as a nasty storm sent hundreds of men rushing to the rail after breakfast.

Friday, 20 October. Just two weeks out of New York, the coast of southern France finally came into view, a ridge of barren purple hills extending out of sight in both directions. We had imagined that the Riviera coast would be flat with sandy beaches and (we hoped) female bathers in skimpy suits. Rounding a promontory, we saw a sea of red tile rooftops shining in the sun. We had finally reached Marseilles. High above the city on a rocky hill escarpment stood the lofty basilica of Notre-Dame de la Garde.

The port facilities of Marseilles had been methodically blown up by the German occupiers before their withdrawal in August, and their remnants had been strewn all over the harbor as if by a posse of angry gods. Upside-down rusting hulls protruded from the water everywhere, systematically sunk in an effort to render the port unusable for Allied convoys. But despite all the enemy's efforts, a passageway had been opened through the cordon of sunken hulks and the battered port facilities were again operable. A screen of anti-Luftwaffe barrage balloons tied together with cables floated above the waterfront like school kids with linked hands dancing around the Maypole. The nearest German air bases were only thirty minutes away in northern Italy.

The familiar shipboard "Voice of Authority" intoned over the loud-speaker, "All troops will return to their compartments immediately and prepare for debarkation." After some incredible confusion in saddling up our packs and other equipment in the confused troop quarters, we hauled our belongings up the steep companionway to the deck. We were each issued two K rations as our meals until next day. One by one our names were called to cross the gangway.

"Gurley," First Sergeant Thomas Mulligan read from his list.

"Franklin L." I replied and headed for the narrow gangplank. Major Barney Lentz, our beloved Battalion Executive Officer, stood beside the gangplank, monitoring our passage, arms folded in his usual Roman emperor's manner.

"Buckle your chinstrap, soldier!" he said. How could I have forgotten to buckle the damn thing? But even if I had forgotten, so what? I thought we had come over here to fight Germans, not to continue Barney's "cadence marching" and other parade ground nonsense.

I had been confident that everything would be different overseas and that Barney Lentz and the others would eliminate the chickenshit, if only as a means of ensuring their own health and longevity. But the Old World so far looked pretty much like our own country, and the Major's reprimand did not sound like an auspicious beginning.

Over the gangway, I found myself crossing the hull (!) of an upended white hospital ship. From there a second gangway led into a battered wharf. After sinking the ships in the Old Port, the Germans had blasted and wrecked the jetties, piers and berth spaces, and booby-trapped the ruins.

Then down many steps, through a bombed out warehouse and out onto the street, I staggered under my horseshoe-roll pack. German and Italian prisoners of war were sweeping and stacking rubble stones under the surveillance of carbine-wielding GIs.

"All right, column of ducks and shake it up!" Lieutenant Mueller shouted. When compliance was slow, the Lieutenant raised a whistle to his lips and sounded a shrill blast. Like Barney Lentz, the Lieutenant apparently hadn't got the message yet that the enlisted men were expecting more democratic treatment overseas, if the officers hoped to preserve their own good health.

"Where'd Junior get that whistle?" someone muttered. "My name ain't Fido."

"During our march to the new staging area," Lieutenant Mueller announced, "there will be no talking with the French population. Nor will any food items be accepted from the locals or given to them. Spies will be trying to learn everything possible about us."

"I thought we liberated these folks," someone said. "Ain't they supposed to be our friends?"

"Those are our orders," the Lieutenant replied. The Battalion moved out in a seemingly endless column of twos along the rough-surfaced street beside the port. It was Act I, Scene 1 of our "Hike to the Reich," a stage production with a cast of thousands being put on in the European Theater of Operations under General Eisenhower.

We passed clusters of troops from many nations standing in groups or reclining along the roadside. There were black colonial troops from Senegal wearing tall red fezzes, dusky-skinned Moroccans called "Goums," and bearded Gurkhas from India wearing turbans. There were also lean, tanned GIs still wearing summer uniforms, who had parachuted into the country during Operation DRAGOON, the August invasion of the Riviera. They were waiting to board the ships we from which we had just debarked.

Our route of march led us out of the waterfront district and upward through the city streets toward the range of purple hills that dominated the city. Charcoal-burning trucks and ancient autos chugged and coughed their way up steep cobblestone streets, pursued by bell-clanging, triple-unit trolleys loaded to overflowing with civilians and soldiery. Children flitted about the feet of our marching columns. "*Cigarette pour papa?! Chocolat pour mamma?!* Hey, Joe, you got any chung-gum?" Robert E. Jones from my squad reached inside his BAR ammunition belt and produced some chocolate bars and chewing gum for the children.

"Hold it, Jones!" Lieutenant Mueller called.

"What's up?" Jones asked.

"Giving things to people is forbidden," the Lieutenant said.

"Hell, these ain't people, these are kids," Jones snorted, but put the gifts back in his ammo belt.

Short-skirted girls demurely observed our passage and the general populace along the road was warm and receptive. Many held out flowers, grapes, tomatoes, and bottles of wine to our still untested foot-sloggers. Lieutenant Mueller seemed as busy as a hockey goalie as he scooted about attempting to block these manifestations of welcome.

"Lieutenant, these folks act real glad to be liberated," someone in the column said. "They're just trying to say thanks."

"Nobody asked you," the Lieutenant said firmly.

The men began to complain of sore feet and overheating as they marched uphill through the sunny afternoon air under the seventy-pound weight of their horseshoe-roll packs.

"I been on that damn ship fifteen days," Robert E. Jones said, "and I ain't got my land legs back yet."

"Keep plugging," Sergeant Gardner said. "Maybe Red Gurley can spell you on the BAR a while."

"Sure," I said.

"Here, let me do it," said Ernie Emmons, Jones' regular assistant.

"No, that's okay," I said, slipping the BAR sling from Jones' broad right shoulder and handing him my M-1 rifle in exchange.

"Thanks, man," Jones drawled. "Now mebbe ah kin look at these French broads without raising my blood pressure and having me a stroke."

"I thought you was married," Ernie Emmons said, eyes blinking mischievously.

"Never said I wasn't," Jones replied.

"How about you, Hershberg?" Lieutenant Mueller said. "Would you like Hogberg to spell you on the BAR?"

"Naaaah," Lennie Hershberg said, laughing. "Hoggie's got bad feet already and will need somebody to carry *him.*"

"That's no lie," Hoggie Hogberg replied. He was limping already and the march had practically just begun. "When do we take a chow break?" Hoggie asked rhetorically, licking his lips.

Despite the instructions about not accepting gifts or communicating with the French, we could sense that we were being treated like VIPs as the people along the road waved and cheered us. If the Camp Kilmer cadres had treated us like princes, the Marseilleans were treating us like kings. These French civilians seemed even more appreciative than our own people back home, many of whom considered the war to be practically won already.

"Take ten, men!" Captain Young called.

Our Assistant Squad Leader, Real Parenteau, wandered into a walled courtyard looking for a drink of water. There an attractive young French woman was delighted to discover that Parenteau spoke French. She had one *"petit"* at her feet and another "on the way." I heard her telling Parenteau that her husband was with General Leclerc's French 2d Armored Division. She disappeared into the house and moments later reappeared with a wine bottle and several small glasses. Members of our squad clustered joyfully around our French-speaking NCO and we were soon clinking glasses. After the long hot march, the wine quickly created a collective mood of euphoria. Just then a whistle blew and Lieutenant Mueller came striding into the courtyard clutching his carbine sling, a grim expression on his face.

"Sergeant Parenteau, you know there is to be no communication with the French population or receiving gifts from them. You are setting a bad example for your men. Get back out on the road immediately."

Real Parenteau's cheeks turned red and his eyes flashed defiance. After several moments of unresolved tension, he shrugged his shoulders and turned away. We glumly followed him out of the courtyard and back onto the road.

The road left the Marseilles suburbs behind and entered farm country. The road was bounded by stone fences and rows of wispy poplars that stood like tall question marks in the twilight. The column moved ever more slowly as soldiers limped, perspired, grumbled, cursed softly, or said nothing.

Pfc. Jack Ogden, the company Mail Clerk, collapsed quietly on the road as though he had been hit by a sniper. He was picked up by a truck put into service to transport those unable to move under their own power.

Farmers in blue denim clothing came forward in the gathering darkness to offer small tomatoes and large bunches of grapes to the marchers. Because of the limited visibility, Lieutenant Mueller was forced to give up trying to block all gifts. Thus we enjoyed the finest grapes from France's vineyards, whose reputation remained intact despite the German conquest of France.

After darkness fell, we heard a faint motor noise in the sky overhead. Captain Young said we were under surveillance by a German reconnaissance plane better known as "Bedcheck Charley." Ground searchlights fingered the dark clouds overhead and we could hear friendly "ack-ack" (anti-aircraft) guns opening up.

"Talking to the local people is the quickest way to let the enemy know where we are," Lieutenant Mueller said, making plain that he felt vindicated by Bedcheck Charley's visit.

Bedcheck Charley's motor sound soon faded from the sky, but a few minutes later a stronger motor was heard, followed by the sound of explosions down the road behind us. Again our "ack-ack" guns were heard, sounding more determined than before. Word traveled along the column that Company D behind us had been the victims the enemy's first air attack on our newly debarked division.

Finally, after eleven or twelve miles of marching, the column was led off the road into a meadow near the village of Septêmes. We bedded down on the ground and were soon asleep.

While the infantry battalions were making the long trek from the port up into the hills that Friday afternoon, General Burress called together his principal officers at Marseilles' Grand Hotel. "Welcome to France, gentlemen," he said with a friendly twinkle. Then he became all business. "The front lines are beyond the Moselle River in the foothills of the Vosges Mountains. Our advance has slowed to a snail's pace. This has its good side in giving us what is called an old lady's sector of the front while our boys get used to the weather and the feel of combat. General Truscott plans to work our regiments in one at a time between his veteran divisions. This will allow our boys to break in alongside units who know all the enemy's tricks."

The divisional staff officers and senior commanders listened with attention. Apart from Bill Miller and Andy Tychsen, none of them had even been old enough to be in the Army during the First World War. "The big problem now," General Burress told his officers, "is removing the cosmoline from your jeeps and trucks and reassembling them for a rapid move of about 450 miles to the front. What do you say to that, gentlemen? How long will it take you?"

"We lack the necessary know-how, sir," said Colonel William Ellis, Commander of the 397th Infantry Regiment. "That's a specialized task for Ordnance."

"I expected a better answer than that from a VMI prof, Bill," General Burress told Ellis, whom he had brought to VMI to teach military science when Burress was serving as Commandant of Cadets there.

"Sorry, sir," Colonel Ellis said with a smile.

"What about you, Nelson?" General Burress asked Colonel Fooks, 398th Regimental CO. Fooks had been a Tactical Officer at West Point, where the cadets had called him (behind his back) "Foggy" Fooks.

"Same problem as Bill Ellis," Colonel Fooks replied. "No trained specialists available."

"Are you in the same boat they are, Chris?" General Burress asked Colonel Tychsen (whose middle name was Christian).

"No, sir!" Colonel Tychsen replied briskly. "My officers and men volunteered to go to a special school in the States to learn vehicular assembly and disassembly. We can do the job, and quickly."

"Good!" General Burress said. Bill Ellis and Nelson Fooks appeared startled. "Weren't you in the Vosges sector in the First War, Chris?" General Burress asked, knowing very well what Tychsen's answer would be.

"I commanded a machine-gun company there in the 88th Division," Colonel Tychsen replied with pride.

"All right, Chris. As soon as you get your vehicles in shape, your regiment will depart for the front. Yours will be the first regiment to meet the enemy."

"I'm looking forward to this," Colonel Tychsen responded. "I asked for a combat assignment nearly three years ago."

"I remember," General Burress said. "One more point. I want all ammo trucks to carry double the prescribed quantity of ammunition."

"But, sir," Tychsen said, "that's far in excess of the limits we were taught to adhere to in training."

"Don't worry, I can assure you the trucks will handle the increased weight easily," General Burress said firmly. "Besides, this is war and we've got to get on with it."

The General's tone of voice made clear that there would be no further debate on that issue. "One disquieting bit of information I just heard," General Burress went on. "The French dock workers won't unload our equipment from the ships during the weekend, and they may go on strike Monday."

"*On strike?*" Colonel Ellis asked. "Don't they know there's a war on?"

"Maybe they think it's over," General Burress replied. "Anyway, if they don't come to work on Monday I want all three regiments to send contingents down to that waterfront, and keep them there till every last jeep and truck are off those ships." Everyone nodded in agreement.

General Burress' aide came into the meeting and whispered something to him.

"Well, ah'll be dayamed!" General Burress exclaimed in his best Richmond drawl. "Gentlemen, we've been mentioned on the radio by the enemy, in fact by no less a luminary than Axis Sally. She welcomes the 100th Infantry Division to the European Theater and promises us a hot reception up at the Belfort Gap in the Vosges Mountains!"

There was a buzzing among the officers. General Burress went on. "Do you know what Axis Sally said next? Get this. She said she was gonna play 'General Burress' favorite song' on the radio."

"What was the song?" someone asked.

"There'll be Some Changes Made!" General Burress said, rolling his eyes and exploding with laughter. . . .[14]

---

[14]Tychsen interview.

Chapter Ten
Marseilles: Delta Base Staging Area

The next morning (Saturday, 21 October) I was awakened by a steady trickle of water down my nose. I had been aware of the dampness for hours, but was too tired to wake up and investigate the cause. It had been raining most of the night, and our equipment was soaking wet. We salvaged some matches and built a fire. Drying out our shelter halves over the flames, Scotty Kyle and I finally pitched our pup tent as we should have done upon arrival the night before.

Unlike us, Captain Young had instructed his command party to pitch tents. However, they had pitched them in a small gully. At dawn, the captain and his CP group were under canvas all right, but they were also sloshing around in one to four inches of water from the natural drainage through their gully. The captain's loud bellowing, as he stood up and shook himself like a wet St. Bernard, informed the entire Regiment of what had happened.

Scotty Kyle and I bartered a Baby Ruth bar for a raincoat full of straw from a local farmer. We used the straw to make a floor for our "pup tent." In fact, we did such a thorough job that our Squad Leader Jim Gardner told us to police up our excess straw that littered the area.

"What do youse boids think this is, Barnum and Bailey's Soicus?" Sergeant Gardner croaked. People unfamiliar with Bronxese might not have recognized "Soicus," but he meant the traveling animal and trapeze artist show.

We had eaten both packages of K rations that had been issued at debarkation, and were now given several cans of C rations. The C rations had two basic meals—corned beef hash or meat and vegetable stew, with a second can containing crackers, sugar, and beverage powder.

"By tomorrow the kitchen should be set up," Sergeant Gardner told us. "Meanwhile, we'll get used to the stuff we'll be eating in combat." We all set to work opening the C ration cans, like kids with a prize. "The Army has just invented an instant coffee powder called Nescafé," Jim Gardner said. "You just heat up water and drop in the powder. The Army wants to know what you think of it. So let me know after you've tried it." It struck me that this was the first time Jim Gardner had ever asked our opinion on any subject. His message in the States had been, "You boids ain't getting paid to think."

Volunteers were asked to go to a town called St. Louis to pick up the company's duffel bags. Although we had all learned you should never volunteer in the Army, a place called St. Louis sounded a lot more intriguing than being stuck in the mud of our meadow. I joined Scotty Kyle and several others on the ride over to St. Louis in a truck and brought it back loaded with duffel bags. While picking the bags up at the warehouse, we also managed to filch a supply of candles, which would come in handy to be able to when trying to write letters at night in our pup tents.

While we were off in St. Louis, Jim Gardner and Real Parenteau went to the local bistro in Septêmes. It was Saturday and that evening the proprietor loaned Real Parenteau his fiddle. Parenteau soon became the center of attention as he reeled off one old Canadian ballad after another. They returned to camp in the early hours, a bit the worse for wear. When Sunday's dawn graced our damp meadow, we could hear them stirring about and arguing inside their little pup tent.

Lieutenant Mueller happened to be passing their tent at the precise moment when Real Parenteau emerged, eyes bloodshot and hair tousled. "Hey, Junior!" Real Parenteau called, seeking to steady himself on his pins after many hours under canvas. "Hey, Lew-ten-ANNNT!" he called again. "What's the big rush anyway? C'mere a minute."

"I'm in a hurry, Sergeant," Lieutenant Mueller said, pausing to give the disheveled French-Canadian a disapproving look.

"Oh no, you ain't in no hurry, SIR," Real Parenteau persisted.

"Hey, Real, come back here!" Jim Gardner croaked, his grandmotherly Gallic face thrusting itself through the flap of the pup tent.

"At ease, Sergeant Gardner!" Real Parenteau said. He reshuffled his legs and established a precarious equilibrium. He began waving his arms about like the blades of a helicopter.

"Now, Lew-TEN-ant, the question is, why do the men call you Junior or Dagwood the minute your back is turned? I thought you and me should discuss this matter in the best interest of the platoon . . ."

"You're in no condition to discuss anything, Sergeant Parenteau," Lieutenant Mueller said. "Get back in your tent."

"Yeah, c'mere," Jim Gardner coaxed from the tent flap. Our pup tents were pitched so close together that most of us were able to hear every word of this incredible exchange. We couldn't believe our ears at Sergeant Parenteau's drunken challenge of the Lieutenant's authority. If this kind of thing continued in combat, which man should we obey, our Lieutenant or our Assistant Squad Leader?

"You know where we are now, sir?" Real went on. "We're *overseas*. You start treating my boys like men, and you and me is gonna get along just fine, I guarantee you that! Ask your Sergeants—we'll all be glad to help you."

"Sergeant Parenteau . . ." Lieutenant Mueller said. Parenteau ignored him and went on. "From here out, you be a good boy and don't go issuing any orders you don't really mean. Like yesterday coming up the road when that lady slipped me and the boys a little wine. Anybody who tells me I ain't gonna talk to the French people is gonna get his ass in a sling so far as getting along with me goes. I ain't no angel myself, understand, but I was at Guadalcanal and I been in a the Army a few years and I seen certain things."

At this point Jim Gardner crawled out of the tent and dragged Real Parenteau off to the water point, where we could see Parenteau getting a good dousing. Lieutenant Mueller disappeared without further comment to anyone.

Mass was announced for 1000 hours and I went off in the rain with Private Eddie Cook, Lieutenant Mueller's radio man and runner. Chaplain Thaddeus Koszarek had set up a portable altar just inside the doors of a low stable. It looked like old Bethlehem, complete with a donkey swishing his tail in the background. After mass, Eddie Cook and I were picked out by First Lieutenant White, one of Captain Young's two Executive Officers at the moment, for a detail hauling belts of machine-gun ammo. "Did you hear about Parenteau's run-in with the Lieutenant?" I asked Eddie Cook.

"How could I miss it?" Cook said in his Sedalia, Missouri drawl. "You could hear it halfway to Marseilles."

"You must know the Lieutenant pretty well," I said. "Do you think he'll try to get Parenteau punished?"

"I doubt it," Cook said. "Mueller knows Parenteau is well regarded by Captain Young on account of his Guadalcanal experience."

Like Lieutenant Mueller, Lieutenant White had joined the company only a few weeks before leaving Fort Bragg. He was a good-looking man of medium height and dark hair, but was acting irascibly this morning. He tried opening the cases of machine-gun ammo by hacking at the steel bands with an ax. When this didn't work, his solution was to issue a stream of expletives. In the middle of one of these colorful operatic solos, along came Father Koszarek, the Chaplain. He took the ax out of Lieutenant White's hand and showed him how to pry open the steel bands from underneath. Then he handed the ax back to Lieutenant White without a word and went on his way. Lieutenant White scratched his head and acted more irascibly than ever, but he had at least learned to do the task at hand.

Monday morning a training schedule was set up to get us back in physical shape after the long idleness of the sea voyage. Captain Young said it was important to be in top shape for what he ominously called "coming things." We fired our weapons at targets at a hastily improvised rifle range, loosened up tight muscles with intensive sessions of calisthenics, and conducted close order drill to sharpen our reflexes and restore unit cohesion.

That same day, the Division was visited by Lieutenant General Jacob L. Devers, the Sixth Army Group Commander, responsible to General Eisenhower for the U.S. Seventh Army and the French First Army. He rode past in a jeep with Pinky Burress beside him and Chris Tychsen in the front seat. General Devers had a ready smile and looked as though he had eaten lots of Wheaties, "Breakfast of Champions."

Scotty Kyle and I wrote letters home that night by the illumination of our pilfered candles. Scotty wrote to his folks,

> *Somewhere in France*
> *October 23, 1944*
> *We are not allowed to criticize our allies (French) in our letters, therefore I leave much unsaid. We disembarked in the afternoon and woke up next morning in the rain. For one day we lived in a sea of World War I sticky French mud. Today it is starting to dry out and all is nice and sunny. Red Gurley and I are pup-tenting together.*

The next morning, Tuesday, 24 October, half of the Company went to Marseilles to unload ships while the other half continued to train. The French dock workers had made good on their threat to strike. Captain Young led us on a march which he claimed was a "four-mile stroll," but it felt more like seven or eight by the time we came limping back to camp.

"The 36th Infantry Division hasn't had a day off the line since the Riviera invasion." Captain Young told us. "They're up near the Belfort Gap now, still wearing summer uniforms and with only one blanket per man."

My heart went out to those 36th boys and I was anxious to be on our way to their relief. Most of us were looking forward to combat, at least a month or two of it to test what we had learned. We were trained for it, we were needed, and besides, how many generations of Americans had an opportunity to fight in a famous war and go down in the history books?

The boys who went to Marseilles to unload the ships reported that the striking French workers claimed they couldn't live on the $42 per week they were earning ($7 per day for a six day week).

"Let's see," said Scotty Kyle, whose calculating ability may have come from his Scottish blood. "$42 a week is about $175 per month. That's three times my $64.80, which includes $50 base pay, $10 for being overseas, and $4.80 for being Pfc."

"Sure, but you're getting free food and housing," someone said.

"K rations and a pup tent?" Scotty Kyle said. "Those must be worth at least 50 cents a month."

While unloading the ships, our boys had taken a razzing from German prisoners who were sitting around doing next to nothing while waiting for the ships to be ready for *them* to sail royally off to some POW camp in the U.S. South.

Scotty Kyle and I waited patiently until Wednesday for passes to be issued so we could visit Marseilles. We decided that unless passes materialized by the next morning, we would take matters into our own hands. We had to plot our escape from camp carefully. The normal rule, unless instructed to the contrary, was that we would fall out in the morning in whatever the previous day's uniform had been. Luckily, yesterday's uniform had been olive drabs, perfect for visiting a city. (If we had set out for the city wearing green work fatigues, it would have branded us unmistakably as AWOL).

In the Thursday morning chow line, Kyle and I were indistinguishable from the other men who were also wearing ODs. As soon as breakfast was over, we would depart. But before morning chow was over, First Sergeant Mulligan announced that we would change to fatigues for PT immediately after breakfast. Kyle and I couldn't walk around Marseilles in fatigues without being picked up by the MPs, so it was now or never to make a break while we still had on our ODs.

Sergeant Gardner was only feet away from our pup tent, shouting to our squad to "fall out in fatigues, rifles, belts, and helmets and make it snappy." While his back was turned momentarily, we crawled out the back of our tent and headed for the Company CP. Dropping some letters in the mailbox, we said "Good morning!" to First Sergeant Mulligan and slithered out the other end of the large pyramidal tent before anyone knew what we were up to.

We reached the Marseilles highway without detection. Two lieutenants from a local medical unit gave us a lift to the outskirts of Marseilles sixteen kilometers away. We proceeded to explore the city, ogling girls, clinging to the outside of the blue streetcars, and buying perfume for the women back home (in my case, my mother). Senegalese soldiers playfully stood in the path of the onrushing streetcars until the very last moment, when they leaped aside to escape death by an inch or two. At the outdoor market, we bought bread and grapes and drank wine from paper cups on a park bench.

In the early afternoon, we suddenly came upon most of the non-coms of our platoon and a few of their Pfcs standing in a cluster like grapes and gaping at us as though we were a mirage or odd specimens in a zoo. Chuck Stanley and Sam D'Arpino were there as well as Jim Gardner and Real Parenteau from our squad and Jim Amoroso, Carlos Daledovich, and Leonard Hershberg from the 1st Squad. I forget who else was there.

"Hey, youse boids missed PT and Close Order Drill!" Sergeant Gardner shouted.

"Yeah, we were sorry to miss it," Kyle called back, as though those unspeakably boring pursuits had been a tempting social engagement we simply had been forced to cancel at the last moment.

"Do youse boids realize you're AWOL?" Sergeant Gardner shouted, his grandmotherly face turning beet red.

"They're too damn big for their britches!" chimed in Sergeant Parenteau, that staunch defender of military order and discipline (as Lieutenant Mueller would certainly attest after their Sunday morning run-in.).

We said nothing and our silence apparently riled up Sergeant Gardner even more. "Youse two boids know you can be *court-martialed!*" he exploded.

"Go ahead," I called back. "We'll miss combat."

Now it was the non-coms' turn to be silent. We could see them whispering among themselves. They had had no trouble getting a pass to see Marseilles, but what would Scotty's and my chances have been as buck privates if we had patiently waited our turn? Some of the boys who were behaving themselves back at camp right this minute might not be alive to see Marseilles later. After all, our employer was the U.S. Army Infantry, not Thomas Cook's Travel Service.

"Listen, boys," Chuck Stanley said. "There's a big square two blocks down that way. There will be trucks waiting there all afternoon. Be sure you're on one of them."

"Yes, Sergeant!" Kyle and I said in unison and departed before sterner measures could be decreed. Sergeant Stanley hadn't said when to catch the trucks, so we continued our Marseilles tour. We climbed a long flight of steps to the Basilica of Notre-Dame de la Garde overlooking the Old Port. The parapets around the church's exterior had served the Germans as machine-gun nests during the Riviera fighting last summer. Mazes of barbed wire were still in evidence and shell holes and bullet pockmarks were everywhere. I bought a blue rosary for my mother from some nuns at a souvenir stand. Inside the church were paintings of sailors in stormy seas, with the Madonna's face looking down from the sky overhead and preserving them from the raging elements.

Afterwards, we found the trucks and rode back to our Septêmes encampment in style. As punishment for our AWOL caper, Scotty Kyle and I were put on "all night guard" at the company water point for an indefinite period. However, we arranged with the cooks to wake us up at 0500 when they arose, since no one in authority was awake to see what we were doing before then. So as a practical matter we missed only about two hours of sleep before the rest of the company crawled out of their pup tents at 0700.

Our water point duty came to an end, Saturday morning, 28 October, eight days after debarkation. The 399th's vehicles were now all unloaded and their cosmoline removed by Colonel Tychsen's trained volunteers. We were told we would leave for the front before dawn the next day. In his final letter from southern France, Scotty Kyle wrote,

> *I talked to a German civilian prisoner. He wants the Americans to get to Berlin before the Russians. He said, "You are getting ready for the last round, aren't you?" meaning Germany couldn't win now. Word may come from me seldom from here on, but have faith. I'll be okay. I did it before and I'll do it again.*

Chapter Eleven
Moving Up

Colonel Tychsen stood beside the road in the early morning half-light, waving to each departing truck as we left the staging area for the front. "Old Spit and Polish" seemed to take an almost paternal interest in what we were doing this morning, Sunday, 29 October. The other regiments would follow as they could, but many would have to be transported by slow old fashioned "40 and 8" troop trains dating back to the First World War.

The truck and jeep convoy rolled due north to the provincial city of Aix-en-Provence. There we turned west toward Avignon in the Rhône River Valley. It was very cold in the trucks, especially for the "air guards," the men detailed to stand up in the wind behind the truck cab holding the cold stock of a BAR as they scanned the sky for German fighter planes.

There were seats for eighteen men and "standing room only" for seven more, who squatted against the tailgate or stood clinging to the wooden bows which looped over the open trucks at regular intervals. Lieutenant Mueller, clutching his carbine like a conductor's baton, sat in the cab with the driver. Many of the drivers belonged to the 36th or 45th Infantry Divisions, and were on special duty to bring the neophytes of the 100th Infantry Division to the front.

In the first stage of the trip, there was constant jockeying for one of the eighteen seats. But by mid-morning the situation changed and all twenty-five of us wanted to stand. The reason for the reversed priorities was the unexpected discovery of French women along the route.

We were amazed at the warmth of the welcome as we rolled through France. The people of Marseilles had been nice enough, but still had not prepared us for today's reception. In every crossroad, hamlet, village, town, and city we rolled through, the entire populace seemed to be either in the streets, on the front steps, or leaning out of tricolor-draped windows, screaming their joy and throwing flowers and kisses. As we entered each town, solid walls of noise exploded on both sides as the French people gave vent to their feelings of joy and gratitude at being liberated after years of occupation and repression. Most streets were quite narrow, and the shops and apartments above them bordered directly on the street. By leaning over the sides of the truck, we were scarcely at arm's length from a host of animated faces, red lips, and flailing arms.

We developed a routine that seemed to make a hit with the French. We would point to Eddie Cook, who looked about fifteen or sixteen years old (actually he was a few weeks short of nineteen) and cry, "*Il est petit garçon*" or "*Il est bébé!*" The French girls in the windows seemed to understand it as a joke and they laughed and clapped their hands. Several raised a friendly eyebrow as though they would have liked to hear more about the good looking youth from Sedalia, Missouri, who was Lieutenant Mueller's runner and radio man.

At the ancient papal city of Avignon, our convoy turned north on National Route 7 along the Rhône's east bank. Between Orange and Montélimar, evidence of the late August fighting was everywhere. Mangled German tanks, half-tracks, trucks, mobile artillery pieces, flak wagons, and even entire wrecked trains were strewn across the valley. In what resembled an open air military museum, we saw several American and German tanks that had dueled to their mutual destruction in a large open gully. A row of burned-out German tanks lined the north side of the gully, facing a semi-circle of seven or eight equally dead U.S. Sherman tanks. The German tanks were streaked with camouflage paint and had long cannons like vipers' necks. The U.S. Sherman tanks were painted a dull green with small white stars on the sides. The opposing rows of rusting armor made one think of two species of prehistoric dinosaurs which had destroyed each other millions of years ago in a fateful, final confrontation.

We stopped for the night in a bivouac area a few kilometers south of Valence. Colonel Tychsen and his regimental staff spent the night at Valence's cavalry school, which had seen its last horses long ago. A small caretaker detachment of aging "*anciens combattants*" (old fighters) from the First World War looked after the 399th men's needs. Colonel Tychsen instructed his staff to treat the old veterans with the courtesy and respect they merited.

"The GI bastards will probably make us pitch pup tents," Scotty Kyle said. He proposed we simply spread out our shelter halves and blankets on the ground, as we had done with such disastrous results the first night at Marseilles. But this time there seemed no threat of rain whatever, so I agreed to Scotty's proposal. To our surprise Lieutenant Mueller said we could "pitch tents or don't pitch tents, as you wish." Scotty Kyle and I talked it over once more, weighing the pros and cons (tent gives better protection against wind, unexpected rain, etc.) and finally got out the tent pole, pegs, and shelter halves and set up our pup tent, feeling slightly like fools.

Lieutenant Mueller said no one was to leave the bivouac area except those Catholics who wished to attend Sunday evening mass in the village a few hundred yards down the road. Shortly before the 1900 Mass time, the men of Company A left the bivouac area virtually *en masse*, bound ostensibly for the local church. The guards stared as the "Catholic" horde strolled past their guard post at the edge of the camp.

Conducting the mass was our Polish-American padre, Captain Thaddeus Koszarek, who had shown Lieutenant White how to open ammunition crates the previous Sunday near Marseilles. The Germans had positioned some antitank guns inside the church, and they had fired through the windows. Two wrecked Sherman tanks stood in the church yard in tribute to the good aim of the German gunners. The American tanks had then apparently blown out most of the church's interior in rooting out the German crews.

The next morning our route took us through Lyon, where the Rhône River left us as it swung eastward toward Switzerland. We then followed the Saône River north to Chalons, Beaune, and Dijon, and spent the night within Dijon's vast city park.

Scotty Kyle and I took a walk along the street bounding the park before turning in. We came to a large ornate iron gate where guards were posted.

"Who goes there?" a voice called out.

"We're A Company," I said. "Just out taking a stroll."

The guard told us that behind the large iron gate was the *Collège des Jeunes Filles* (Girls' High School).

He said, "When Colonel Tychsen drove up to this gate this afternoon, he remembered passing this same gate in 1918, riding a horse."

Scotty Kyle snorted. "Then it's time they took down the sign 'Wanted for statutory rape, American officer riding a horse with a rod on'."

"Who had the rod, the nag or the Colonel?" the guard said, lowering his voice to avoid a sudden transfer to the stockade.

"The horse, of course," Scotty Kyle said.

The guard laughed and opened the gate. "I'll show you a shortcut back to your company area."

"Thanks," we said.

On the third day we crossed the Moselle River at Epinal and continued northeastward. In the late afternoon our journey finally ended in gently rolling terrain where open fields and meadows alternated with patches of woods. Lieutenant Mueller said we had covered over 450 miles in three days. There had been sunshine throughout the trip, but the ground here was wet as though it had rained recently. Clambering stiffly out of the trucks, we followed the lieutenant down a path into a wood. C rations were distributed and we sat on our packs munching corned beef hash and crackers like picnickers.

Around us under the trees we found old German foxholes, funny-looking German helmets, potato masher grenades and empty ammunition canisters. Although the sun was still shining outside the wood, it was already becoming dark inside where we were. The enemy foxholes had an unhealthy aspect as though they might contain snakes or worse. For the first time since coming overseas, no one among the ordinarily curious GIs was interested in taking a stroll.

We pitched our pup tents and were soon asleep. I was awakened by a series of loud explosions. *"Whoom-whoom!! Whoom-whoom-whoom-whoom!!!!"* Huge daylight-restoring flashes of light flared up nearby, followed by thundering crashes of what sounded like heavy artillery. By some miracle I was still alive. Taking a rapid inventory of arms, legs, etc., I raised the tent flap and peeked cautiously outside. Just then something hurtled past me from inside the tent at only slightly less than the speed of sound. Then I heard the crashing of underbrush and a loud splashing sound, followed by complete silence. Scotty Kyle had apparently jumped or fallen into one of the old German foxholes.

All around me arose a great clamor and clattering of shovels and picks hacking and clawing at the earth. Large-bored guns hammered out a mighty concert punctuated by great weird flashes of light which shredded the illusion of night. After a while, I reasoned it out that the artillery must be our own, since nothing was actually striking near us. Scotty Kyle crawled up out of the German foxhole, which he had fallen into without realizing there were several inches of water in the bottom.

Captain Young confirmed next morning that the nocturnal roars and flashes had been from the field artillery of the 45th Infantry Division. He said our company had lost one of its squad leaders -during the night, when Sergeant Lollander's rifle discharged in the darkness and put a bullet through his foot. "He was an ideal soldier in garrison," The captain said somberly, adding "I wonder what actually happened?"

The captain informed us that we could expect to stay where we were for about three days. He said today was 1 November and we might get paid soon ("the eagle will scream tomorrow" was how he put it). He added that we would be paid in French francs.

Scotty Kyle and I rounded up Eddie Cook, Herb Rice, and Ray Sholes (all five ASTPers) and took off across a long open meadow leading down to a stream. There we had our first good wash-up since Camp Kilmer. We watched a quartet of P-51 Mustang fighters scoot past overhead, giving us a wonderful feeling of security. But then they were suddenly chased off by an equal number of dark-winged planes, and we felt less secure.

Colonel Tychsen reported to the CG (Commanding General) of the 45th Infantry Division, who turned out to be Major General W. W. "Bertie" Eagles, an old friend and classmate of Tychsen at the Command and General Staff School at Fort Leavenworth. General Eagles said Tychsen's regiment would go on the line in a few days, relieving a regiment of the 45th that was understrength and in need of rest and refurbishing. Our regiment would be under General Eagles' direction temporarily until further notice.

"Sandy Patch at Seventh Army and the new VI Corps Commander, Ted Brooks, have asked that our Divisions work together closely at all levels to help your Regiment adapt rapidly to combat conditions," Eagles told Tychsen. "In practical terms, this means our officers and men will give aid and advice to yours in matters of bivouac, assembly areas, available cover and shelter, routes of advance, enemy order of battle, intelligence, and standing operating procedures in the Corps."

"Fine," Colonel Tychsen said.

A moment later, General Eagles was called to the telephone. When he put down the receiver, he said to Colonel Tychsen, "Bingo! That was Ted Brooks' Operations Officer. Plans have changed, Andy. Brooks wants your regiment in the fray at the earliest possible moment. You will go up tonight to relieve Colonel Jack O'Brien's 179th Infantry Regiment sooner than we had anticipated."[15]

"I know O'Brien from Jefferson Barracks days!" Tychsen said.

"Good," General Eagles said. "I'll ask Jack to leave his regiment with yours for a few hours before pulling back. That way his boys can shoot the bull with yours and hopefully answer some of their questions about front line conditions."

"Much obliged," Colonel Tychsen said. "I certainly appreciate all your helpful advice, Bertie," Colonel Tychsen said as they shook hands.[16]

"Say, listen!" Eddie Cook said. We heard what sounded like Sergeant Gardner's voice calling from far away.

[15]Ibid.
[16]Ibid.

"Come on, youse boids, hurry it up!" We ran across the meadow toward the wood. "The company's pulling out!" Jim Gardner screamed. "Why don't you *tell* somebody when you take off like that?"

"Captain Young said we were staying here three days," Scotty Kyle replied.

"Ah shaddup!" Gardner said.

Captain Young was waiting in a clearing as the company assembled. It was late afternoon and the fragile autumn light was already starting to fade. "Men," Captain Young said, "orders have been changed. We're going up tonight to relieve the 179th Infantry Regiment, 45thDivision. I want to share a few thoughts. I know we're ready for what lies ahead, in terms of training and leadership at all levels. I also know each of you will give a good account of yourself. My personal goal in combat is to go all the way through to the end without losing a single man." No one's attention wandered. You could have heard a pine needle drop in that forest clearing as we listened to our oversized captain. Knute Rockne or Frank Leahy might fire up a Notre Dame team to win a big football game. But the stakes were much greater today and those mythical giants were not in the same league with Captain Young's address to our green infantry company about to move into line.

"The key to success in combat is the ability to work together," Captain Young said. "Do you remember the story about, "For want of a nail, the shoe was lost; for want of a shoe, the horse was lost; for want of a horse, the rider was lost; and for want of a rider, the battle was lost?" It's going to be like that in combat. A chain is no stronger than its weakest link. We're all going to depend on one another, and we can't afford any weak links."

Captain Young announced that the platoon leaders would conduct their own briefings while awaiting the signal to move up. Our platoon moved off to another part of the clearing for our last minute instructions. Lieutenant Mueller looked fit, even eager, for the big challenge that awaited us. "I have nothing special to add to Captain Young's comments," Lieutenant Mueller said. "Instead, I'd rather you heard some words of advice from the NCOs. Sergeant Stanley, would you like to say something?"

All eyes turned to the platoon Sergeant. "No, sir," Chuck Stanley grunted. "Nothing in particular for the time being."

"How about you, Sergeant D'Arpino?" Lieutenant Mueller asked, "Could you comment on the kind of fighting we might expect?"

"Very well, sir," said Sam D'Arpino, rarely at a loss for words, even in the cannon's mouth. "First, I'd like simply to remind the men of my two principal responsibilities or functions as Platoon Guide. First, I'm responsible for seeing that the platoon has sufficient ammunition at all times to enable it to carry out its assigned missions. Second, I am responsible for assuring that there are no stragglers, which means men who either hang back or try to go back when faced with enemy fire." After pausing to let his last message sink in, Sam D'Arpino continued, "A word on the type of fighting we might expect. Some days you'll be firing all day from your foxhole, whereas other days you will probably fire your rifle only an hour or so."

Sam D'Arpino's description sounded to me like the usual theoretical picture of the front lines—Americans and Germans holed up in opposing rows of foxholes three or four hundred yards apart, potting away at each other with small arms fire. I didn't know what it would actually be like either, but I was skeptical about Sam D'Arpino's version. I would have amended his statement to say, "Most days you won't have to fire your rifles at all, while on busier days you may have to fire for about an hour."

Sergeant D'Arpino next reminded us of the importance of "water discipline"—voluntary restraint of water consumption—and of the necessity of adding halizone tablets to water taken from streams to kill dangerous flora and fauna before they lodged in our guts.

Sam D'Arpino turned the forest floor back to Lieutenant Mueller, who next invited the squad leaders to address the platoon. Jim Gardner and the other two squad leaders, James Amoroso and Gilbert Moriz, demurred, shaking their heads.

"At least we might hear something from our only combat veteran," Sam D'Arpino suggested. "Real Parenteau, you fought on Guadalcanal. Can you give the men some tips based on your personal experience?" It was not a coincidence that Lieutenant Mueller had not been the one to invite Parenteau to speak. Eddie Cook told me the lieutenant had stayed away from Parenteau since their Sunday morning run-in at the staging area at Marseilles.

Real Parenteau stepped forward a step or two before speaking. "It's important always to have one man awake in the foxhole at night. If you are on guard and start feeling sleepy, remember to shake the other guy and tell him you can't hack it any more. Then the other guy takes over and the two of you straighten out the hours later so everybody does his fair share."

"That's a very useful tip, Real," Sam D'Arpino said. "Anything else?"

"That's about it," Real Parenteau said.

This didn't sound like very earth-shattering advice, so I asked a question. "Sergeant Parenteau, did you actually fire at the Japs?"

"Aw, we heard something in the bushes in front of our foxhole one night, so we fired at where the noise was coming from," Parenteau replied. "Next morning we found out it was just a bunch of cows. We didn't hit any."

"All right, thank you," Lieutenant Mueller said, without asking Real Parenteau if he had finished. "The squads will now organize themselves and wait for the signal to move up."

"Listen, boys," Jim Gardner told his eleven charges when we had assembled. "From now on, the toid squad is family. The other squads, the other platoons, the other companies are your foist, second, and toid cousins. But everyone else can go to hell in a Shoiman tank."

"In a what?" Scotty Kyle asked.

"You hoid what I said, wise guy," Jim Gardner replied with a grin. "Okay, everybody check over your stuff once more," referring to our cumbersome equipment and gear.

As darkness settled into the forest clearing, a shadowy convoy of two-and-a-half ton trucks rumbled quietly into the area. We clambered aboard and stacked our horseshoe roll packs on the floor between our knees. As soon as we were ready, the trucks rolled quietly forward again, the drivers straining to see in the scant cones of faint light emitted by the blackout drive lights. Normally driven in a noisy and undisciplined fashion, tonight the drivers kept their vehicles under strict control, shifting gears quietly under their weighty human cargoes, and idling the truck motors as softly as cats purring in the gathering gloom.

If the trucks were quiet, their helmeted human cargoes were even quieter. For once, like the trucks themselves, we were neither noisy nor undisciplined. Most of us were lost in thought, asking ourselves questions for which we had no answers.

"What will it be like?"

"How will I act under fire?"

"Will I still be around tomorrow night?"

"Will I chicken out like Sergeant Lollander and shoot myself in the foot?"

"Will I see my girl and my parents again?"

"Will I screw up and let Captain Young and the others down?"

"Will the experience we're about to go through change my personality and outlook?"

I did some silent praying and could feel that others were doing the same. Scotty Kyle and I stood upright behind the truck cab and warned the others whenever a low-hanging evergreen branch came along. The road was unpaved, very narrow, and bordered by thick evergreen walls.

"Duck! Branch!" I whispered loudly a dozen times. Everyone lowered their heads as the branches slapped across the truck's ribs. Fate seemed to be drawing us along on long invisible ropes in the darkness. The trees wouldn't tell us anything but seemed to be whispering among themselves. The trees must know the answers, for hadn't the war gone right through here? They knew; now it was our turn to learn.

If this truck movement had taken place back in training at Fort Bragg, the truck drivers would have gunned the motors loudly or forgotten to turn off the lights or smashed into trees or driven off a cliff into a lake or through some farmer's chicken coop roof. But here in the real world of war, there was no unauthorized noise or light, and no collisions, confusion, or screw-ups. The trucks rolled inexorably forward toward the unseen front line that lay somewhere ahead in the black night.

Finally, the ride ended and we dragged our horseshoe packs off the truck. Beyond this point, it was feared that our truck motors might give away our presence to listening enemy ears. We were led up a forest path through the evergreens. Beside the path we could make out ghostly silhouettes of tanks and tank destroyers parked under camouflage nets. Their guns were pointed toward where the enemy must be. Others were fighting in the war too and nobody seemed too excited about it. So why should we be afraid?

During a short rest break, an artillery major came out of a small net-draped bunker beside the road to chat with us. "We have two ways of delivering counter battery fire," the Major explained. "One way is to get a sound ranging of the enemy guns, unless the wind is blowing *toward* the enemy, which it often does in the Vosges. Another even better way is to line up the position of the enemy gun from its muzzle flash unless the gun has flash defilade behind a steep hill. Despite the large number of hills here, we can usually see enough of the flash to be able to apply the triangulation technique."

"What's that, sir?" I asked.

"Once we get two or more different fixes where the gun's flash is coming from, we can calculate its location and wipe it out promptly. It's that simple."

Through the major's triangulation technique, I supposed, it would be only a question of time before the enemy's artillery would be completely eliminated. Without their artillery, how long could the Germans hold out? It was a comforting prospect. American technology was a wonderful thing, in war as in peace. I half wondered why their artillery hadn't been knocked out already if it was so easy. But basically I hadn't the slightest doubt about the Major's story.

The climb continued. We were perspiring heavily. Men began to go down under the weight of their loads. "It's Smith. Somebody stay with him until a medic can get here." The man who folded was always somebody else. Nothing could happen to *ME*. Other guys might get killed, although I hoped they wouldn't, but not *ME*.

In the Army, and especially in the Vosges, the hills seemed to go up but not down. When finally we reached what seemed to be the top of the long ascent, we were led off the road among the trees. After the squad leaders conferred with Lieutenant Mueller, Jim Gardner gave us the straight poop. "We're not going to relieve the other outfit till morning." This brought murmurs of approval. "There's a little town about a mile down in front of us," Jim Gardner went on. "If it was daylight youse could see it from here. The Fifteent' Infantry of the Toid Division is going to take the town tonight. In about fifteen minutes, you'll hear the most tremendous artillery barrage you ever hoid in your life. After they take the town, we'll relieve 'em and move into the houses." We dug shallow slit trenches in the pliant Vosges soil. Then we rolled up in our shelter halves and blankets and were soon asleep.

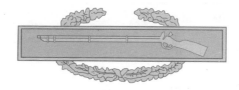

Chapter Twelve
Into the Line

When we were awakened at 0500, I asked if anyone had heard the "tremendous artillery barrage" Jim Gardner had promised. No one had.

Sergeant Gardner had sold some product or service back in the Bronx before being drafted. In the Army, he continued "selling" whatever he came in contact with, which at the present moment happened to be his side of the war. He probably could have sold the enemy on laying down their arms if he had had a safe conduct pass through the lines and a little basic German grammar.

It was drizzling slightly in the High Vosges forest where we had spend the night. It was Thursday, 2 November. We kicked dirt into the slit trenches that had served as our beds, honoring the training principle of "leaving the area in the condition we found it in."

Somehow the company's kitchen jeeps managed to come forward up the narrow trail we had marched along the previous night and served us hot dehydrated eggs and real bacon before we continued moving up. Hot chow undoubtedly lifted our morale, but to some of us, the meal had overtones of the favor done a prisoner before taking "the long walk." The final leg of our trek to the front led along a winding mountain road, past camouflaged tanks. Tall evergreens stood high and mighty over our heads.

This morning there was hustle and wisecracking, but no special fears or heavy thinking or questioning. The fear, thinking and questioning had apparently been creatures of the night. It was now raining steadily and the woods were full of mist. During the rest break, Jim Gardner explained that the 3d, 36th, and 45th Infantry Divisions of VI Corps were holding the front lines in our sector. He said the 45th had been squeezed out by the others, and that while they were still out of contact with the enemy, it was decided to insert our division to relieve them.

Finally we reached the front lines and met the men we were to relieve. They were friendly, rugged-looking guys, with beards and camouflage netting on their helmets. We stood around chatting beside their foxholes while they awaited the order to move to the rear. The rain seemed to run off their

3d Squad   2d Squad   1st Squad

Squad Leaders
S/Sgt Gardner S/Sgt Moriz S/Sgt Amoroso

Assistant
Squad Leaders
Sgt Parenteau Pfc Rybiski Sgt Daledovich

Assistant
Squad Leaders
CPL Gilbert

Platoon Aid Man
Tech 5 Woodard

First Scouts
Pfc Rice Pfc Adair Pfc Jeske

Second Scouts
Pvt Gurley Pvt Price Pvt Cash

Platoon Leader
Lieutenant Mueller

Automatic Riflemen
Pfc Jones Pfc Haskell Pfc Hershberg

Assistant
Automatic Riflemen
Pvt Emmons Pfc Hema Pfc Hogberg

Platoon Sergeant
T/Sgt Stanley

Ammo Bearers
Pfc Kyle Pfc Lorenze Pfc Vickers

Runners
Pvt Cook

Riflemen
Pfc Swartz Pfc Piltzer Pfc R. Fields

Pfc Munty

Pfc Day

Pfc DeRubeis Pfc Wade Pfc C. Fraley

Pfc Montgomery

Pvt Case Pfc Sholes Pfc L. Fraley

Pvt Talley Pfc Pederson Pfc Boban

Platoon Guide
S/Sgt D'Arpino

Pfc Ecblom Pvt Rule

Pfc Watson

**1ST PLATOON
COMPANY A
399TH INFANTRY REGIMENT**

2 NOVEMBER 1944

helmets onto their raincoats and onto the ground without getting them the least bit wet. It was our first look at combat men and we were duly impressed.

"We waited seventy-nine days since the Riviera invasion for you guys," one of them said with a grin. "Where you been?"

"We got here as fast as we could," I said. "We only left New York October 6th."

"That's pretty fast", he acknowledged.

"Twenty-five days from Manhattan to the front," I added. "We were the first convoy to come direct to France from the U.S."

"Are you guys from the 100th?" he asked.

"Er, yes," I admitted, fearing this might be a punishable breach of security. But I feared even more that this authentic combat man would consider me an idiot if I didn't reply.

"Where are the front lines?" I asked my new friend.

"Front lines? You're them," was the answer.

"Then where are the Germans?"

"Jerry? Oh he's out there somewhere, don't know for sure where."

"You mean there's nobody between us and them?"

"That's roger."

"My squad leader said your division got squeezed out," I said.

"Not that I know of," he replied. "Say," he said, "what do you plan on doing with those fancy full field packs and those horseshoe rolls? I even saw one of your boys with an extra pair of shoes dangling from his pack."

"But that's all standard equipment," I said. "We lugged that stuff all the way from Fort Bragg. Where are yours?"

"Threw 'em away long ago," he replied with a grin. "How do you expect to chase a Jerry when you're loaded down like a Penn Station Red Cap?"

"But how can you sleep without blankets?" I asked.

"We have small sleeping bags which the kitchen carries around and hands out at the end of the day's fighting."

"But what about towels, washcloths, underwear, soap, razor, toilet articles, stationery?"

"This isn't a beauty contest," he replied, "If we take a town or get relieved like today, we wash up and shave. Otherwise, no."

"Have you got a toothbrush?" I asked.

"Nope."

"What about pup tents?" I said.

"I pack the shelter half in with the bedroll, but I haven't seen a tentpeg since I forget when."

"Did you ever get a bayonet charge by the Germans?" I asked him.

"In Sicily one day we did," he replied. "Some gung-ho Kraut outfit came out of a gully waving bayonets at us like we were a bunch of rookies. I let 'em get close, about seventy-five yards maybe, and then I really creamed them with my BAR."

"Not bad," I said.

"You know," he said, "seeing dead Krauts lying around don't make any more impression on me than leaves laying under the trees. But when I see one GI lying there cold, it really busts me up inside."

"Have you had many casualties?" I asked.

"We've been pretty lucky coming up the Rhône Valley," he replied. "Since the invasion we only lost ten men from the platoon." A platoon at full strength normally had forty men including one officer, so these "lucky" guys had already lost about twenty-five percent of their strength in less than three months.

He explained that the rhythmic artillery sounds we were hearing overhead that ended in distant explosions far off were "our stuff." The occasional ear-splitting crashing sounds we heard behind us were enemy shells, landing in our rear areas. German artillery smoke was black and American artillery smoke was white. In the small arms category, the enemy weapon that was fired in nervous short bursts was called a "Burp gun." The German machine gun also fired very rapidly, while our machine guns made a slower, pounding sound.

I noticed that their rifles were "preserved" under a coating of what appeared to be rust.

"Do they fire?" I asked timidly.

"Sure they fire," was the reply. "We run a patch through the bore once in a while and keep the chamber clean. The M-1 is a good gun and doesn't need too much maintenance."

He pointed to a young soldier walking past the foxhole. His only equipment seemed to be a rifle and a single bandolier of ammo slung on the outside of his raincoat. The young soldier had landed in France as a Pfc. and was now up for a battlefield commission.

"He's our new Platoon Leader," my friend said. "He's still nineteen."

Another 45th man observed cheerfully, "If Jerry pulled a counterattack right now, we'd really be laying for them. We've got double strength all along the line." They chuckled at the delicious thought of the enemy falling into such a trap.

"Hey you guys, keep it down to a low roar, will you?" their youthful platoon leader said. The men complied, lowering their voices respectfully.

"He's right," one said. "The Kraut forward observers can hear a pin drop sometimes."

One-man foxhole protects against tanks, from Field Manual 7-10, *Rifle Company, Infantry Regiment* (18 March 1944), p. 239.

One of the 45th guys reminisced about the advance up from the Riviera. "Over on our right at night we could see the lights of Switzerland," he said. "It was a beautiful sight."

I raised the question of the best way to fight a tank. I said we had been taught that when a German tank bore down upon you, you first tried to stop it with antitank grenades or a "bazooka." If this failed, you scrunched down in the bottom of your foxhole while the tank rumbled over the hole. The tank's weight would usually cave in the sides of your foxhole but not deeply enough to crush you in the bottom. Then, as soon as the tank had passed beyond your hole, you were supposed to stand up quickly and hurl a "Molotov Cocktail" (a gasoline-filled bottle with a fuse) onto the tank's rear deck. If all went according to plan, the Molotov Cocktail would explode upon impact and the enemy crew would burn to death as their tank was enveloped in flames.

"Is that what they're teaching back at Benning?" one of them asked.

"At Benning and Bragg and everywhere else," I replied.

"Here's how it actually works," he said. "It won't be a one-on-one duel between you and that tank, because the tank will usually be accompanied by *panzer grenadiers* (armored infantrymen). Those babies will do everything in their power to prevent anyone from firing a bazooka or tank grenade. As far as hiding in the bottom of your hole while the tank goes over you, the first problem is those *panzer grenadier* boys who'll flush you out of there like an old possum. Even if they don't, the top soil here in the Vosges is very soft. A tank running over your foxhole will crush in the sides so deep that it'll finish you off ninety-nine times out of a hundred."

"So what's the right solution?" I asked.

"There's no solution," he said. "When we see a tank bearing down on us, we drop everything but our rifle and head for the hills like big-ass birds. Those *panzers* will chase one lonely GI through the trees, so you have to outwit them the way a rabbit does on a rabbit hunt."

"So who stops them?" I asked.

"Stronger medicine than you," he replied. "57 mm anti-tank guns, M-4 Sherman tanks or maybe tank destroyers with a three-inch gun or 90 millimeter. But never an M-1 rifle like you got."

That was enough to remold completely my ideas on how to fight tanks. A year of training in the States had taught us the Ft. Benning solution, but a few sentences from a real fighting man was enough to wipe out every false preconception.

Finally the order came for the unit we were relieving to move out. With much well wishing on both sides, they saddled up their modest belongings and left the Germans exclusively to us. Their farewells could not have been warmer if we had known them for several years instead of only two or three hours. There was, it seemed, no cause or room in the combat infantrymen's world for jealousy, selfishness, or other vices of the spirit.

"I wonder if the Krauts know we're here?" Doc Emmons, the erstwhile Company Barber, asked Robert E. Jones. Now that we had reached the front lines, Doc Emmons was no longer the barber, but was engaged full time as assistant BAR man to Robert E. Jones.

"Naw, doubt it," Jones replied. "They'da pulled a counterattack already if they know'd a bunch of 4-Fs is now agin 'em."

Like the rest of us, Captain Young had mostly listened during a lengthy meeting with the CO of the company we were relieving.

"We started with 187 men and we're now down to 90," Captain Young was told. "You can't afford to be too discouraged if the same thing happens to you." Captain Young pondered the numbers and said nothing.

"Another thing to remember," the other CO said, "is that it isn't your fault if men are wounded or killed. You have objectives to take, and it's your job to take 'em. Casualties are unavoidable, but if you put the blame on yourself, you won't be able to do your job any more."

Captain Young pondered the other man's words. Then he said, "You saw us come up to relieve you this morning. What were your impressions of our discipline, deportment, equipment, and morale generally?"

"I'll be frank," the other CO said. "When my men first saw your boys hunched under those horseshoe packs, they said, '"Boy, those poor lambs are going to get slaughtered!"'"

"I suppose we've got a lot to learn," Captain Young said. "My Division and Regimental commanders were over here in the First World War and my Battalion CO is a West Pointer. You'd think somebody would have clued them in about how much equipment is reasonable and necessary up here."

"The School of Hard Knocks is the only reliable teacher," the other CO said. "There's always a wide gap between garrison doctrine and actual combat conditions."

They shook hands and the other CO moved off through the woods toward the rear. Captain Young told his Communications Sergeant, Sergeant Lou Nemeseck, to get in touch with Battalion on their newly installed telephone wire.

"Lou, we've got to find out what the situation is, and what's to happen next," Captain Young said. "Try to find out from Battalion what we should be doing."

"Yes sir," Nemeseck said quietly. This was the first time he had seen Captain Young in less than full control of a particular situation. It was also the first time the Captain had called him "Lou" during the year they had been working together.

Now that we had reached the front, we were paired off according to military function rather than personal affinities. Since I was the Gardner Squad's Second Scout, my new "foxhole-mate" was First Scout Herbert D. Rice. My previous tent-mate, Scotty Kyle, who was part of the Jones-

Emmons' automatic rifle team, was now bunking with Corporal Woody Gilbert, a "spare" NCO. Corporal Gilbert was third-in-command of our 3d Squad under Jim Gardner and Real Parenteau.

Herbie Rice and I dispersed our equipment in the foxhole and underground foliage where enemy eyes couldn't easily spot it. Herbie was a good-looking, intelligent, nineteen-year-old ASTP man with pink cheeks and a line of friendly banter. He had spent summers at his grandparents' farm outside Peoria and knew a bit about life in the country and hunting.

Our foxhole guarded a junction of two forest trails. Close by the foxhole, a 57mm antitank gun was burrowed beneath a load of damp pine boughs. Like its crew crouching in a foxhole less than a yard away, the gun must have been nearly invisible to anyone approaching from the direction of the enemy.

We were told to keep one man on guard in each foxhole day and night around the clock. I took the first two-hour trick while Herbie Rice went off somewhere. Standing there in the foxhole, I was wondering what would happen next. I quickly got an answer. Thirty or forty yards away from the direction of the enemy, ten or a dozen people suddenly materialized out of a patch of mist left over from the last shower. They weren't wearing uniforms and looked like refugees of some kind. They saw me soon after I spotted them, but continued moving toward me without any of them saying a word.

What was I supposed to do now? If they had been enemy troops, I would have opened fire. If they had been enemy tanks, I would probable have run away in accordance with what I had learned this morning. But they were neither. Should I step out and block their passage, shout that they were under arrest and lead them back to the rear in my custody? Would they understand English? Should I speak to them in French? Despite hundreds of hours of French classes at Newton H.S. and Harvard, no useful phrases sprang to my lips except *"Bonjour, Monsieur,"* or perhaps, *"Où pensez-vous que vous allez?"* ("Where do you think you're going?")

While I pondered these questions, the group simply kept advancing, advancing, advancing, until they had passed our foxhole and passed out of my sight into our rear area. Shouldn't they at least have stopped at the sight of a large, heavily-armed American and explained who they were, where they had come from and why they wished to pass through our lines? But they had simply ignored me.

Things were quiet for several minutes. Then Corporal Woody Gilbert arrived. "Hey Red," he said, frowning, "why didn't you stop that group of people who came through here?"

"There were so many of them," I stammered, improvising as I went along, "that I thought the best solution would be to let them go through to where we could be sure they couldn't escape."

"They didn't escape all right," Woody Gilbert said. "They walked right into Captain Young's CP. The Old Man really blew his top."

"Gee I'm sorry," I said.

"All right now, shape up!" Corporal Gilbert said sharply and left me alone again.

I felt depressed for a while after Woody Gilbert's chastisement, but then my mood changed. We were securely installed on the front lines and hadn't seen a single German yet. The only sign of life from the enemy side was an occasional ugly "crack" back in our rear area as one of their shells landed. But this "incoming mail" was insignificant compared to the reassuring overhead rustling of our own "outgoing mail," whose delivery was announced by a series of "Whoom-whoom-whooms" far off ahead of us somewhere.

Yesterday I would have said the war was a contest between democracy and Nazi tyranny. But the 45th Infantry Division boys usually called the enemy "Jerry" as though he was no Aryan monster at all, but just an old possum who lived in the woods the way we did. Our daily task was not so much to wipe out Nazi tyranny as it was to simply try to put one over on Jerry before he put one over on us. The 45th Division guys hadn't expressed any hatred, ideological or personal, for the enemy. They made it sound more like an old-fashioned game of cowboys and Indians, cops and robbers, or capture-the-flag.

Up front here I began to feel a strange new freedom. There would be no more "details" or chickenshit. We were here to fight, and until we were attacked or the order came to advance, we could take life easy. Also, I somehow doubted that Major Barney Lentz or any others of our ball-breaking superiors would want to come up here to inspect my uniform and equipment and tell me to "buckle my chinstrap." They would, I thought, cherish their own safety too highly for that.

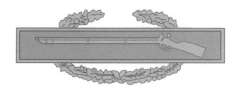

Chapter Thirteen
Action at St. Remy

The rest of 2 November passed without further incident. Just after noon the next day, Lieutenant Mueller announced that the platoon had received its initial mission, a contact patrol to the positions of the 3d Infantry Division in a village called La Bourgonce. Captain Young had told him to take Jim Gardner's squad. The Lieutenant oriented us at great length, with the aid of a map, about the route we would follow and the possible dangers the patrol would entail, and generally about his vast responsibility in being given this important assignment by Captain Young.

Herbie Rice and I, First and Second Scouts respectively, passed through the front lines and emerged from the dark forest into a beautiful green valley bathed in sunshine. A church spire and the red roofs of a town were visible in the distance. Our job was to lead the squad into the town along the route Lieutenant Mueller had indicated. Around three sides of the valley ahead of us, stolid green hills stood high and sinister, masters of all they surveyed. The hills were covered with evergreens, which along the crests resembled Indian headdresses or wigwams. Beyond the village of La Bourgonce were two cone-shaped hills called "*Les Jumeaux*" (the twins) on Lieutenant Mueller's map. We weren't sure which of the many summits ahead were still in enemy hands, but Lieutenant Mueller had warned that concealed German artillery observers might follow our progress through high-powered glasses. Faint sounds of machine-gun and rifle fire drifted down from the higher hills, punctuated by occasional thumps of artillery rounds landing. Now and then I could make out the distant "Rrrrpp!" of a German burpgun. Smoke or mist (or both) was rising from the hills everywhere, and we could not tell if the vapors were being caused by war or nature.

I followed Herbie Rice at a fifty-yard interval as instructed. I looked back and saw Jim Gardner's crouching figure come slinking out of the woods about fifty yards behind me. Finally the Lieutenant left the shelter of the woods, still studying his map like a Boy Scout leader. Arm and hand signals were scrupulously passed forward and back from Lieutenant Mueller to Sergeant Gardner to me and on up to Herbie Rice. At least five or six times I relayed the signal to Herbie Rice that he should "Continue straight ahead." Rice shot me a look that said, "Why keep telling me to go on doing what I'm already doing?" A detached observer might have wondered what there was to signal about anyway, since the roofs and spire of La Bourgonce were as plain as the noses on our faces. All we had to do was keep walking and we would fall into the town.

Soon we reached the edge of the town and stepped carefully over a partly disassembled enemy roadblock. Suddenly two GIs came bursting out of a house, wearing wool-knit caps and carrying no weapons.

"What outfit you from, fella?" one of them asked Herbie Rice. Rice stood silent, boots anchored in the mud.

"Hey, what outfit you from?" the man repeated.

"Don't tell 'em, Herb," I called. Herbie Rice remained silent.

"We watched you come across that field," the GI continued. "Whatta you, on maneuvers or something? The town was taken days ago."

By this time, Sergeant Gardner and Lieutenant Mueller had reached the roadblock. More arm and hand signals from them indicated that we should continue to the center of the village, which appeared to be our only option anyway. We resumed our advance and after a few minutes, Lieutenant Mueller located the CP house he was looking for. Still clutching his map, he disappeared inside with Jim Gardner. He was in contact with Headquarters Company, 1st Battalion, 15th Infantry Regiment.

Other 3d Infantry Division men came over to chat with Herbie Rice and me as we waited for our leaders' return. They said their division had made a big attack through the hills near La Bourgonce and were now in an exposed position out ahead of the divisions on the left and right.

"The fighting is still going on in those high hills to the right of the Tits," one man said, pointing toward "*Les Jumeaux*."

"Our line companies say the Krauts are fighting as hard up there as they did at Anzio, maybe even harder."

"Do you expect to reach Strasbourg soon?" I asked. In the *Stars & Stripes* I had seen a map showing Strasbourg on the Rhine beyond the Vosges Mountains, at most fifty or sixty miles from where we were now standing.

"Where?" he said.

"Strasbourg," I repeated.

He shook his head as though he had never heard the name before. I was beginning to suspect that this war had a "big picture" and a "little picture" and that we were in the process of leaving the former behind and becoming immersed in the latter.

"Hey, what have you guys been eating lately?" he said.

"K rations," I replied.

"Bring your boys into the barn," he said. To our astonishment, they proceeded to broil steaks for us.

"Where did you get these steaks?" Scotty Kyle asked.

"A pleasantly plump cow was slaughtered by the artillery just out back," the cook said with a grin. "We didn't know if it was ours or Jerry's that hit her, but it was a good day for us. I hope she gets the Purple Heart." They poured red wine from a tall bottle into our canteen cups, and fried some potatoes to go with the steak.

The cook looked up from his stove. "Whoever said 'War was Hell' forgot about Elsie the French cow," he said. "Here's more stuff for later." He began emptying a carton of ten-in-one rations, handing us cans of ham and eggs and "Charms" hard candies. From the standpoint of our stomachs at least, our first patrol had already been a smashing success.

Finally, Lieutenant Mueller and Jim Gardner emerged from the battalion CP. The lieutenant seemed quite full of himself. "Let's go back, men! Same formation as before!" He clutched his carbine sling eagerly, his map now back in its case. He apparently felt he knew the way this time. We crossed the fields again and reentered the forest where our comrades were manning their foxhole line in the eternal twilight of the evergreens. Lieutenant Mueller went to report to Captain Young and our first patrol was over.

The next morning, 4 November, we received our first attack order. We were going to leave our dripping, gloomy woods behind and join the war.

"B Company will take La Salle," Sergeant Gardner told us. "Then C Company will take St. Remy, and after that A Company will pass through C Company and take a third town. I'll get the name later."

We liked the idea of being the *last* of the three rifle companies to be committed against the enemy.

"You'll hear a lot of artillery today," Sergeant Gardner continued. "Of every ten shells overhead, nine will be ours. And our L-5 spotting planes will be up there plotting the muzzle blasts of the Jerry guns so that our artillery and air force can knock them out."

Our generals had apparently thought of everything. Saddling up our huge horseshoe packs and other gear, we started off through the woods in double columns and then onto a dirt road with a ten-yard interval between men. The interval was soon changed to fifteen yards, then twenty-five, then back to ten yards. We were told to leave the road and march parallel to it through the trees at a distance of twenty-five yards, then to get back on the road, then to march fifty yards away from the road. Finally we were told to halt and "dig in." Herbie Rice and I took turns digging and within half an hour had a three-foot-deep foxhole-in-progress.

"Everybody back on the road!" Sergeant Gardner called. The situation was "normal"—all fouled up.

Finally the trees began to thin out and we could see open ground and some burning farm buildings ahead. Someone said the buildings were part of La Salle. Just then a wet muddy column of GIs hurried toward us from the direction of the burning settlement and came into the wood we were about to leave. We recognized them as Lieutenant Jack Reid's platoon from Company B, fresh from the capture of La Salle. We were tremendously impressed by the rangy, confident step of that little group, who seemed to know exactly what they were about. They had already been tested in the crucible of "action" and had acquitted themselves honorably. When would our turn come, and how would we perform?

Our double column emerged from the woods and proceeded across open ground to the left of the burning farm buildings. Our marching interval was increased from ten to twenty yards due to our increased exposure in the open terrain. A mile or two ahead, across rolling farm fields, we could see a church steeple which someone said was in St. Remy. I thought I recognized the open ground to our right as part of the green valley through which our patrol had advanced yesterday. Our destination of yesterday, La Bourgonce, was apparently over beyond the burning farm buildings of La Salle. Beyond St. Remy were those same angry hills we had seen yesterday, covered with pointed evergreens like quills of porcupines. Clouds of mist swept across the slopes of the dark-treed hills as though they were on fire.

La Salle's smoking cluster of buildings receded and disappeared behind us. The tall grass of the marshy meadowland concealed dangerous ruts in the ground which caused a few men to stumble and fall under their heavy loads. After a while, the company echeloned off toward some woods on the left and we continued our advance within the shelter of the trees. Artillery activity increased and we heard the rhythmic whisperings of American 105s overhead, followed by loud "crumps" off to our right front somewhere in the general direction of St. Remy. The 105s gave us a sheltered feeling, like carrying a large umbrella in a shower.

The American artillery had apparently irritated the enemy, for whistles were soon heard overhead coming from the enemy's direction. Fortunately for us, the whistles continued a few more seconds beyond where we were before exploding with loud ugly "cracks" like doomed souls landing in hell. We saw distant wisps of black smoke rise above the trees to the west of us, marking where the shells had fallen.

"They're looking for us but don't know where we went," Sergeant Gardner said. "Wait till our air force gets after those Heinies!" He could almost make an enemy shelling sound like an attractive business opportunity.

We continued our advance along the edge of the woods for well over a mile before receiving the order to dig foxholes. From the edge of woods,

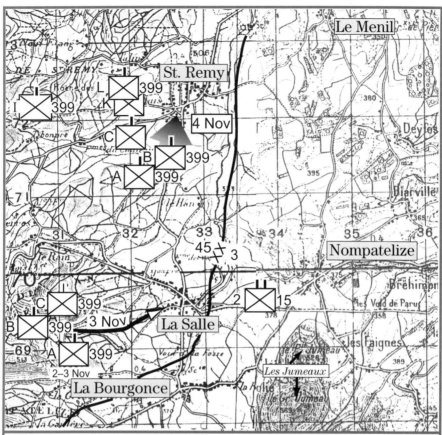

399TH INFANTRY REGIMENT OPERATIONS
AGAINST ELEMENTS OF THE
716TH VOLKS-GRENADIER DIVISION
IN THE VICINITY OF LA SALLE AND ST. REMY
2-4 NOVEMBER 1944

US Infantry Units

Advance of B/399th

Attack of B/399th,
   supported by Company C

Scale: One grid square = One kilometer (.62 miles)

| Company |
| Battalion |
| Division |

we could see a few buildings of St. Remy across a field. It was now late afternoon. Farther along the edge of woods a Sherman tank came waddling out of a black wall of pines and started whamming away at some target in St. Remy.

I dug for fifteen or twenty minutes in the damp pliant soil and then Herbie Rice relieved me for a spell. To cool off I walked along inside the edge of woods to see how the others were doing. Most foxholes were already a foot or two deep. I stopped to chat with Sergeant Moniz's scouts, James Adair from Louisville, Kentucky, and Hugh Price from Oklahoma City. Adair was an ASTP boy and Hugh Price was an ordinary draftee with eternal good nature and a deadly shooting eye.

Although we had been on the front line only three days, Jimmy Adair had managed to pick up a second weapon already. On one shoulder he carried a carbine, and on the other an all-metal submachine gun called a "grease gun" or "Zip-gun." The greasegun's sling draped over the shoulder in such a way that the muzzle always pointed forward. To fire, all he had to do was press the big trigger and send anything up to thirty .45-caliber slugs flying out. As a fellow member of the scouting fraternity, I thought that sometime I should try to pick up one of those grease guns, too.

"Where did you get it, Jim?" I asked.

"One of the 45th boys gave it to me," he replied. "He said it had belonged to a friend."

As I turned to exchange some joke with Hugh Price, Jimmy Adair glanced at a letter before tucking it back inside his shirt. I noticed the words "My dearest Sweetheart" in flowing green ink at the top of the page. Although I didn't have a girlfriend of my own at the moment, I was happy for Adair and not the least bit envious of his good fortune in love. Adair acted very happily this sunny afternoon of our first day in combat, treading lightly through the trees with his new grease gun.

I moved along to Sergeant Amoroso's squad and chatted with his scouts, John Jeske and Garland Cash. Jeske, an ASTP boy, had been voted the "Most Handsome Senior" at Chicago's Pulasky High School. Garland Cash hailed from Henderson, North Carolina.

"Have a turnip?" Jeske asked, cutting me a chunk off a huge dirty light-colored vegetable. I tasted it and spat it out.

"I been telling him that stuff is for hogs," Garland Cash said.

"It's food, isn't it?" Jeske said. "Hoggie Hogberg has been eating it with no complaints."

"I told you it was for hogs, didn't I?" Cash asked again.

I returned to our foxhole just in time to relieve Herbie Rice who was beginning to grow weary. I took over the digging task and soon we had gone down four feet. Just then Sergeant Gardner told us to saddle up and be ready to move out. The houses of St. Remy across the field were becoming harder to see now as twilight settled in.

"Listen closely, men," Lieutenant Mueller said. "Our mission is to search the houses on both sides of the road leading into town from here. Do you see that little shed over there at the edge of town? Leave all your equipment except rifles, ammunition, and grenades behind that structure. We'll go back for it later. The 3d Squad will search the houses on the left side of the road; 1st Squad search the right side; and 2d Squad remains in reserve with the CP group. No lights to be used even after it gets dark. Any questions?"

Herbie Rice and I advanced across an orchard and dropped our equipment behind the shed as instructed. Soon we were approaching the first house on the left side of the road. Smoke hung above the house and blended with the deepening twilight. We hoped to Hell the Jerries had pulled out, but we couldn't be sure.

"Okay, boys, you all know what to do," Sergeant Gardner said. It was a drill we had practiced dozens of times in training in the mock village at Fort Bragg. The three non-coms and the BAR team covered the doors and windows with their weapons, while the scouts, followed by our riflemen, rushed in a zig-zag pattern toward the front door. Herbie Rice burst into the house, with me following four or five steps behind. Rice went into a room on the left and I dashed into a room on the right. There was no sign of life in the house. Rice and I led the squad out the back door as Jones covered us with his BAR from the kitchen window.

"Okay, boys," Sergeant Gardner said. "Let's hit the second house." We went through the same procedure again without incident and were soon approaching our third dwelling.

I was advancing along a shallow depression beside the road, about fifteen yards behind Rice. Suddenly across the road, I saw a dim figure step around the corner of a building. Amoroso's squad on the right side of the road had fallen behind us so I knew this was not one of his men. Although the light was poor, I was fairly sure it was a GI, so I saw no cause for alarm.

"Who's that?" he called. I had no reason to think he was calling to me, so I continued advancing while keeping an eye on him just in case.

"Who's that?" the dim figure repeated. I saw him lean against the corner of the house and brandish what appeared to be a weapon.

"Hey, are you talking to me?" I said, suddenly afraid.

"You're damn right I am. What's your outfit?"

"A Company."

Apparently satisfied, the murky figure came storming forward toward me but no longer brandishing his weapon at me.

"Do you know I almost shot you?" he cried.

"I'm not scared!" was my brave, if inane, reply.

He identified himself as Lieutenant Joseph Majeski, Executive Officer of Company C.

We searched the third house and again found no Jerries. Out back of the house we discovered several GIs from Company C sitting on the ground eating K rations.

"Aw, we already searched that house," one of them said.

Just then John Jeske came across the road from where his squad had completed searching the houses on their side.

"You know what happened?" Jeske asked in that fast Chicago way he had of talking. "Cash and Ammo and I didn't walk in through the front gate because it could have been booby trapped. Instead we took wire-cutters and opened a hole through the wire fence. I rushed the house with Cash two steps behind and Hersh and Hogberg covering us with the BAR. I was about to go up the front steps when Ammo called to wait. He remembered the training film where the GI walks up the steps of the house and gets blown up. He tells me to leap like a broad-jumper over the three steps and land at the top. I did and pushed the door open. Then I go outside and say to Ammo, 'Do you like dead men?' "

" 'What do you mean?' Ammo asks me.

"So I take him inside and show him my dead man, slouched in a chair. Finally Ammo lit a match, even though it was against orders, and we heard what we thought were German voices in the next room. We opened the door a crack and peeked through. You know what we had found?"

"What?" I asked.

"Captain Campion and the whole Charlie Company CP group. Campion and Ammo were friends from the old days when Campion was our Company Executive Officer. We still called him "Our Man in C Company." He told Ammo we had captured the Charlie Company CP and asked what we plan on doing for an encore."

I said, "You captured everybody but Lieutenant Majeski who tried to shoot me out in the yard."

"What about the dead man?" someone asked.

"It was just a sleeping GI," Jeske laughed.

Eddie Cook, Lieutenant Mueller's runner, came up and told us to go back to get our equipment at the edge of town. It was now completely dark. I passed the company CP group and saw Captain Young trying to interrogate an elderly couple. They acted terrified of this roaring giant who leaned his great hulk down over them and waved his carbine in their faces.

"Who can speak French around here?" he finally roared in frustration.

"I know a little," I said when none of the rear echelon types in his CP group volunteered.

"Good, Red. Go ahead and talk to them."

"What should I ask them?" I asked.

"Dammit, you're the one who speaks French!" he said. Then, upon reflection, he added, "Tell 'em we'll shoot 'em if they don't cooperate."

"*Bonjour*," I said to the old couple. "I mean, *bonsoir*," I corrected myself.

"*Bonsoir, Monsieur!*" They returned my greeting with relief.

"*Où sont les Allemands?*" I asked.

"*Ils sont partis dans l'après-midi*" they replied. "*Ils ne reviendront pas!*"

I told Captain Young, "They say the Jerries left this afternoon and won't be back."

"Okay, thanks," the Captain said. "Tell them we'll set up my CP in their house." I did so and the old couple asked me to tell the captain how happy they were to be liberated and that they wanted to offer apples and wine to everyone.

"Tell them thanks," the CO said, "but skip the wine. My boys are disoriented enough already."

When word got around that I knew a few words of French, I was soon called upon to mediate a second dispute between Sergeant Ralph Harrington of Lieutenant Ballie's platoon and a French family barricaded behind their door. Harrington had called for them to "Come out with hands up!" When they failed to comply because they hadn't understood him, he fired a burst of twenty rounds from his grease gun into the door. That had started them screaming and word went out that an interpreter was needed.

"*Vous ne serez pas attaqués!*" I shouted through the door. "*Mais il est nécessaire pour vous d'ouvrir la porte!*"

Slowly the door swung open and a nose appeared.

"*Bonsoir*," I said. "*Quelqu'un est blessé?*"

"*Heureusement non, Monsieur*," was the answer. I was relieved, but hoped Sergeant Harrington would prove a better shot when he met a real enemy. This was perhaps Harrington's noblest moment since the time he betrayed Sergeant Bull by tripping him into the sawdust pit at Bragg while scores of VIPs watched.

Captain Young set out from his new CP on some mission which took him past the village cemetery. There Doc Emmons stepped out to warn him of a local hazard.

"Don't step off the road in that field beside the cemetery, Captain," Emmons said. "The civilians say the Germans got it mined."

"*Don't* call me Captain! Call me *Young!*" the captain roared.

"All right, Young," the unflappable Doc Emmons replied.

We all understood operational security—that we should not make it obvious to the Germans that Captain Young was our CO—but the idea of calling him simply "Young" was odd and somewhat amusing to us. As the weeks wore on, Doc Emmons took full advantage of this admonition.

Although the town was now clear of Germans as far as anyone could tell in the darkness and overall confusion, German shells continued to hum vindictively overhead before exploding in loud crashes in all parts of the town. We heard that Companies A, B, and C were now all in town as well as our Battalion CO, Lieutenant Colonel Zehner.

Although Company A's miscellaneous adventures that day seemed quite exciting and fraught with dangers, the fact remained that we were the "reserve company" behind Baker and Charlie, both of which had actually engaged the enemy and suffered casualties.

That morning, a patrol from the 45th Infantry Division had entered St. Remy and ascertained that two German units were defending the town. Responsibility for taking the town was assigned to the 399th's Company C. Captain Campion sent Lieutenant Jack Jenkins into town with a seventy-man patrol. As the patrol moved through the town without drawing enemy fire, a throng gathered and followed them until the scene soon resembled the Pied Piper of Hamelin leading a long procession. The civilians led them to a field where the gruesome corpse of a German soldier lay, already several days dead and putrefying (they referred to the dead man as "*Boche*"). They plied Jack Jenkin's men with apples, wine, schnapps, cheers, and enthusiastic embraces. Jenkins decided he had better rejoin his company in the woods outside the town before the men became drunk.

Unknown to Lieutenant Jenkins, a German machine-gun crew was hidden in a house a few feet away from the celebrating throng, but withheld its fire apparently because the soldiers were intermingled with civilians. As the patrol left town they could see Company B advancing across a field toward the town. Suddenly the hidden German machine gun opened up and pinned Baker Company's attack force to the ground.

When Lieutenant Jenkins reached the safety of the woods, he found that Captain Campion had already left for town by a different route. Jenkins turned around and led his seventy-man patrol back to town as the sun was setting. Meanwhile, Company B had already lost two men killed and two wounded to the machine gun fire and was still pinned down. Colonel Zehner came along and, seeing Baker Company's demoralized condition, stepped out front and led the way to town as the German machine gun continued firing in his direction. The men of Company B rose from the ground and followed. At the edge of the town, Colonel Zehner entered a house and, unexpectedly finding himself in a room with four German soldiers, exited through a window.

I never learned why Captain Campion's Company C and Captain Young's Company A were both told to clear the same part of the town, getting their wires crossed in the process as Sergeant Amoroso's squad captured Captain Campion's CP and Lieutenant Majeski almost fired his carbine at me. Majeski told me much later, "I was looking for somebody to shoot at and you looked like the one."

Captain Young showed Lieutenant Mueller on the map the sector of the town which our platoon would occupy and defend during the night. He said the deep stone cellars under the farmhouses should be used for protection against artillery fire, with sufficient guards posted around the buildings to deal with a possible counterattack.

Our squad was assigned to a farmhouse, where we awaited Lieutenant Mueller's visit. I served as Sergeant Gardner's interpreter with the farm couple who showed us where the blankets, bedding, candles, and blackout curtains were. Finally Lieutenant Mueller arrived with Sergeant Parenteau who had been doing some interpreting for him at the platoon CP house.

"Sergeant Gardner," he said, map spread out on the table under candlelight, "I want you to put two men in the little farm building across the street, four men in two foxholes out back of this house, a two-man foxhole at the crossroads, and keep four inside here."

"Gee, Lieutenant," Sergeant Gardner said, "The way I get it, our big risk tonight will be from enemy shelling, not from a counterattack. So if we put the men in the stone caves under the houses, nothing can touch them. I'd recommend two guards, one in front of and one behind the house, and keep the other ten inside."

"I'm sorry, but that's it. "Lieutenant Mueller said. "I wouldn't rule out a counterattack as much as you seem to. Besides, the Fort Benning book says foxholes are good protection. And that little building across the street is even better protection than foxholes."

"Hmm," Sergeant Gardner said thoughtfully, sensing that further efforts to change the lieutenant's mind would be a waste of time.

The pill was sweetened a few minutes later by word that the company jeep had arrived with hot chow. Six men were sent to the company CP with double mess kits to pick up chow for the squad. As we ate, Sergeants Gardner and Parenteau and Corporal Gilbert discussed the lieutenant's directive about the squad's tactical posture for the coming night.

"That little building across the street looks too flimsy to me, at least compared to this one," Sergeant Gardner said. "Let's forget it." Sergeant Parenteau and Corporal Gilbert nodded their assent.

"Now what about putting men at the crossroads?" Sergeant Gardner asked his board of advisors.

Woody Gilbert replied, "We know Jerry has mined the crossroads so he certainly won't send a counterattack through there tonight."

"It's a cinch the Germans zeroed in the crossroads before they pulled back," Real Parenteau added. "That means they'll drop stuff right on that spot tonight."

"Okay, no foxhole at the crossroads," Sergeant Gardner decreed. "What was the other one?"

"Putting four men in two foxholes out back," Woody Gilbert said.

Real Parenteau spoke up again, "Too exposed out there. The men are safer inside the house."

"Real's right," Woody Gilbert said. "It's foolish to expose men to artillery fire in the open when we have a solid building to protect us."

"All right," Sergeant Gardner said. "If we get caught it'll be my ass, but I'm paid to get kicked in the butt once in a while by the Brass Hats." Sergeant Gardner said we would take turns standing guard in our hour shifts at the door of the stone stable attached to the house and facing the crossroads. The eleven men not on guard could catch some shuteye in the "salon" where four men draped themselves across a bed, two squirmed onto a sofa and the other five men stretched out on the floor.

The French woman, who looked to be fifty-five or sixty, urged us to join them in the cellar ("*la cave*") where it was safer. I explained that we hadn't spent a night in a house since the States and wanted to enjoy the night in the living room.

At 0250, L. C. Talley prodded me for guard. Putting on my field jacket and grabbing my rifle and ammo, I followed Talley through the black interior of the house to the little stable.

"Did you hear them explosions a little bit back?" Talley whispered in an awed tone.

"No, I was sleeping," I said.

"Three or four of them 88s come right in here close to the house," he said. "When I hear 'em comin', I just lay me down agin' the wall and the blast bounced me up and down. I'm telling you, I was praying."

"Gosh, you had a rough time," I said.

"I'd best be hitting the sack," Talley said, disappearing inside the house.

I stuck my head cautiously outside the half-open stable door and surveyed the damp night which hung over St. Remy like a wet blanket. The good weather of yesterday seemed to have gone away and the air felt humid again. Distant black farm houses were outlined against a flashing sky every five or ten minutes as enemy barrages dropped their freight, but in our immediate locality everything was quiet. It was almost too quiet, I thought. Death seemed to be lurking somewhere outside. It was an inexplicable feeling to me at the time.

The minutes crawled by. At 0350, I stumbled back inside the dark house, shook the bundle of blankets which most resembled Scotty Kyle, and informed him he was on guard. He finally woke up, grumbling as he crawled out of his inner sanctum.

To my surprise, the lady of the house had come up from the cellar, and wanted to chat. I found a couple of Nescafé packets I had been saving from our K rations and she heated a kettle of water on a little wood-burning stove in the kitchen. She said her husband had a heart condition which was not being helped by all the shelling.

"You shelled us for a whole month," she said. "What were you waiting for? Why didn't you come?"

I said we had just arrived on the front lines two days ago and didn't know anything about the troops who were in the vicinity before that. I added that one month ago my division was still in America, so we couldn't have been responsible for the delays and shelling.

She said her father had been sixteen when the Germans came through town in 1870. A French corps had fought a delaying action and killed many Germans. The dead were loaded onto the St. Remy farmers' wagons and taken back to Germany for burial.

She said she had a daughter living in St. Dié, not far from there. The daughter's husband was in the *Forces françaises de l'intèrieurs* (the FFI, or French Resistance movement) and was captured in September by the Germans at a place called Mon Frère du Rouge Vêtu. He was deported to Germany and they had heard nothing further from him.

After about half an hour, Madame went back down into the stone cellar and I hit the sack with four others who were stretched out on the floor of the living room.

Sergeant Gardner had us all up by 0530. He went off to the platoon CP and returned with some bad news. "Mueller had Sergeant Moniz send four boys out close to those crossroads last night," he said. The four were First Scout Jimmy Adair; Second Scout Hugh Price; BAR man Carlyle B. Haskill from Deer Island, Maine; and Ellahugh Sluder from Tookland, Virginia. They had had time to dig foxholes only about a foot in depth when the barrage struck. Hugh Price, who had learned to sense the approach of tornadoes on the Oklahoma plains, had picked up the 88s' whistle soon enough to sound a warning before rolling into the shallow foxhole and safety. Standing outside the foxhole, Jimmy Adair was killed instantly. In the other foxhole, Carl Haskell was wounded seriously in the back, while Ellahugh Sluder's leg wound was less serious. The wounded men had been

Major General Withers A. Burress, Commanding General, 100th Infantry Division. He was highly regarded by fellow VMI alumnus, General George C. Marshall, and brilliantly led his division from activation through the end of the war. His prior experience as Commandant of Cadets at the VMI may have heightened his genuine concern for the welfare of the thousands of young Americans who served under his command in combat.

The 100th Infantry Division was activated at Fort Jackson, South Carolina, on 15 November 1942. The Division left Jackson in November 1943 to participate in Second Army No. 4 Tennessee Maneuvers, and went on to Fort Bragg, North Carolina, for post-maneuver supplementary training. At Bragg, the Division was stripped of its well-trained soldiers who would refill units already in combat, and received and amalgamated thousands of non-infantrymen, including ex-ASTP men.

Colonel (Later Brigadier General) Andrew Christian Tychsen, Commander of the 399th Infantry Regiment from activation through the first two months of combat. After distinguishing himself as a combat leader in this capacity, he was promoted to Assistant Division Commander, and eventually assumed command of the 100th in the summer of 1945 when General Burress moved up to assume command of VI Corps.

Lieutenant Colonel Elery Zehner, Commander, 1st Battalion, 399th Infantry. Shown here handling a Thompson submachine gun, Colonel Zehner was a brave, aggressive leader who wore a red scarf in combat so his men would be aware whenever he was "up front" . . . which was most of the time.

Captain Richard Young, Commanding Officer of Company A, 399th Infantry, who ably led us from Fort Bragg into battle in the crucible of the High Vosges. In six months of combat command, his company never failed to seize an assigned objective. He was awarded the Silver Star for his outstanding leadership and valor during the battle for Hill 462.8.

Lieutenant (formerly Technical Sergeant) Rudoph Steinman, D/399th Infantry, the "unneutral Swiss" receives the Distinguished Service Cross (DSC) from Lieutenant General Wade Haislip who was the commanding general of XV Corps during the 100th's attack into the High Vosges. Sergeant Steinman, a WWI veteran of the French Foreign Legion and a lifelong profesional soldier, earned the DSC for his actions on 16 November 1944 on the *Tête des Reclos*.

An extract of the 399th Infantry Regiment colors. The musket and powderhorn on an infantry blue shield (on the eagle's chest) was the same as our distinctive insignia, which we wore on our dress uniforms. Our regimental motto is emblazoned on the scroll in the eagle's mouth, and, as with all units of the Organized Reserves, the the Lexington Minuteman crowns the insignia, facing "to the proper" (right). In April of 1775, the author's ancestor, Phineas Gurley, marched with his militia company from Connecticut to join Washington's army encircling Boston, just after the battle at Lexington Green.

Four noncommissioned officers of Company A, 399th Infantry partaking in timeless soldierly recreational endeavor, imbibing beer and smoking cheap cigars, in this case, at the legendary Town Pump saloon in Fayetteville in the summer of 1944. From left, they are Sergeant Jim Gardner, Squad Leader, 3d Squad, 1st Platoon; Staff Sergeant Sam D'Arpino, Platoon Guide, 1st Platoon; Sergeant Lou Nemeseck, Company Communications Sergeant; and Corporal Jim Amoroso, Squad Leader, 1st Squad, 1st Platoon. Note that the latter soldier is wearing his ranger tab under his 100th Infantry Division patch. Except for D'Arpino, all of these men became casualties to German rifle fire in November 1944, in the Vosges Mountains.

Lieutenant Ballie, Platoon Leader of Company A's 3d Platoon, whose ardor for combat was sated by the ferocious fighting on Hill 462.8.

The WWII version of the Army Ranger Tab, with white letters on a red field. The 100th was one of nine divisions to send many of its men to the Army Ranger Course at Camp Forrest, Tennessee, to enhance their individual combat skills.

Sergeant Gil "Moe" Moniz, Squad Leader of our platoon's 2d Squad. During the battle for Hill 462.8, he wordlessly pinned his Good Conduct Medal ribbon and his Expert Infantryman Badge to his filthy field jacket in a bizarre gesture that suggested either a departure from the ranks of the sane or the most unflappable sense of humor in the company. Subsequent events indicated it was the latter.

The Expert Infantryman Badge

Technical Sergeant Walter Bull, Platoon Sergeant (and, after Lieutenant Harry Gullborg was wounded near Neufmaisons, Platoon Leader) of Company A's 2d Platoon. At Fort Bragg, Bull added the Army first-ever Expert Infantryman Badge to his Soldier's Medal, and later added a battle-field commission to his impressive WWII accomplishments. Not a terribly successful speculator in certain sectors of the petro-chemical sector, he did enjoy a remarkable life in the Regular Army, ultimately serving in Korea and Vietnam.

Sergeant Real Parenteau, Assistant Squad Leader of our platoon's 3d Squad shown here clowning around with a liberated German World War I helmet. Sergeant Parenteau was the only member of our platoon to have served in combat prior to our baptism of fire in the High Vosges; he had served with the Americal Division on Guadalcanal.

Lieutenant Ed Casazza, *left*, Transportation Officer for 1st Battalion, 399th Infantry Regiment, whose level-headed attitude toward combat balanced the exuberance of Lieutenant Ballie and some other officers in our outfit.

Lieutenant Ray Landis, *center*, Executive Officer of Company A, whose demonstrated commitment and concern for his soldiers was an inspiration to all of us. Seeing his outnumbered comrades on Hill 462.8, he volunteered to serve on the hill as a rifleman from 17–23 November 1944.

Major Barney Lentz, *right*, our battalion Executive Officer. A lawyer by civilian profession, he eschewed the Judge Advocate General Corps for the infantry, like his father before him. (The elder Lentz had once been Colonel Tychsen's boss in the Regular Army.) An "Army brat," Major Lentz was nevertheless famous for his unusual marching style.

Lieutenant Jack Harrell, our highly competent Texan platoon leader who helped us ASTP men rapidly and effectively assimilate into the infantry in general, and our company in particular. Not sure that the 100th would ever deploy to combat, at Bragg he volunteered for parachute duty, unknowingly leaving us to the tender mercies of Lieutenant Mueller.

Captain Park Brown, our Battalion Operations and Training Officer (S-3), as well as former Big Six 880-yard and cross-country champion at Northwestern University.

Lieutenant Henry Majeski, Executive Officer of Company C, who was wounded in the 1st Battalion's assault on the *Tête des Reclos*. As he was being carried off in a litter, he spotted his friend, Dick Young, and exclaimed, "Dick, you look awful!"

Captain Ronan Campion, Commanding Officer of Company C, 1st Battalion, 399th Infantry Regiment, and former commanding officer of our own Able Company. Captain Campion led Charlie Company from Fort Bragg into combat in the High Vosges forests, after which he was wounded and transferred.

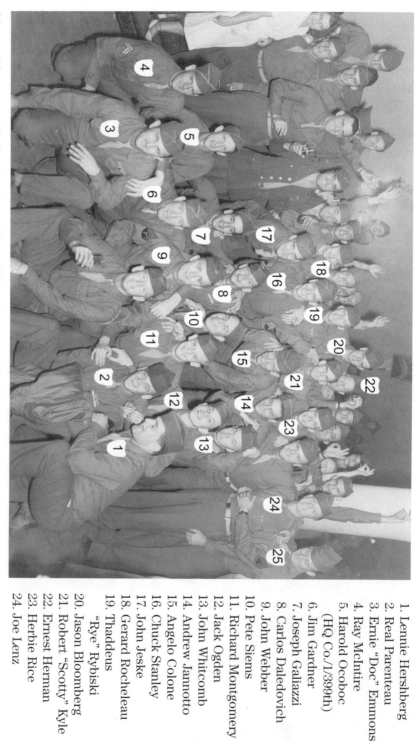

Many of Company A's finest at the hallowed Town Pump on their last Saturday night in Fayetteville before shipping out for the ETO.

1. Lennie Hershberg
2. Real Parenteau
3. Ernie "Doc" Emmons
4. Ray McIntire
5. Harold Ocoboc
(HQ Co./1/399th)
6. Jim Gardner
7. Joseph Galiazzi
8. Carlos Daledovich
9. John Webber
10. Pete Siems
11. Richard Montgomery
12. Jack Ogden
13. John Whitcomb
14. Andrew Jannotto
15. Angelo Colone
16. Chuck Stanley
17. John Jeske
18. Gerard Rocheleau
19. Thaddeus
"Rye" Rybiski
20. Jason Bloomberg
21. Robert "Scotty" Kyle
22. Ernest Herman
23. Herbie Rice
24. Joe Lenz

Robert "Scotty" Kyle, our squad's Ammo Bearer for the BAR gunner. An ASTP alumnus, he became "drunk with power" when he was promoted to Pfc at Bragg and the author wasn't. By the time we got to France, he had recovered sufficiently to go over the hill briefly with the author for a quick tour of Marseilles, before going in to the line near St. Remy. Wounded on 8 December 1944, and evacuated to England, in this post-war photo, he is sporting his Combat Infantryman Badge.

Five Company A stalwarts get together at the Town Pump for one last night on the town prior to deployment to the European Theater of Operations. From left to right: Joe Maneri, Carlos Daledovich, John Jeske, Herbie Rice, and Robert "Scotty" Kyle. Within forty-five days, all would face the enemy in the freezing gloom of the Vosges Mountains.

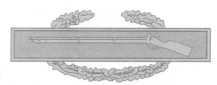

The Combat Infantryman Badge

First Sergeant
Thomas Mulligan

Thaddeus "Rye" Rybiski

Richard Montgomery

Ray Fields

Ernie "Doc" Emmons

Garland Cash

George Lorenze

Bob "Hoggie" Hogberg

Bob Jones

evacuated to the Battalion Aid Station. We were all tremendously shaken by the news of our friends' misfortunes, especially Adair's death which we couldn't even begin to assimilate. We felt we now had a personal score to settle with the Krauts.

Sergeant Gardner said the small farm building across the street where the lieutenant had ordered two of our men be outposted had received two direct 88 hits and was a shambles. If we had put men there and at the cross-roads as the lieutenant wanted, we might have lost half our squad. We all felt gratitude that the lieutenant's orders had been weighed and partly disobeyed by our non-coms. I wondered why Sergeant Moniz had simply swallowed the orders without better analyzing the risks..

I remembered Jimmy Adair the day before, striding confidently through the woods, a carbine on one shoulder and a Buck Rogersish grease gun on the other. Poor Adair had never even had a chance to lead his squad as First Scout.

When Sergeant Angelo "Babe" Colone of the Second Platoon learned of Adair's death, he said, "My God, the Army's gonna make us *die* in alphabetical order too!" Since he was a "C" himself, Colone probably didn't feel too secure.

At the Company C CP, Captain Campion and Lieutenant Jack Jenkins hadn't been able to fit in the stone cellar with the rest of the men so they had slept on the kitchen floor. Or *tried* to sleep, because the two old maids who lived there wanted to drink with them to celebrate their liberation. When barrages fell several times during the night, Campion and Jenkins took refuge under the kitchen table, while the old crones went on talking to them as though nothing had happened.

Jack Jenkins, a Clemson graduate, had worked for the government as an engineer until he was drafted and sent to Australia and New Guinea. He was rotated back to the ZI (Zone of the Interior) in January 1944 and given a safe job as an instructor at the Infantry Training Replacement Center at Camp Croft, South Carolina, near Spartanburg. The CO of the training regiment there invited all the officers to a party one Saturday night in June, but Jenkins didn't like the colonel and didn't like the Army and didn't go. The next week he found himself transferred to the 100th, bound for parts unknown—like St. Remy, France.[17]

---

[17]Jenkins, Jack. *19 Days in Combat.* MS. at USAMHI.

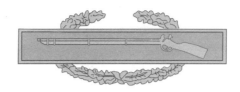

Chapter Fourteen
Bayonet Charge at Woods Six

Sunday, 5 November. The roads of St. Remy, still muddy from recent rains, were churned by hurrying boots and grinding jeep wheels in the predawn darkness. A chaos of scurrying shadows slowly converged into organized platoons and companies. Soon Company A was assembled and ready to go, just beyond the last house on the east side of town. We were told to stack our horseshoe roll packs beside the road, to be able to march and fight without undue encumbrances.

"Come on, you guys, get some damned interval!" bellowed Captain Young. "You want one shell to wipe out the whole lot of you? Come on Mueller, get your scouts out!" A strong wind reeking of turnips blew into town and it had started raining. "We've got to reach that woods before it gets light," Captain Young said.

Since Companies B and C had borne the brunt of capturing St. Remy yesterday, today it was apparently Able Company's turn to lead.

The lieutenant pointed to the distant high ground which appeared to be around three-quarters of a mile east of St. Remy. "That's the woods," he told Rice and me.

"Mueller!" bellowed Captain Young, "If we don't get in that woods before daylight, we'll be caught like dead ducks in the open!" The Old Man was really nervous this morning.

Herbie Rice led the company's advance across the rutted pasture which was an ocean of mud, complete to the wavelike furrows. Beyond Rice's silhouette, I could see the distant patch of woods that was our objective. The wood stood on a balcony dominating St. Remy, and between them the land fell away and then rose again.

Herbie Rice went down a shallow draw leading to the bottom of a large perpendicular valley through which flowed a stream which had to be crossed. Rice and I waded through the cold water which came up to the tops of our shoepacs. Rice seemed to have shipped more water than I for he began losing momentum as we climbed the open slope beyond the stream toward the wall of sinister black evergreens on the crest far up ahead. Every step he took looked like a log being yanked out of the mud by a winch. I could see a little light now behind the evergreens and began to fear that Rice was going too slowly to win the race against daylight for that patch of woods. We were like fugitives from justice as the first flicker of the police car's spotlight pokes around the corner into the street where we stood huddled against a building.

I began to close the twenty or thirty yards separating me from Rice with a prolonged succession of long strides. Soon I drew even with the First Scout who was breathing heavily. Without thinking or asking permission, I plunged out ahead of Herbie Rice, who said nothing but kept plodding ahead as best he could.

Up the long pasture we climbed—Gurley, Rice, Gardner, Mueller, Young, and 185 others, furtive shadows of the night seeking refuge before being caught by the rays of daylight. I finally reached the edge of the wall of dark, silent pines and entered among the trees. Sergeant Gardner told us to continue to the far edge of the wood.

I led the way with Herbie Rice fifteen or twenty yards behind me. I had traversed most of the woods, which seemed to be about seventy-five yards deep, when Sergeant Gardner told us to "hold up." I knelt on one knee and peered ahead, trying to see what lay ahead. Suddenly in front of me, I heard someone cough.

"Herb," I whispered, "I heard a cough up there. Pass it back."

Rice crept back and told Sergeant Gardner what I had heard.

Then I heard the cough again. The owner of that throat had to be German and could not be more than ten or fifteen yards ahead of me, probably occupying a foxhole at the wood's rear edge. Piqued by old-fashioned curiosity to learn the cougher's identity and take appropriate action if he was enemy, I began to creep through underbrush and vines up a slight rise. Miraculously, no twig broke under my carefully planted shoepacs (a kind of insulated boot that helped keep feet warm, but had the disadvantage of trapping moisture).

But did I really want to know that badly who the cougher was? If he or one of his friends riddled me with 9mm slugs, where would that leave me? I stopped my forward crawling. Hell, I was no hero. I would wait for instructions from my squad leader.

A minute or two later Rice whispered, "Pull back out of the wood. We're going back." Astonished, I crept back through the trees behind Rice and soon was out in the open once again.

It was now almost light enough to see normally. Ahead of me I saw Able Company withdrawing in some disorder back down the slope Rice and I had led them up, as though they had lost a battle. It was incomprehensible to me why we were pulling back. Beyond the deep draw ahead I could see the spire and roofs of St. Remy, which when viewed from the east seemed to be standing on a hill. Yesterday, when we had entered the town's west end, it had seemed to be situated on a flat plain.

We waded the stream at the bottom draw again, getting our socks, boots, and trousers wet a second time. On a little rise of ground off to the left of the crossing site we were told to dig foxholes in a copse of trees that looked down on the stream. It appeared to be a good defensive position.

As we passed the CP group I heard Captain Young say, "I guess I had my map bent. That wood was Hill 372 but we aren't supposed to be up there till tomorrow. It's my fault"

It was now broad daylight as we began digging in. Everyone was sweating buckets and feeling a general let-down after the strenuous, tension-filled movement from St. Remy up the hill and back down again. Our squad was on the left flank of the company position in a little neck of small trees and brush where the wood ended in green soggy meadows. Nobody was really in the mood yet to dig in, so we contented ourselves with making a few passes at the ground with our little collapsible shovels while discussing the events of the morning.

Rice and I, who were on the extreme left of the position, had just managed to excavate a few scoops of top soil from the rocky clay terrain when a breathless rush of air materialized above us. *Boom!* A loud explosion and the *whee-ee-ee!* of hurtling shrapnel filled the air. We couldn't believe it was aimed at us, and felt there must be some mistake. Our muscles quickly forgot their weariness of the morning's adventures and a frantic excavation followed like dogs seeking buried bones. We could hear the other members of the squad hacking away for dear life with picks and shovels at the stubborn clay soil.

After the first explosion, everything was calm for perhaps another minute. Then they came again, this time in volleys. Clearly, the German forward observers were verifying the range and deflection. *"Whirr-rr-RR Boom zing-g-g-g twang-g-g! Whirr-rr-RR Boom zing-g-g-g twang-g-g!"* We gave up digging and tried to burrow into the hard ground. One doesn't just assume it's impossible for a pliant human body to force its way into an unyielding hard ground surface, at least until one has made the effort. When that failed, we tried praying. No matter how many shellings a soldier goes through, none remains so vivid in the mind as the first one, like first love. I would never forget those warning rushes of air, the cracking explosions, and the sizzling shrapnel. Viscerally, I couldn't believe the Germans would actually want to kill us, when we hadn't done anything to them. Also, why would they want to massacre such a nice bunch of guys as our squad, our platoon, our company? If the

Germans weren't cowards, why didn't they come out and fight like men instead of sneakily trying to murder us from positions of concealment?

Based on what had happened to Adair and the others last night and what was happening now to us, the enemy's artillery and mortars seemed to have eyes which followed wherever we went, day or night. Like a seasoned major league pitcher, Jerry's very first mortar had been "in there," a perfect strike. Finally, after what seemed an unbelievably long time, the *Whirr-booms* stopped and a deathly stillness prevailed. Then we head timid calls from up the line, "Everybody all right?" This was passed along until it reached our foxhole on the extreme left flank. It turned out that no one in the platoon had been hurt by the shelling.

Captain Young, whose CP group was bracketed by the same mortar barrage that had hit us, also thought there must be some mistake. Convinced that the mortars had come from the American side and had landed in our lines through some observer's error, he called Colonel Zehner to demand that the shelling be stopped.

"Dog Company made the same assumption as you," Colonel Zehner replied. "But those aren't our mortars, those are Jerry's."

"Oh my God," Captain Young said, incredulous. Then he told Colonel Zehner how we had advanced to Hill 372 by mistake earlier in the day, before he caught his map-reading error and pulled us back to our present position.

"But why didn't you stay up there and try to hold that woods?" Colonel Zehner asked. "After all, you got up there without taking any casualties."

The men needed no further encouragement to concentrate their energies on excavating foxholes four and even five feet deep. Ernie Emmons said that his foxhole mate, Scotty Kyle, went through much gesticulating with the shovel, but without removing much dirt or making their foxhole appreciably deeper.

When Herbie Rice and I had finished digging, we gathered tree branches to make a roof for our foxhole. We covered the roof with dirt and leaves to keep rain out and to create the desired camouflage effect. We fashioned a parapet of dirt covered with leaves on the downhill side of the foxhole and placed our rifles, six bandoliers of ammo and six grenades on the parapet.

Around mid-day the enemy started throwing stuff our way again. A mortar round exploded down in the stream bed fifty or seventy-five yards below the platoon's position. Several seconds later, a second round landed about ten yards behind our line of foxholes. After another several seconds, a third round landed on the crest of the little hill behind us. The three rounds had marched through our position on a perfectly straight line. What was the enemy up to anyway? A few minutes later, a barrage of three or four mortar shells flew overhead to explode ineffectually two hundred or more yards behind our position. The same pattern was repeated at intervals for the rest of the day. Sergeant Gardner said the enemy was trying to interfere with the supply of ammunition and food to our front line positions. I remembered Sergeant Gardner's statement that we would have nine shells in the air to every one of the enemy's. So far today, all we had heard was flying Krupp steel.

The enemy shelling forced Captain Young to cancel plans for the kitchen force to hand-carry large cans of hot food to our front line position. Instead, we received a carton of "ten-in-one" rations for the squad, supposedly enough to feed ten men one meal provided they had a nice stove and other cooking amenities. Actually we were twelve starving Armenians with no stove to cook green beans and pork and eggs from a can, so we divided the stuff in its cold state and each man took a small bite of everything like birds at a picnic. We almost felt hungrier at the end than when we started.

Herbie Rice and I cleared out enough branches in our little scrub patch so we could throw grenades out onto the green meadow below. The tops of most of the bushes around our foxhole had been sheared off by some force of nature which I didn't understand. Before us we had an unobstructed view of the stream and the slopes beyond leading up to patches of woods. We felt we could hold off the world in this position, provided they came at us in reasonable doses. We were thirsty but didn't dare to expose ourselves by going down the slope to the stream to fill our canteens. Maybe this was what Sergeant D'Arpino had been talking about when he lectured us on "water discipline."

Off to our left rear about 150 yards away we could see the last two farm buildings of St. Remy along the slope leading down to the stream. At about 1500, we saw troops assembling around the buildings, and a short time later they moved down across the stream. It was Charlie Company, starting up the long open rise toward Hill 372, where Herb Rice and I had led our company earlier.

Captain Campion stood beside one of the farm buildings, a sound powered telephone in each hand, directing the movement of Company C's platoons up the slope. Lieutenant Jack Jenkins, whose seventy-man patrol had been first into St. Remy yesterday, was in reserve today. He was with Captain Campion now.

At about 1530, as a bit of pre-twilight pink was suffusing an otherwise sodden sky, all hell broke loose on the slope where Company C was advancing in a long skirmish line. We heard what sounded like a 4th of July celebration. German machine guns, burp guns, and rifles opened up, as orange tracers criss-crossed in the sky. The men of Charlie Company responded with a chorus of deep-throated roars from M-1 rifles, and the factory-like pounding of BARs. Soon a .30-caliber machine gun from the Weapons Platoon went into action, adding bursts of its staccato hammering to the cacophony of battle. As I stood in our foxhole listening to the show, a chain of red tracer bullets rose from the enemy position into the sky. The red arrows hung suspended in the sky for what seemed several seconds before angling downward and coming straight for where I was standing. The bullets clipped the saplings and bushes over our foxhole as I ducked down into the hole for safety.

The Company C skirmish line had reached a point about one hundred yards from the wood I had gone into at dawn, when the German defenders opened fire. One of Charlie Company's scouts, Bud Steelman, succeeded in entering the wood, but came staggering back out a minute later with a bloody neck. Private Gordon S. Porter, a former ASTP student from South Arlington, Virginia, was struck across the middle by shrapnel from a mortar round that landed just in front of him and nearly cut him in half.

Gordon Porter was so well built, so handsome, and brimming over with self-confidence that I was certain that, whatever my own deficiencies in combat, Porter would come through as an indestructible man of steel. One Sunday in May at Bragg, I remembered Porter demonstrating the high polish on his belt buckle to his mother, a handsome Southern belle. He had practically lifted himself off the ground displaying that shiny buckle to his mother. Now he was dead of massive shrapnel wounds in the same midriff section where his shiny buckle had been worn on his garrison belt.

The enemy shelling continued, killing a second man and wounding several others.

Company C was pinned down and at risk of demoralization when Lieutenant Paul "Dutch" Loes rose and cried, "*Come on!*" He led the way toward the nearest machine-gun nest, which he and Scout Charley Hoak eliminated with carbine and rifle fire, and hand grenades. Charlie Company advanced another fifty yards to within half a football field of the wood's edge before digging in on orders from Captain Campion. Captain Campion felt that this was a less dangerous option than trying to move forward into the enemy-held wood or withdrawing to St. Remy.

Charlie Company spent the night pinned down on Hill 372 before the wood Herb Rice and I had entered before dawn without drawing any more violent reaction than two "coughs" from an unseen enemy. In retrospect, I

399TH INFANTRY REGIMENT OPERATIONS
IN THE VICINITY OF HILL 372
5-6 NOVEMBER 1944

⊠	US Infantry Unit	
⊠ (V)	German *Volks-Grenadier* (Infantry) Unit	
I	Company	
XX	Division	

A/399th's advance and withdrawal, 5 Nov

Attacks in support of C/399th, which was pinned down on 5 Nov

Scale: One grid square = One kilometer (.62 miles)

* I/399th Inf relieved in place byB/399th on the night of 6 Nov

figured I had done the right thing in not investigating further the source of those coughs.

Due to the interdiction of our company supply lines by enemy mortar barrages, it proved impossible to bring up our packs or bedrolls. Instead, Herbie Rice and I slept in our raincoats, with one man awake at a time on a three-hour shift. It rained on and off throughout the long night. I heard noises (or imagined them) and saw enemy shadows (or thought I did) creeping, stalking, lurking, bending, and aiming guns at me from down by the creek bed, always advancing. I watched what appeared to be one Jerry in particular who held his weapon out from his body at a right angle and always seemed about to charge up the slope from below. It was my most jittery night so far overseas. On the parapet in front of the foxhole, I kept my rifle an inch from one hand and a grenade in the other, ready to pull the pin on a moment's notice.

At one point, eight shots from an M-1 rifle rang out in rapid succession on my right, and then all was silence again. A while later, a single shot rang out, followed by scuffling sounds and again silence. Had the platoon been wiped out silently one at a time? Were the Krauts now creeping up on our foxhole? What was that fellow doing with the weapon held out from his body at a right angle? He was still there; he hadn't tried to come up the slope yet.

Come the dawn, we saw dim forms standing in the other foxholes, probably wondering, as we were, what the hell had gone on during the night. By full daylight, when a few brave birds honored nature's ritual by chirping in the little trees of the grove, I saw that the "Jerry with the rifle" who had been stalking the stream bed in front of me all night was in fact a bush with a branch that jutted out like a readied rifle. Glancing up at the sheared off tops of the bushes near the foxhole, which I had first noticed yesterday, I finally realized that the shearing must have been caused by artillery before we moved into the position. The super-quick fuses of modern artillery projectiles are detonated as soon as they hit anything, even the uppermost branches of trees; hence, the massive pruning of the trees in this area.

The author of the nocturnal outburst of M-1 fire turned out to be Sergeant Moniz's First Scout Hugh Price ("promoted" from second to First Scout after Jimmy Adair's death twenty-four hours earlier). Hugh Price said he had seen a Jerry near the stream and had fired eight times at the intruder.

"Are you sure you saw somebody?" Moniz asked. "I don't see any corpse down there."

"You're right I saw somebody," Price replied in his Oklahoma drawl. "Why else did I fire?" The other single shot I had heard while on guard had been fired by Sergeant Chuck Stanley. After receiving a call from Captain Young, Lieutenant Mueller had sent his runner, Eddie Cook, to tell Sergeant Stanley to alert the platoon to be on guard for a counterattack. Eddie Cook stumbled around in the dark looking for Chuck Stanley's and Sam D'Arpino's hole. Stanley heard the stumbling noises nearby, but instead of calling out the challenge and giving Cook a chance to reply with the password, he simply leveled his rifle and fired. After almost killing Cook, Stanley grappled with him for several seconds before finally recognizing him. Eddie Cook, who was scarcely two yards away when Stanley fired, had powder burns on his neck marking the bullet's close passage.

We were all very hungry now. The next best thing to actual food, I supposed, would have been a story about food. A story was, in fact, all we got. The kitchen commandos of Company A had allegedly started across the fields headed for our position with large marmite cans containing hot vittles. Suddenly an enemy machine gun or sniper (or perhaps it was an unfriendly gnat or mosquito) opened up from somewhere and they dropped the marmite cans and fled for their precious lives back to the shelter of the kitchen.

If the powers-that-be had been unable to feed us, they hadn't forgotten that we were needed to help the battalion earn its own daily bread that day. The battalion objective was "Wood Six," whose capture would outflank the German force that still had Charlie Company pinned down on the exposed slope of Hill 372. Company C men were weeping and sick from exposure after their long night ordeal and their foxholes were half full of water which they bailed out with canteen cups.

Before our company could advance, however, a foot bridge had to be built across the stream down in front of us. Since our platoon would be in reserve in the first phase, the "bridge-building" task fell to us. Sergeant Gardner's squad was selected and Real Parenteau picked five of us to help find a likely place to cross the rain-swollen stream and construct a ford. We slid down the damp slope to the stream and waded in water nearly up to our waists. Behind us on top of the slope we could see rifles, BARs, and machine guns protruding from behind every tree as our friends covered us.

Real Parenteau supervised us as we lashed some puny-looking tree logs and branches together with two pieces of rope he had been given for the mission. Finally we completed a narrow, slippery, log bridge which a well trained tight rope walker in tights might be expected to get across about half the time without falling in and getting drenched. The other platoons would certainly cuss out the patrol which had selected this asinine site across deep water and had fashioned such a ridiculous looking bridge.

While we were about it, we drank our fill and filled our canteens from the stream. For over twenty-four hours we had gazed down at the water but had not dared to descend the slope for fear of being dispatched by an alert sniper or mortar observer.

"Don't forget to put Halizone tablets in that stuff!" Sergeant Gardner called down to us from behind a tree. If Jerry didn't poison it he probably pissed in it!"

To our inexpressible surprise and joy, the 2d Platoon managed to cross our laughable log bridge without a man falling in or drawing enemy fire. The 3d Platoon followed them across and soon it was our turn. Once across the surprisingly sturdy "Parenteau Bridge," Company A advanced up the opposite slope through waist-high weeds which drenched the soldiers up to the ammunition bandoliers draped across their chests. We climbed a steep, defiladed draw past a small quarry up onto the next flat area. Ahead lay an eerie landscape of alternating open fields and tightly packed evergreen forests.

As we came up past the little quarry, the thought occurred to me that we were more or less back where man started from, slogging around in a primitive world of living in caves with little food and crude weapons to fight other tribes with. Surprisingly, my reaction to this primal regression was not one of disgust or despair, but a fierce sort of pride. We were discovering that we could still stand up to some of the old challenges that our caveman ancestors had had to overcome to hand us our comfortable modern world.

We halted along a muddy trail between two pine groves. While we waited for the signal to move forward again, a 3d Platoon man came along the trail escorting three enemy prisoners with hands on their heads (in the prescribed POW manner) and fear in their eyes. For our benefit he said as he sloshed by, "Humph, they don't look like Supermen to me."

Word filtered back that the 2d Platoon had sent a patrol into Woods Six which came upon enemy machine-gun emplacements and withdrew after being fired upon. The enemy then laid in mortars on the wood from which the 2d and 3d Platoons were preparing to attack. Captain Young responded by directing 4.2-inch chemical mortar fire against the Woods Six area where the machine guns had been identified. The German mortar barrage ceased.

The action against Woods Six was slowly building toward a climax. Captain Young appeared and went into a huddle with Lieutenant Mueller and Sergeants Stanley and D'Arpino. Off to our left front, we could see the dark tops of Woods Six across an open field.

Just after Captain Young left, I was sent by Sergeant Stanley through the woods to the right to contact Company G of the 3d Infantry Division's 15th Infantry Regiment. The 3d Division Joe I found was also out looking for contact with us. He wore a camouflaged helmet and a dark beard and carried a Thompson submachine gun casually in the crook of his arm. He looked at me in a protective way, almost like an older brother, although I had never seen him before and never would again.

"Company A is getting ready to attack Woods Six," I told him.

"Okay," he said. "Tell your CO that G Company is about two hundred yards to your right. We'll come over to help out if you run into anything bad."

"Thanks a lot," I said. He faded off among the trees like a seasoned Indian fighter in buckskin who had just steered a newly arrived greenhorn onto the safest trail.

Returning from my liaison mission, I reported to Lieutenant Mueller and Sergeants Stanley and D'Arpino, who seemed pleased at my report. Eddie Cook was sent off to inform Captain Young.

Finally at twilight, the order came, "We're going to attack Woods Six." Lieutenant Mueller was running around in circles shouting, "Get your stuff on! 1st and 3d Squads will advance abreast with the 2d Squad in support. Our objective is to take the left side of Woods Six by frontal assault. Captain Young and the 3d Platoon will attack Woods Six from the right."

I suggested to Lieutenant Mueller that we fix bayonets, since by the time we reached those woods, it might be too dark for us to aim our rifles properly. I felt a bit old-fashioned in making the suggestion, since bayonets were often the butt of jokes as being useless implements "except for cutting branches or opening a can of beans."

Nevertheless, the next thing I knew, the Lieutenant cried, *"Fix bayonets!"* I was proud that my suggestion had been acted upon. There was a tremendous clanking and rattling as the men complied with the order. Nobody said the order was silly and we were a truly impressive group with the long steel showing above the muzzles of our M-1s.

"Scouts out!" Lieutenant Mueller ordered. It was over the top, World War I all over again. Out of the woods we went, onto the open field, like ducks on a pond. Woods Six looked to be three or four hundred yards away. Herbie Rice and I were on the right, John Jeske and Garland Cash of Ammo's squad were on the left, with Lieutenant Mueller's CP group midway between the two squad leaders. I hoped that either (1) there were no longer any Krauts in Woods Six, despite previous reports of machine guns and mortars; or (2) they would be eating an early sauerkraut supper and wouldn't notice the subtle approach of thirty-five running men laden down with BARs, rifles, carbines, grease guns, bayonets, grenades, and bandoliers of ammunition.

One month ago today, Scotty Kyle and I had watched the Statue of Liberty glide past our ship.

Today we would make a bayonet charge.

We had gone perhaps fifty yards when we heard shouting from the rear.

"Hey wait for me!" Lennie Hershberg cried, brandishing his BAR aloft like a toy. "I got held up by a case of the GI runs!"

We advanced about two hundred yards out into the field, a bit over halfway to Woods Six and just far enough so it would be disadvantageous to turn back if fired upon. At that precise moment the enemy machine guns opened fire. The air around us was alive with dancing chains of red-orange tracer bullets, pirouetting a ballet of death. No one in the platoon needed to be told to hit the dirt. I landed flat in a furrow and began burrowing like a mole. It is truly amazing how much untapped energy a person has inside when he starts letting it out. Pushing a dirt wall up in front of my prone body with my hands and at the same time wriggling my body down into the damp earth while crunching feet and legs into the dirt, I was only doing what I supposed everybody else was doing. For the first time in my life, I felt sympathy for the wooden ducks in a carnival shooting gallery.

When I became tired of burrowing, I cautiously raised one eyebrow to see what was going on above the earth's surface. The enemy guns were still firing tracers which seemed to sail high, wide, and handsome over our cowering bodies as though they didn't know how to aim. However, I quickly became aware of the sound of non-tracer bullets striking the sod all around us. Apparently Jerry was using the high tracer fire of one gun as a decoy, hoping we'd be dumb enough to stand up only to be "sat down" again by the grazing fire of the other gun. The issue was now joined between our force and the enemy—we wanted the wood he was occupying, and he had seen us coming and had pinned us down with machine-gun fire. Who would come out the winner in this head-on confrontation?

"All right, get up! *Let's go!*" Lieutenant Mueller bawled. Was he insane? Had he been taken in by the decoy tracers? The four scouts rose and ran forward, crouching as low as we could. One machine gun continued to chatter but nobody seemed to be hit. After we had advanced another fifty or seventy-five yards, the fire tapered off and suddenly stopped altogether.

Just then I became aware of the reassuring whirrings of friendly mortars overhead, which exploded along the front edge of the wood and kicked up black geysers of dirt and smoke.

When we reached a point about fifty yards from the wood, I heard a rush of air above us in the gathering shadows. Enemy mortars! *"Boom! Whirrr Boom!"* Once again, we became part of the pasture as we were when the machine guns had opened up, but too scared this time even to burrow ourselves a mole's hole. Dirt was kicking high all around and showering down on our backs when, as suddenly as it had started, the barrage was over.

Captain Young (whose voice was so powerful he often didn't need a radio to contact his units) yelled from somewhere to our right front, "Mueller, where the hell are you?"

Lieutenant Mueller responded by crying *"Go!"* and we charged the last fifty yards to Woods Six. In among the black tree trunks, our bayonets clanked against wood. Any Jerry in my path would have gotten stuck good, but they had apparently pulled back minutes or seconds before we charged.

Doc Emmons was nursing a bloody thumb from a mortar round's explosion that had blown his left glove off. He seemed to be our squad's only casualty from our charge across the field. Captain Young and the 3d

Platoon had entered the right end of the wood and worked their way through the trees to join our force just after we had crashed into the tree-line with our bayonets. Private John McCarthy, an eighteen-year-old from Waltham, Massachusetts, was killed in the 3d Platoon's assault on Woods Six, and Staff Sergeant Frank Soldano of Boston was wounded.

We consolidated on the objective, forming a defensive line among the trees against a possible Kraut counterattack. We had to lie within a yard of the next guy or he was invisible or out of touch. It was the old hand-in-front-of-the-face story in these dark Vosges woods. Then Captain Young told us to move through the woods to the far side, where we formed a new line of defense looking out across a field toward another wood.

Our successful attack against Woods Six relieved some of the pressure on Company C, which remained pinned down on Hill 372. Off to Charlie Company's left, Item Company stormed across the road leading northeast out of St. Remy at approximately the same time we were attacking Woods Six. Their company's point man, Ulysses Henry, was killed by machine-gun fire and fifty others were killed or wounded. Captain Travis "Hoppy" Hopkins' Company I "Greyhounds" (as they were called) had been trained by Hoppy at Bragg on a diet of running and forced marches. At St. Remy they were as fleet as ever, but fifty-one of them couldn't move as fast as the machine-gun bullets and flying mortar fragments that brought them down.

Although Company I's attack was probably a debacle *per se*, it also contributed to relieving the pressure on Charlie Company which at 2300 was able to withdraw to St. Remy for rest and refitting after being pinned down for over twenty-four hours in the rain and bullets.

Suddenly Herbie Rice and I realized how tired we were from the day's activities and the food we hadn't eaten for the past two days (except for those uncooked ten-in-one "snacks" the previous morning). Our total bedding consisted of raincoats and wet field jackets. It was raining as I dug our foxhole while Herbie gathered wet pine boughs for "blankets." Mix muddy foxhole with cruddy doughfeet, place wet pine boughs on top, subtract guard duty, sprinkle with rain, stir thoroughly, and you have a rather odd prescription for a good night's sleep. Nevertheless, Rice's pine boughs actually did produce considerable warmth and we managed to sleep quite well when not on guard.

Captain Young asked for volunteers to run a contact patrol to the 3d Infantry Division unit I had contacted that afternoon. Sergeant Gardner and Doc Emmons volunteered to go.

"But I understand you got hit," Captain Young said to Emmons.

"Naw, it's just a scratch, Young," Emmons replied. He had bandaged his thumb and was wearing gloves to hold the bandage in place.

"Don't you want Battalion Aid to look at it?" the Captain asked.

"Naw, Young," Emmons replied. I wondered why he wasn't calling him "Captain Young" with due military respect until I remembered their conversation at the St. Remy cemetery two nights ago and the captain's specific injunction against use of rank.

Sergeant Gardner and Doc Emmons set off in the rain and darkness.

"Halt! G Company?" Gardner called several times into the wet wind. The smell of evergreens came strongly into their lungs but there was no response to Gardner's calls. It was like exploring a haunted house.

Finally they identified someone moving at the edge of a copse about fifty yards away.

"Hallo! Is that you G Company?" Sergeant Gardner, pride of the Bronx, called out in his most engaging manner. "Friends, are you there?"

There was no reply and the movement ceased. About half a minute later three mortar shells whooshed in close and exploded. Apparently the only G Company they had found so far was "G" as in "Germans." They decided to abandon their mission and return to Woods Six to report to Captain Young.

Captain Young had a problem evacuating the wounded. He sent a runner, Private John Day from Salem, Oregon, to find Scotty Kyle. When Kyle heard Day call his name, he "kept his trap shut."

Sergeant Stanley said, "He's over here." Day delivered his message and Kyle reported to the Captain.

"Kyle," Captain Young said. "I want you to drive some wounded men back to St. Remy."

"What's the matter with the regular jeep drivers?" Scotty Kyle replied. He had already put in more than a full day's work of foot-slogging and now those "rear echelon jerks" wanted him to do their work to boot.

Captain Young's helmet loomed down over Kyle. "How would you like to be court-martialed?" he roared at the spindly Oregonian. Kyle had never been talked to that way in his life.

"I'm going, sir," he sighed, totally deflated.

"Don't call me 'Sir!'" Captain Young said.

"All right" Kyle said.

Scotty Kyle made four trips back to St. Remy evacuating wounded and picking up needed ammunition. On one trip, Captain Young told him to stop off at Battalion Aid in St. Remy and find out if Lieutenant White were there. White had disappeared during the day's operations.

Kyle recalled later, "The sergeant in the aid station, a building in the town, was not going to tell me anything. I aimed my rifle at him. After all, *Captain Young* wanted the information. (Incidentally, you were not supposed to go armed into an aid station.) The medic Sergeant changed his tune and said the Lieutenant had combat fatigue. I'm sure "cowardice" was the word Captain Young and I equated that to mean.

"After four trips and the coming of daylight, I left the jeep with the cooks headquartered between the creek and the woods by a small hill. An engineer came back with his vacuum sweeper type of minesweeper and told me they had found three or four Teller mines in the road. Had we hit a mine it would have been a disaster for all of us on or near the jeep.

"When I rejoined our platoon, Frank Gurley said 'My God, Scotty, you look twenty-four years old!' " (Kyle was eighteen)

One of Kyle's Purple Heart passengers on his runs to St. Remy was Sergeant Carlos "Dale" Daledovich, Ammo's assistant squad leader. Dale told Kyle he had been sitting in a foxhole while Ammo leaned against a tree dragging on his pipe. When mortars started falling, Dale shouted for Ammo to get in the hole, but Ammo refused to move until he finished his pipe. A mortar round landed close to the foxhole and a hunk of jagged shrapnel found its way down into the hole where it embedded itself in the back of Dale's left leg. Ammo, although completely exposed to the effects of the blast outside the foxhole, had not been touched or injured in any way.

"Dale always told me that if we soldiered by the book, we'd come through combat all right," Scotty Kyle told me the next morning. "Taking Dale back to St. Remy, I thought I had had a good demonstration of what the book was worth, namely nothing."

When daylight came we had our first good look at Woods Six which we had crashed into at nightfall when visibility had been poor at best. At the corners of the wood there were machine-gun emplacements. Scattered inside the wood were large, well-camouflaged dugouts containing general and sleeping quarters. The dugouts were so elaborate that the German defenders must have planned on a long stay here. But when Captain Young's crazy company came charging at them with fixed bayonets, they apparently decided to move out without leaving a forwarding address. Like crafty Indians, the Krauts had fired at us from camouflage, and when about to be overrun had simply vanished deeper into the forest. Unfortunately for us, the Kraut brand of Redskin was not limited to bows and arrows, but was equipped with machine guns, mortars, burpguns, and snipers' rifles, most of which were said to be superior to our own weaponry.

Most of the platoon crowded inside the lieutenant's dugout which normally had room for only eight or ten men. Everyone was feeling chipper, despite the lack of food and dry clothes, because there was a fire burning in the stove and there was straw to lie in. The was a lot of German equipment in the dugout, but nobody touched anything out of fear of booby traps.

I noticed that Lieutenant Mueller had picked up a second canteen some-where. He was in fine fettle this morning and didn't seem particularly tired despite our collective exertions of yesterday.

"This dugout must have been built by French slave labor," the Lieutenant said. "According to what I heard in St. Remy, the Germans have built a winter line somewhere up ahead and French conscripted laborers worked on that too."

The conversation drifted round to the fact that we had not yet run into German tanks and what would happen when we did. Lieutenant Mueller recounted with enthusiasm how he would crouch down in his foxhole until the treads of the Tiger or Panther tank had run over his hole without injur-ing him, and then run after the tank with a grenade in his hand (he sound-ed like David chasing Goliath with a paper clip for a weapon). He'd jump up on the back deck of the iron monster and beat on the turret with his car-bine butt. When they opened the hatch he'd drop the grenade in their laps and quickly leap clear before the tank was consumed by flames and inter-nal explosion. He made it all sound so simple that I could picture him tak-ing a whisk broom out of his pocket and sweeping the pieces neatly off to the side of the road afterward.

A week ago I would have agreed with the lieutenant's dissertation on how to kill a tank. But the 45th Division boys had wised us up, and we now knew that the Benning school solution to the problem was totally imprac-tical, if not suicidal. As a practical matter, if you hung around long enough for that tank to run over your foxhole, you were already a dead man. If the tank's treads did not finish you off by collapsing the walls of your foxhole, the German infantry accompanying the tank would apply the *coup de grace* as you emerged from the debris of your foxhole like a blind mole. Unfortunately for him, Lieutenant Mueller hadn't yet been clued in on the realities of the tank problem. In delivering his outdated lecture he suc-ceeded only in making a fool of himself in front of most of the platoon. The sad thing about it was that he didn't even realize what was happening.

I wondered why it was I couldn't seem to relate to the lieutenant the way I did with, for example, Chuck Stanley, Sam D'Arpino, and Jim Gardner. If the ASTP men in the platoon shared college backgrounds with the lieu-tenant, it didn't seem to bring us closer together. On the other hand, I had never heard Eddie Cook, who shared a foxhole with him, complain about him. It was difficult to define what the lieutenant's problem was. Kyle said that the lieutenant ("that jackass") came from the same town as he

(Medford, Oregon) and that Kyle did all he could to play down their common origin.

Perhaps the lieutenant was too sure of himself and talked too much, rather than listening once in a while. If he had listened to the 45th boys, for example, he might have learned that the way you fight a German tank was not to engage in outdated heroics but to run away and live to fight another day.

Two hot rumors reached Mueller's CP dugout. First, they were sending up two five-gallon cans of cold coffee from the kitchen in St. Remy. Second, we might get relieved this afternoon. As to Rumor No. 1 (perfectly accurate at the time we received it), the 2d Platoon had first crack at the five-gallon cans of java and drank every drop. I didn't drink coffee as a rule, but couldn't think of anything I looked forward to with such keen anticipation as that cold coffee. It would have tasted as good as water, for which we were also thirsting.

We had better luck with Rumor No. 2. At about noon we were relieved, and started our trek back over the captured ground of the past few days. It was pouring as we sloshed back around woods and across muddy pastures. It was heart-rending to see men slip and fall in puddles of water with all their equipment and then struggle to get up again. I felt great sympathy for my fellow foot-sloggers, who resembled a row of poplars in winter, their finery gone, bowing wearily to the will of wind and rain, yet somehow remaining upright. Their green raincoats and olive-drab field trousers had merged into a generalized tone I would have called mud-colored. I was certain I wasn't the only one who was completely sick of all the war we had witnessed in such a short time.

We passed Hill 372 and the fateful wood where I had outfooted Herbie Rice and briefly became the company's point man three dawns ago. In the muddy field in front of the wood was a row of abandoned foxholes partly filled with water and surrounded by empty K ration cartons, bandages, bandoliers, ammo clips, and the other usual flotsam and jetsam of an infantry unit tossed by the seas and squalls of combat. Here the men of Company C had gone through thirty hours of wet hell before being relieved. The German defenders had enjoyed a magnificent commanding view of the long slope leading down to the stream and up the far slope to the houses and church spire or St. Remy. I wondered how we had gotten in and out of that wood without running into the Jerries who later made Charlie Company's existence so miserable.

Finally, we reached St. Remy and were billeted one squad to a farmhouse. Our house had a cellar, two chilled rooms and a small kitchen where the farm's only heat came from a small wood-burning stove. For security against shelling we spent most of our time in the cellar, which had five-feet standing clearance, dirt walls, rotting log rafters, a potato bin, apple bin and large brown earthen jugs along the wall connected by mazes of cobwebs. Our entire stay was spent attempting to dry our ski sox, gloves, shirts, trousers, field jackets, bandoliers, undershirts, longjohns, sweaters, and everything else we owned, without exception. The farm family rigged up clotheslines in the kitchen for our things to dry out near the stove. Most of us walked around wearing only shoes and raincoats as our uniforms dried out. The family also provided us blankets, comforters, burlap bags, and a couple of mattresses for our sleeping comfort in the cellar.

Real Parenteau cut an Army blanket into twelve equal strips to provide a home-made scarf for every member of the squad. Parenteau also took the K rations we were issued upon our return to St. Remy and made a gigantic "K Ration Stew for Twelve" consisting of pork and egg yolks (the breakfast K unit), cheese (the dinner unit) and corned pork loaf (the supper unit) plus the crackers that came with each unit. On the stove he had a large cauldron of Nescafé boiling lightly.

Whatever rations were left over from Parenteau's gala stew were collected and placed on the kitchen table for the family—green boxes, blue boxes and brown boxes, some still unopened and others with various parts of the rations inside. We showed them how to open the K ration boxes by biting into the corner of the box. They acted as happy as children at Christmas at receiving the rations.

Of all the war's unsung heroes, one of the greatest was probably Hersh's assistant BAR man and the platoon's undisputed champion chow hound, Bob "Hoggie" Hogberg. Hoggie had (like the rest of us) gone seventy-two hours with very little to eat but never complained as far as I knew. He wrote to his folks that evening,

> *Nov. 7, 1944 Somewhere in France*
> *I've been on the go for quite a while and haven't had a chance to write. I'm feeling fine. I don't get enough to eat, but that's something that isn't unusual. Send me some cookies, candy, and maybe chocolate bars. I'll ask for packages in my letter as I'm always hungry.*
> *I think this French weather is for no good. It always rains and is very cold at night. You should see the beard I've grown. You wouldn't recognize me.*
>
> *Your loving son*
> *Bob*

Not wishing to attend the "88 concert" that night, we all opted to sleep in the cellar. Our devil-may-care attitude of our first night in St. Remy, when the squad had slept at ground level in the salon, had changed completely only three nights later. We finally convinced our non-coms that it was too wet outside either for us to stand guard or for the Krauts to pull a counterattack. Besides, we argued, we had pushed the enemy back from Woods Six and there seemed little likelihood that they would try to return.

We slept for sixteen hours, from 2000. until noon the next day. Drying our clothes completely was impossible but we managed to get luke-wet socks and trousers out of the mass drying operation.

We stuck our heads out of the house to find that the rain had stopped. Low dark clouds were scurrying by as usual but were not dropping their loads for the moment. St. Remy had been shelled during the morning and we were told to remain indoors where we would be safe from all but direct hits.

After a K ration brunch, I slipped outside to have an unauthorized look at St. Remy, which we had entered at twilight on the 4th, left before dawn on Sunday, the 5th, and only seen briefly yesterday, the 7th, in a heavy downpour. No shells were falling and if one did, I would be the only one to pay the price for ignoring the order to stay indoors. I found the house where we had spent the first night, and the crossroads where Jimmy Adair, Carl Haskell, and Ellahugh Sluder had been hit. Across the road from the house was a stone war memorial surrounded by an iron grill fence. The monument had been erected through public subscription and dedicated in 1910, the fortieth anniversary of the beginning of the Franco-Prussian War [the war began in the summer of 1870 and ended in early 1871]. Many St. Remy men had died in that war, at places like Sèvres and Neuilly in the Paris suburbs. Ironically, only four years after the monument's dedication, German shells from the war of 1914–18 began taking gouges out of the monument's stone faces and corners. The long list of St. Remy men who died in that war was in alphabetical order by year—1914, 1915, 1916, 1917, and 1918—five years of fighting and dying. The monument had received additional nicks and gouges from both sides in our war, and now the retreating Germans were getting in what appeared to be their last licks of World War II. As I thought of the German victory in 1871, their defeat in 1918, and the excellent prospects for another defeat in the present war, a silly sports headline popped into my head,

Krauts cop series opener, then drop two

Back at the house, the farmer's wife told me there would be additional names added to the monument from our war. Two St. Remy men had died in combat so far, four had been shot by the Germans, while nine had been deported to Germany. The mayor and six other civilians had been victims of the fighting in the St. Remy area.

Her fifteen-year-old son was afire with an enthusiastic hatred for the "*Boche.*" He came down into the cellar and explained to the 3d Squad's twelve wet old men how anxious he was to fight.

"*Non, non!*" I told him, laughing. We all appreciated his patriotic sentiments, but also felt that anyone who volunteered for combat was plain crazy. You'd have thought we had gone on the line seven years ago instead of only seven days. Before going on line, the consensus among my friends had been that we'd like to see a month or two of action. Now, we had already had more than enough. We had all become anti-war, except as an unavoidable necessity.

At about 1400 we were told to get ready to move. The lady and her son waved good-bye to us.

"It's only four hours on foot from here to Germany!" she (over-optimistically) cried, pointing east.

"*Au revoir!*" I said, laughing at the irony that our column seemed to be heading *west*, at least for the moment.

We left town the same way we had entered four days earlier, passing the wood where Jimmy Adair had been so at peace with the world with his new toy-like grease gun. Leaving the exposed open ground, we reached the shelter of rows of pines cascading one upon another. The rumor went up and down the column that we would reach a rest area in an hour or so.

We passed an ammunition point among the trees where wooden crates of shells, grenades, machine-gun belts, and rifle ammo were piled in perfect neat rows in contrast to the wildness of the surrounding woods. The dark woods held everything we associated with war's horrors except Jerry, who was absent today. Whoever was leading the march led us up one hill and around two others, until we had lost all sense of direction. Instead of reaching our destination with ample daylight to dig foxholes, we finally stumbled into the bivouac area as it was getting dark.

Herbie Rice and I thought over carefully the order to dig in. Since it would be rough trying to dig a foxhole in the dark, we decided to dig a one-foot deep foxhole to be in formal compliance with the order, but then to pitch our pup tent elsewhere. Herbie had acquired a tent pole and pegs somewhere, after we had burned our original ones the first day on the line.

The next morning, 9 November, at 0600 hours, our regiment reverted to the control of the 100th Infantry Division after nine days of being attached to the 45th Infantry Division. When General Burress had set up his first CP in the Vosges village of Padoux on 1 November, the local residents were very hospitable. The local people wore wooden shoes outside their homes, due to the mud and various exotic types of animal manure that covered the village's unpaved roads. Some of the 100th men bought wooden shoes as souvenirs and mailed them to the States.

The owner of the house selected by General Burress for his CP watched the Signal Corps bring in all sorts of wiring for electricity, generators, telephones, and other technical marvels essential to the functioning of a modern army. He soon began to worry that his home would be burned to the ground through a power overload. On the third or fourth day, he became so overwrought that he blew up in General Burress' presence, expressing the wish, "*que les Américains partissent!*" General Burress smiled in his kindly way, but ignored the man's objections. Finally, to the owner's inexpressible relief, the 100th left Padoux for the larger town of Rambervillers on the day it assumed command of all divisional units.[18]

The only sounds of war in our bivouac area (called the *Forêt de St. Benoît*) were American artillery firing toward distant targets and the occasional deafening roar of a concealed German land mine. The explosions of the land mines caused many to dive into foxholes in the mistaken belief that the Germans were shelling us, but Herbie Rice and I were never fooled.

One outdoor trick Herbie Rice had learned on his grandfather's farm was how to build a fire. After we had completed the excavation of our foxhole, Herb started rubbing the two proverbial sticks (wet, M-1) together, supplemented by a small book of wet matches. After four or five fruitless attempts, he finally kindled a tiny spark which soon matured into the life-restoring flame we needed to dry our clothes and heat some Nescafé.

Just then a land mine exploded with a tremendous roar, probably transporting someone from here to wherever we all go ultimately. A second earth-shaking explosion followed and about a minute later, Captain Charles E. Beaver, Headquarters Company Commander, came running up to Rice and me.

"Put out that fire!" he shouted. "Can't you hear we're being shelled?"

"Captain, that's just a couple of land mines," Herb said.

"That's an order. Put out that fire!"

Herb had no choice but to comply.

Captain Beaver moved off through the trees looking for other arsonists like us. He was about six foot three, flabby, and almost girlish looking. I wondered how he'd perform under non-simulated combat conditions.

---

[18]Lyons memoir.

Five or ten minutes later Captain Beaver was back.

"Light 'em up, men. It was only a false alarm."

Herbie Rice tried again several more times, but even his farm boy magic wasn't adequate this time to ignite the thoroughly wet wood.

It was rumored that the Regimental Plans and Training officer (S-3) was responsible for moving our battalion into this lethal bivouac area without first conducting a mine search and certifying the area free of danger to the lives of the troops. Lennie Hershberg volunteered when four sturdy men were sought to carry Lieutenant Paul Loes of Company C, the victim of the two explosions that had led Captain Beaver to cancel our fire a short time before.

It was the same Lieutenant Paul "Dutch" Loes who had risen and called out "Let's go!" to his demoralized men at Hill 372 before knocking out an enemy machine gun. This morning, he had been looking around in the St. Benoît woods seeking a better spot for some of his men, who were placed in an unfavorably located gully because of the limited visibility at nightfall when we had arrived there. As he walked among the trees, a mine exploded under him, blowing off his right foot. Still conscious and attempting to wrap himself in an overcoat one of his men threw to him, he touched off a second mine which nearly severed his left arm. The aid men who moved him expected that every step would be their last. From there, Hersh and three other volunteers put Lieutenant Loes on a litter and carried him downhill to the Charlie Company CP. As he began his litter journey, Hersh head him say, "Does anyone want a good ear? There's one lying right over there." While waiting for a jeep to evacuate him, Loes turned to Lieutenant Joseph Majeski (my nemesis who nearly shot me in St. Remy) and said, "Guess I fouled up." He turned to Ray Engel and grinned. "Keep your nose clean, Engel." Hersh said that despite Dutch Loes' jocular attitude, he seemed worried that he would look funny after the war with only one ear.

That afternoon we had our first snowfall, flurries of white crystals cascading down through the filtered air below the pine roofs, fusing a little life into the soggy air. Chaplain Koszarek came up in his jeep to our "evergreen retreat" to say Mass. A lofty roof of pines supplied the chapel, a K ration carton served as an altar and the silently descending snow added appropriate atmosphere. It wasn't Notre Dame, but perhaps proved that the Mass didn't need lavish properties or calculated pomp to be meaningful. Everyone knelt down in the wet pine needles even though they knew their pants were wet enough already. Eddie Cook and I were a bit surprised to see Sam D'Arpino, Jim Gardner, Real Parenteau, Jim Amoroso, Moe Moniz, and other company non-coms who hadn't attended at Marseilles or coming up the Rhône Valley.

By our second night in the St. Benoît woods, Herbie Rice and I had finally roofed our foxhole with logs to our satisfaction. We rigged up shelter
halves over the opening so we could light one of the candles we had converted to our own use (i.e., stolen) while guarding an Army warehouse
near Marseilles (thank God we had had the foresight to steal them!) Herbie
wrote to at least six people and stuck the V-mails in his shirt pocket. But
by the time he was ready to mail them a few days later, they were smeared
so badly with Vosges mud and stains that they were unfit to mail.

We knew we weren't allowed to say we had been in combat, but at least
we could try to get the idea across that we had been digging a lot of foxholes. That would leave it to the folks back home to figure out what made
a fellow dig so many holes in the ground. Could it be recreational in
nature?

I wrote to my folks,

Novembrrr! 9 1944
Dear Ma & Pop,
*I have passed the 1,000,000 mark in digging foxholes, I guess. I'm
writing in one now—at night. In one small town, our squad stayed in
a house; I talked to the elderly couple and got us all set up for beds, fire,
blackout curtains, etc. Felt like an interpreter, b'gosh. In Marseilles, they
ate only bread and grapes. Here they haven't seen bread in four years.
We gave them coffee, too—another forgotten food.*

*I think I'm lean and hard. We've had three Masses since hitting
France and I've received communion twice. Once was in a stable like
Bethlehem, complete to the mule. Next in a community church, completely barren and devastated by war. Today it was on a mountainside
under pine trees in a snowstorm, with an upside-down box for an
altar. Even our atheistic Sgts. have turned religious. C'est la guerre! I
could line up the armchair generals and mow 'em down, s'help me!*

*Stars & Stripes today says Roosevelt won. Good! Now bring all "the
red-headed Franklins" home, Mr. Pres, huh? Please write often.*

Roosevelt had defeated Thomas E. Dewey in the Presidential election
on 7 November.

One thing I had learned from our first week on the line was that we
weren't simply spectators in this war, as I (and I believe everyone else in
the platoon) had naively assumed we were. Sailing into European waters
past Gibraltar and later trucking up the Rhône Valley to the cheers of the
populace, we were a gang of happy tourists on a government-paid "Cooks'
Tour." This state of bliss lasted until Jimmy Adair was killed and we took
our first mortar barrage outside St. Remy. Each of us had come wrapped

in an imaginary six-foot encasement of bullet-proof cellophane material tied with a ribbon and a card reading, "Just out after experience; not responsible for anything going on; immune to fire from both sides; just passing through; please don't fire at me till I fire at you; etc." That first mortar barrage had finally broken open all our wrappers. We knew we had to wake up quickly to reality and be prepared to kill or be killed.

Another thing I had learned that first week on the line was that our Fort Bragg training, although it had taught us many of the fundamentals of how to fight as infantrymen, had failed to communicate at least half of the true picture of combat. What we *hadn't* been taught at Bragg was that while we were storming up a French equivalent of Gaddy's Mountain under live artillery support, the enemy would not be idle. Instead, he would be waiting in skillfully camouflaged entrenchments to greet our approach with concentrations of machine-gun, rifle, mortar, and artillery fire. Even when we were not trying to advance, he would shower us with pre-registered artillery and mortars as he had done the night Jimmy Adair died and the next morning in our exposed position above the brook. Also, at Bragg the simulated "fighting" usually lasted about three days, after which we returned to barracks to wash and catch up on sleep. Over here there were no breaks in our combat exposure, unless one considered a gloomy death trap like the St. Benoît woods as a rest cure.

Other unpleasant surprises which training had not prepared us for were the necessity of going for long periods with little or no food or water; sleeping in damp, cold foxholes with only raincoats and wet pine boughs for warmth; and everlasting rain that drenched all our clothing and kept it drenched. The guys who had been with the Division before us—on maneuvers in the mountains of Tennessee from November 1944 through early January 1945— understood the rigors of protracted field duty much better, but we whiz-kids who arrived from ASTP had missed that due to our arrival late in the 100th's pre-combat life."

Perhaps there simply was no field manual in existence that could teach men what combat was really like, without their actually experiencing it first hand. As I was falling asleep with Herbie Rice standing guard above me in the foxhole, I had a final thought, you do not get a sense of belonging to the land, and of the land belonging to you, until you have been shelled and have made your first attack in the face of enemy fire.

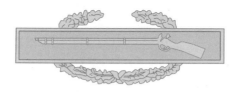

Chapter Fifteen
Our "Super-Secret" Move to the Baccarat Sector

In the mid-afternoon of 10 November, after two days in the misty chamber of horrors identified on the map as the *Forêt de St. Benoît*, we were told to saddle up for a "super-secret" movement to a new sector. We were not unhappy to be leaving our lethal "rest area."

To my amazement, it was Lieutenant White who led Able Company through the woods toward a road where trucks would pick us up and haul us to our new destination. This was my first awareness that Battalion Aid had rejected Lieutenant White's request for "battle fatigue" asylum the night he had ridden back to St. Remy with Scotty Kyle. Lieutenant White was carrying a carbine on his shoulder and that was the extent of his "equipment"—no pack, no coat, or other weighty encumbrances.

"He's going like a racetrack rabbit," someone complained under one hundred pounds of gear. "How the hell are we expected to keep up?"

Snow fell on the trail as Lieutenant White led the long column through tall evergreens. The march was mostly uphill, as most marches seemed to be. At the end of the trail the sun appeared briefly in the western sky and the snow stopped. A long silent convoy of trucks was lined up along the road waiting for us. By the time our truck was fully loaded, Moe Moniz had to sit with his butt over the tailgate, but Moe was a very bouncy little fellow and didn't even seem to mind.

After about an hour, our convoy rumbled across the bridge over the Meurthe River into the city of Baccarat, known for making quality crystalware. In October, Allied aircraft had attempted to destroy the bridge, but their bombs had gone astray, destroying the church instead and killing the priest in the middle of the Mass. Now the powers-that-be had reason to rejoice that our bombers had missed and the bridge was still intact. We would have loved to stay there in houses, but it was not in the cards, apparently because of the "highly secret" nature of our move.

Much later, we would understand what the "secrecy" had all been about. The Germans were expecting us to cross the Meurthe River and to try to capture the key road junction town of Raon l'Etape on the east bank. Raon l'Etape was one of the bastions of the enemy's "Vosges Advance Position," their line of fortifications in which they intended to hold out until at least the spring of 1945 But General Burress and the hierarchy above him decided instead to *feint* a Meurthe crossing by the 398th Infantry Regiment, while sending the other two infantry regiments (the 397th and our 399th) across the Meurthe on a bridge at Baccarat north and west of Raon l'Etape. Then, starting 12 November, the two regiments would strike south toward Raon l'Etape and would attempt to capture it from the west and north, which were less heavily defended. It seems probable that the "secrecy" exercised within the 100th Infantry Division contributed to the success of the overall operation.

We unloaded from the trucks in a wooded area about a mile to the east of Baccarat and were told to dig in. We found ourselves in a pleasant setting of yellow, tan, and russet-leafed trees where frosted autumn leaves covered the ground like a colorful blanket. Before dark, Herb and I had completed a solid log roof over our foxhole.

Our esteemed squad leader, Sergeant Jim Gardner, briefed us on what we might expect in the hours ahead.

"Tomorrow is Armistice Day," he said in his finest Bronx croak. "To celebrate, at precisely midnight every gun on the Western Front will open up and give the enemy holy hell. Then at dawn, the whole Western Front will jump off *except us* in a big offensive. With any kind of luck the war might be over by tomorrow night."

Sergeant Gardner's often rosier-than-reality "briefings" were not supposed to be solely creations of a fertile Gaelic imagination, but were presumably based on information he had received from Lieutenant Mueller, who in turn received his information down the links of a lengthy chain of command extending up to General Burress and beyond. The briefings we received were always oral and never written, so we more or less had to rely on what Sergeant Gardner told us, at least until observed facts contradicted his predictions. Most of us didn't want to believe that Sergeant Gardner's fantastic predictions could be hokum this time, so we hoped and prayed that he had the straight scoop for once. But we could never be certain how much of his poop came down from Division HQ and how much was added seasoning of his own creation.

I was particularly interested in Sergeant Gardner's prediction of a generalized offensive along the Western Front, since I had been wondering what had ever happened to General Patton's Third Army. In October, as we had crossed oceans and continents in our pell-mell rush to the front, we feared that General Patton would reach Berlin before we had a chance to see action. Now in November, after a week of combat, we ardently wished to see General Patton unleashed immediately so that he could end the war and send us home.

"Jeez," said Scotty Kyle afterward, "Georgie Patton is a pessimist compared to our Bronx Bombaster. Georgie says he'll make Berlin by December 15, but Gardner will end the war tomorrow afternoon before tea!"

The engineers taped off the areas that had been cleared of mines, but some of the guys got their signals mixed and patronized the wrong side of the white tape. It was a good thing the place was mineless (unlike the St. Benoît woods where Lieutenant Loes had lost leg, arm, and ear two days ago) or the taping would have been not only pointless but positively counterproductive.

Sergeant Gardner delegated the supervision of night security duty to Sergeant Parenteau, who said that the men in each of our six foxholes would pull a two-hour relief of guard duty, from 1800 to 0600. Herbie Rice and I had the 2200 to midnight trick, but were very tired after roofing our foxhole and couldn't keep awake. This meant that the midnight to 0200 shift was never awakened, thereby causing the squad's security to collapse completely for the rest of the night.

"Which of you bastards fouled it up?" Sergeant Parenteau wanted to know. He had fire in his eye. All that was necessary would have been for the others to say we had failed to awaken them and Herbie Rice's and my own goose would have been cooked but good. But nobody stooled and Sergeant Parenteau was unable to place the blame where it belonged.

Sergeant Gardner's midnight bombardment and war-winning final offensive across the Western Front had apparently not taken place. Or if the Western Front *had* jumped off at dawn as Sergeant Gardner had predicted, the Armistice Day battle was being fought with silencers on the weapons because it was as quiet as a church where we were. Someone asked Sergeant Gardner what was going on (or not going on). Sergeant Gardner, unfazed, replied that something "big" was brewing and that there would be a briefing later.

It seemed ironic that the Armistice, which had capped so many years of trench fighting and so many millions of dead, was now a hollow celebration as a Second World War raged on into its sixth year. Our fathers had managed to win the first one, but hadn't known how to make the peace stick. Germany had come bouncing back off the floor to refight the entire

match. Well, we were going to demonstrate both to our fathers and to the
Jerries that this war would be won unconditionally and we would not
allow the peace to come unstuck.

At eleven minutes after 1100 on 11 November 1944, General Burress' new
Division CP opened in the village of Sainte Barbe, a few kilometers west of
the Meurthe River in the vicinity of Raon l'Etape. During the preceding
forty-eight hours when the CP was located in Rambervillers, it had rained
incessantly. The Meurthe was reported to be at its highest level since 1917.

As General Burress looked out the window of his new HQ, he saw a file
of French war veterans march past proudly bearing flags and wearing all
their medals. A small band played "*La Marseillaise.*" The Western Front
was today roughly where it had been twenty-six years earlier, when he and
Andy Tychsen had been young officers in the American Expeditionary
Force. It had taken nearly three years after Pearl Harbor to get back here
to where they had left off in 1918. They were now ready to finish the business
that had been left unsettled when the guns were hushed exactly
twenty-six years before.

There was an announcement that religious services would be held at the
end of Armistice Day morning for all three faiths. Since tomorrow was the
Sabbath, holding church services a day earlier seemed to portend that we
would be elsewhere tomorrow. Perhaps Sergeant Gardner's latest prediction
about something "big" happening soon was right for once.

"You don't have to be Jungle Jim Griffith to figure out we're attacking
tomorrow," somebody said.

Lieutenant Griffith was the Battalion S-2 (Intelligence) officer.

Old Reliable, Chaplain Koszarek, showed up as he had two days previously
in the St. Benoît woods. This time he said Mass on the hood of his
jeep, as bright periods of sunshine alternated with snow flurries. There
were so many non-coms in attendance that I was afraid some of the trees
would be asked to move. But somehow everyone managed to fit into the
Chaplain's natural chapel.

Returning from church, Eddie Cook was telling me how inconvenient
the war was in terms of delaying his career plans. He and his girl friend,
Doris, planned to complete college, get married, and start an interior decorating
business for new homes built in the housing developments that

would surely spring up with GI Bill money. They were both impatient to get started, but the war had placed them miles apart and Eddie's college plans were on indefinite hold.

I had a different view of the war, regarding it as a once-in-a-lifetime experience of supra-human scope and dimensions. While I had quickly had a stomachful of combat, participating in the war would nevertheless set us apart from all the generations which had not gone through this awful miracle or would not in the future. Now, hearing Eddie Cook say that the war was interfering with his personal plans startled me a bit, making me wonder whether he was being short-sighted or if perhaps I was taking the whole thing too seriously.

Eddie Cook gently blew the whistle on our "esteemed" (with reservations) platoon leader. Lieutenant Mueller, he said, was a blanket-grabber who frequently tried to pull rank at night when they were sharing a foxhole, in an effort to get the lion's share of the coverings. But Eddie Cook's Missouri egalitarian/populist attitude, which recognized all men as equal with no special consideration to officers, didn't let the Lieutenant get away with more than his fair share of the warmth (which wasn't all that abundant to begin with).

The company kitchen brought up hot chow from Baccarat in marmite cans. After lunch, Sergeant Sam D'Arpino took the ammunition report, noting how much ammo each man was short of basic load. New bandoliers were given out to each man along with a fresh supply of green and yellow hand grenades. No one doubted now that we would be launching a big attack of some kind in the morning.

Sometimes when I'd get to thinking that "things are pretty tough" for me personally, I'd take a look around to see if somebody else wasn't having it a mite tougher than I. Corporal Woody Gilbert, third in command of our squad, had a king-sized case of the "Government Issues" (the GI's GIs as they are known) that day in the Baccarat Woods. Every ten or fifteen minutes, he had to answer a call other than to colors, and it was really pathetic to see him go off all doubled up that way.

Mail call brought "*beaucoup de*" mail, the largest delivery since we arrived overseas. Eddie Cook got twelve letters plus a birthday locket from Doris (his birthday was coming up on the 19th). Herbie Rice of course got umpteen letters from Peoria and vicinity as usual. Scotty Kyle did all right too, while I got one or two short notes from his non-writing Boston acquaintances.

That evening, auspiciously heading our V-Mails "Armistice Day 1944," we wrote everybody and his brother to whom we owed letters. We used our usual blanket-over-the-foxhole, write-on-your-knees system, which was more of an endurance contest than a literary performance. I wrote to my French teacher, Miss Waldmyer, at Newton H. S., describing for her the beauties of France, and pausing between sentences to curse out the country and its weather before settling down and penning another lie. It became so cold that Herbie Rice and I had to dig the foxhole another six inches deeper to warm our fingers enough to keep writing. To my parents I wrote,

Another foxhole candlelighter. It's Armistice Night, twenty-six years too late. It's Armistice Day Morn where you are and everyone is probably hepped up about a football game or something. Life is strange. We had C, P & J services this morning and even more sgts. went to communion. War is heaven, as Sherman once failed to remark, etc.

There is not a man in this Division who wants to fight; fortunately, there is also not a man who won't give out with everything when he has to fight. God-fearing men, I calls us.

Lessee, I received the Expert Infantryman Badge on September 24 or so. About thirty-seven days later I became eligible for a wreath and five more rocks per [month]. I bet that's a record.[19]

Herb Rice, fellow scout and foxholer, put a log roof on tonight's dwelling. The woods have on their camouflage suits and are really beautiful. Please send candles and cookies. Hope the Russians do something soon, heh heh.

Love, Frank

Scotty Kyle took advantage of the slightly relaxed censorship rules announced that day to tell his folks for the first time that we had been in Marseilles together,

Red Gurley and I went to Marseilles and rode on the outside of the streetcars, saw a French Movie and the chapel on the hill. I have seen quite a chunk of France. I have been busy. The people are generous and pretty glad to see us. Soon the people we meet won't be so glad.

Here is a little item for anyone going into the service, whether Dick Elmer or any of my friends. The Infantry is rough. Don't get in it. At any cost don't get in the Infantry.

[19]We were awarded our EIBs on 24 September at Fort Bragg, and went into combat at the beginning of November (37 days later), thus beginning the eligibility date for our Combat Infantryman Badges (CIBs). Since we were forbidden to mention that we were in combat in our correspondence, this was my way of telling my folks that we had "seen the elephant." The "combat" badge looked just like the "expert" badge except it had a super-imposed silver wreath, hence my comment we were now "eligible for a wreath."

The French welcome us. Their peace-time life must have been nice. They live simply in homes built before Napoleon's time. There are no wooden structures. The forests are much like Oregon forests.

I'm laying on my stomach to write. Mom, I think of you always and have much to say. I love you more than I ever said. I pray often.

Love, Bob

Bob Hogberg, apparently suffering his usual acute hunger pangs, wrote his folks,

I sure wish I were there. I'm feeling fine. At least as best as can be expected under present conditions. Send me some cookies and candy. Send lots of eats for I sure do get hungry.

My beard is growing to the stage where I can almost comb it. What a rugged character I am. The weather is rotten. We had a sleet storm the other day. I sure don't see where they get the idea "Sunny France." That's all for now. Keep writing.

Your loving son
Bob

Sergeant Parenteau said one foxhole would stay awake at a time during the night—or else. Seeing he meant business, Herbie Rice and I fell into line. Everything was all right during my tour from 2200 till midnight. Then I woke up the next victim, Robert E. Jones, and started back to our hole no more than ten yards away. My first hint that I might by flying off course was when I fell violently into a hole and asked, "Is that you, Herb?"

"Hell no, you damn fool, why doncha watch who you're walking on?" It was *Monsieur le* Private Julius de Rubeis who lived quite a distance downstream from us. After bumping into many trees, none of which I succeeded in knocking down, and adding a few words to my vocabulary I didn't even know I knew, I started hollering at the top of my lungs for Herbie Rice. He finally awoke and escorted me in. If there were any Krauts lurking in the nearby woods, they would sure as hell have known where we were after that performance. It was just another of my one hundred good reasons why I felt that in the interest of overall efficiency, doughfeet should be allowed to grab a little sleep when they could instead of standing guard in rear areas where enemy attacks were extremely unlikely. If I could only get my idea through the Sergeants, Looies, and higher brass up to Ike, maybe they'd do something about it. But then again maybe they wouldn't.

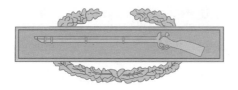

Chapter Sixteen
The Battle of Baccarat Woods

Before turning in, we had lined up our rifles and grenades on the lip of our foxhole together with our packs, to be ready for the planned pre-dawn departure. At 0500 we awoke to find a decorative layer of snow about an inch thick on all of our exposed equipment. We brushed off the snow and rolled up our bedding to be collected by the kitchen jeep. The condemned men then ate a hearty breakfast consisting of dehydrated eggs, bread, and coffee. We were also issued three K rations for the day, which we stuffed in raincoat pockets or under field jackets.

It was Sunday again, and again we would attack. Last Sunday it had been toward the crest of woods on Hill 372 east of St. Remy. Today it would be through the Baccarat woods. What ever happened to the Sabbath as a day of rest? Even God was able to get the world built in six days, leaving the seventh day for rest. Our generals were apparently less well organized than our Commander-in-Chief-in-the-Sky.

Sergeant Gardner assembled our squad for final briefing as to what was in prospect for the morning. "The last ten days we were operating on our own as a Regimental Combat Team," he told us. "Now the other two regiments have arrived on the line, so the 399th is reverting to division control as of right now." He pronounced it "revoiting."

"We're going to attack through some woods," he continued. "Our platoon will be in front and our squad will be point for the platoon. That means Herbie Rice and Red Gurley will be in front. What you can expect to run into are enemy riflemen, some machine-gun emplacements, and possibly some crude pillboxes protected by ditches and barbed wire. The enemy can be expected to use mortars and even bigger stuff once he discovers we're there. I want everyone in the squad to be on the alert today. That applies in spades to Rice and Gurley. Keep your eyes open, boys; you might learn something." Of course, he pronounced it "loin."

I checked over my uniform. Under my raincoat I was wearing two shirts, two pairs of pants, and two field jackets. Outside the raincoat were bandoliers of ammo criss-crossed across my chest, garnished by three green grenades. On my back was a full field pack from which dangled an ammo bag filled with personal stuff like a wayward skiff being towed by a larger boat. I felt like a Walking Fortress, M-1 version (rather than B-17, the "Flying Fortress" model).

Staff Sergeant John W. Hambric of the 3d Platoon guided us along snowy trails to the jumpoff point. The route, as usual, was uphill all the way and Sergeant Hambric was in a hurry. Hambric, an aggressive looking individual with wild, almost hostile eyes, was an American Indian from Flaine, Arkansas.

"Hoggie" Hogberg was lugging his squad's BAR this morning, a result of Sergeant Carlos Daledovich being wounded at Woods Six, and BAR man Lennie Hershberg's promotion to replace him as assistant squad leader in Sergeant Jim Amoroso's squad. Hoggie was whimpering about how his feet hurt as we all hustled and humped along trying to keep pace with our impatient Arkansas Indian guide. After a while, Hoggie's whining began to irritate the other boys and Sam D'Arpino told him to knock it off. Hoggie was doubtlessly in pain, but what could we do about it? When I considered the torture some guys went through with bad feet, upset stomachs, overall weariness, and eternal dampness, it struck me as little short of a miracle that they could keep going that way day and night including Sunday, attacking with whatever resources were required. The next day they went through the same thing—no eating, no washing, no sleeping, and no relaxing, mentally or physically.

John Hambric was not only an authentic Redskin, but a highly proficient infantry non-com who knew he had to deliver us to the IP (Initial Point) by a certain time. After a mile of breathless plodding, we advanced up a snow-lined lane and met Hambric's platoon leader, Lieutenant David Ballie. Ballie and a few of his men were just back from a final reconnaissance patrol. They stood there like snowbirds, completely at home among eerily silent snow-dusted evergreens. Lieutenant Ballie had a short ragged beard and cold eyes. He briefed a small group of us that included Lieutenant Mueller and Sergeants Stanley, D'Arpino, Gardner, and Parenteau, in addition to Herbie Rice and me as the company's point men.

"You go up this road over that little knoll. After you pass a clearing in the pine trees on the right, you turn right into the woods. You'll see a little French sedan and then stop just before the next clearing. That's the LD (Line of Departure). Company D will then lay down supporting machine-gun fire before you cross the clearing. You can expect to run into the enemy 250 to 400 yards beyond the clearing." Lieutenant Ballie paused and fingered his barbed stubble growth. "Remember one thing," Ballie added. "Dead heroes stink."

"Thanks for everything," Lieutenant Mueller said. "Okay, scouts out!"

Lieutenant Ballie and Sergeant Hambric watched us move out. Herbie Rice and I followed Ballie's instructions and after about three hundred yards turned right into the woods. Almost immediately, we saw the French sedan covered with fallen leaves and a fresh covering of snow, looking like all the booby-trapped mock Nazi vehicles we had been exposed to in training exercises in the States. It was probably crawling with trip wires and filled with enough TNT to blow the entire battalion sky-high.

Ahead we saw the clearing where we were supposed to hold up and await the jump-off signal. This was the LD for the attack.

Gardner and Parenteau came up and gave Rice and me our final instructions. Artillery had been laid on the enemy positions at dawn, they said, and Dog Company heavy (water-cooled) machine guns would soon arrive to assure our safe passage across the clearing to the woods beyond. Charlie Company's scouts should be visible advancing parallel to us over on the left. We were told to take off our back packs and leave them to be picked up by the company supply jeep. Our packs contained such things as shaving equipment, washcloths, soap, toothpaste, and writing materials.

The platoon flattened itself against the ground to await the attack order. While lying there doing nothing, I bit open a K ration and made some quick calculations on how to divide it two ways. A long extended arm offered Herb two crackers and half of the cheese which I broke between my gloves. He said it was delicious. I reached back and pulled the canteen cup from where the canteen fit into it. Pouring water into the cup, I added the orange drink beverage powder and sugar, and stirred with the finger of my glove. Again without raising more than an inch above a prone position, I passed the concoction to Herbie Rice for a first swig. A minute later I offered him some Walnetto candies.

"You're quite a chef," he said, munching away contentedly.

"I'm going into dehumanized foods after the war," I said. "I'll call it the 'K Ration Konstipation Korporation'."

Suddenly a torrent of machine-gun fire seemed to explode in our ears. We had been so busy eating a second breakfast that we hadn't noticed the Company D crew setting up a large water-cooled .30-caliber machine gun about fifteen yards away. They blasted away for about five minutes at the target woods, making only slightly less noise than the Chrysler factory producing Sherman tanks on a three-shift schedule. [According to the US Army Aberdeen Proving Grounds series of books, Shermans were mostly built by Chrysler.]

Then a Jerry machine gun let rip with a long, panicky burst of fire, like a watchdog who suddenly awakens at a noise and starts yapping. Their counter-fire did not seem to faze the Company D crew which kept hammering away for another few minutes before completing their mission and departing. *"Whirr-Boom! Whirr-Boom!"* Jerry mortars! We flattened out against the ground and could feel the concussion as the mortars exploded around us for perhaps two or three minutes. The mortars stopped and the wood was silent again. Nobody seemed to be hurt.

"I don't know if that machine gun of ours was helping the cause or just waking up Jerry," Sergeant Gardner said.

"All right, let's go!" Lieutenant Mueller called.

"Say, Sergeant," I said to Gardner, "Is there any objection if Rice and I skirt around the right side of the clearing through the trees rather than exposing ourselves in the open?" I felt a bit guilty to be questioning authority this way, but it seemed dumb to walk out in the open when lives (our own in fact) might be saved by using our heads. Sergeant Gardner passed along my request to Lieutenant Mueller who frowned. Captain Young asked Lieutenant Mueller what was holding us up. When Lieutenant Mueller told him of my request, he said, "All right, go around the clearing." Captain Young was with Lieutenant Mueller, just behind our squad. He apparently planned to direct the company's advance from way up front this morning.

"Scouts out!" Sergeant Gardner said.

"Listen, boys," Sergeant Parenteau added. "Don't be too brave."

Around the clearing we went and into the woods beyond. We clicked off the safeties on our rifles and held them in a vigilant port-arms position in front of us. Forward we went, Rice and Gurley, 3d Squad, 1st Platoon, Company A. Everything was on schedule. We advanced steadily through the trees which were now predominantly deciduous, with few evergreens to be seen. We passed woodpiles stacked neatly beside little trails leading through the trees. Both the woodpiles and the trails had the one inch covering of snow that seemed standard everywhere this morning. The trees had a watchful, expectant, slightly hostile air as we passed through them. The wood was as quiet as a church and the trees stood as tall as interior church columns. The scene was as beautiful as a Christmas card, but there was tension in the air. It was almost like searching a church for pickpockets who had been stealing from the collection plate.

Herbie Rice, who was lightly built and light footed, looked anything but that this morning. His bulky pants made him look like a fat man and his size 13 shoepacs (or Barka boots as we sometimes called them) made him look like a clubfoot. His shuffling feet never left the ground except when absolutely necessary. When he had to negotiate a fallen tree, he didn't clear it by over half an inch.

Soon we spotted elements of Charlie Company advancing in a line of skirmishers far off to the left. Then Herbie Rice said he saw somebody up ahead. I saw the man at the same time. It was a soldier walking across our front not more than seventy-five yards away through the wood. I told Sergeant Gardner what we had seen and waited for the Brains to decide what we should do next. Meanwhile, the soldier we had spotted continued walking back and forth among the trees ahead.

After a minute Sergeant Gardner, who had conferred with Lieutenant Mueller and Captain Young, called up to me, "You think maybe it's C Company you saw?"

"We saw C Company off to the left," I replied. "This is different."

"What did the guy look like?" Gardner asked.

"Like a soldier," I said. "In the woods one uniform looks like another."

"Sit tight," Sergeant Gardner said. What did he think I was planning to do, go off on a bird hunt?

So it went on for several minutes, our entire advance halted while the bizarre Stroller paraded back and forth, appearing and reappearing from behind trees. Rice yelled "Come on out!" in his high boyish voice, but the guy was either deaf or didn't give a damn. Every time we got ready to open fire, somebody behind us yelled that it might be a GI.

Just then two Kraut machine guns cut loose from somewhere up front. Whining ricochets chopped wood above us. Over on the left, the Company C skirmishers had hit the ground. Apparently one of the machine guns had them pinned down. Ahead of us, the Stroller reappeared, and continued to wander across our rifle sights.

"You guys decided who he is?" Herbie Rice called back over his shoulder.

"How about it?" I asked Sergeant Gardner, who didn't answer but looked perplexed.

"Hey!" Herbie Rice called in that boyish voice of his. "Somebody just put a hole in my raincoat collar! If they don't identify themselves pretty fast, I'm gonna open up!"

I heard Sergeant Parenteau's voice. "He-he-he-he-he!" he laughed in his irrepressible French-Canuck way. "Go ahead and open up, Rice!"

Finally, we started firing at the Stroller, who soon disappeared in our gunsmoke and the mist of the wood. The enemy answered our fire with rifles and machine guns. Herbie Rice spotted an adversary behind a tree and they dueled with rifles at seventy-five paces. Every time Rice got a bead on the Jerry, the fellow popped out of sight behind a tree.

"Medic, Medic, Medic!" someone shouted to the left and slightly behind where I was lying behind a tree. I raised up on one elbow and saw a man with a Red Cross brassard on his arm running forward and a helmetless GI running back. They came together and dropped into a sitting position where our aid man, T/5 Charles "Woody" Woodard administered first aid to the injured man. Sergeant James Gardner, our squad leader, had been shot in the arm by an enemy rifleman or sniper.

Sergeant Parenteau took over command of the squad without a hitch. He moved the rest of the squad up on line with Rice and me to form a skirmish line, and sent Scotty Kyle back to guide Sergeant Gardner to the rear. We saw Scotty Kyle go off lugging both his own and Gardner's rifles, but the wounded man was going so fast that Kyle was having trouble keeping up. Doc Emmons, who was lying behind our squad leader, said Jim Gardner became curious about where the enemy was. He moved a shoulder and an arm from behind his tree when a Kraut drilled him in the arm. Sergeant Gardner, who that morning had said Herbie Rice and I might "loin" something today, had apparently "loined" something himself about not exposing oneself unnecessarily when under enemy observation.

A cold drizzle began falling on us as we clung to the snowy leaves and moss on the forest floor. We were startled by clumps of snow falling from the trees until we got adjusted to the sound. After a while, the drizzle changed to snow, and then back to rain again. The early morning spell of an enchanted forest under a layer of fresh snow had now evaporated, leaving only a depressing, cold, wet wood where unseen enemy riflemen and machine gunners remorselessly awaited the opportunity to kill anyone who exposed a head or an arm.

Our trigger hands were becoming cold. Slowly and systematically we were starting to freeze as we lay on the wet moss. The rain stopped and a short time later the snow resumed, incongruously drifting peacefully down through the branches onto the turbulent earth below.

Explosions on both flanks reported the attempts by our bazooka anti-tank weapons to blast holes in the heavy log machine gun emplacements that were said to be holding up our advance. The bazookas proved ineffective against the enemy's solid logs. Artillery would be required to solve the problem.

Captain Young ordered us to pull back about one hundred yards so that Cannon Company (our battalion's own artillery company) could blast the enemy emplacements with 105mm fire. We were apparently now out of rifle range and ate K ration crackers as our regimental Cannon Company's big stuff ripped spasmodically over our trees and crashed into the enemy held sector. The Cannon Company guns made strike after strike, like a champion bowler. Captain Young and a forward observer (FO) guided the Cannon Company guns by field telephone. They began with long rounds and gradually marched them back toward the front lines until they had them adjusted on where the enemy emplacements were thought to be located. Soon the explosions were less than two hundred yards ahead of us, like shooting an apple off the head of William Tell's son. By the time Captain Young and the FO had marched the 105 fire back as far as they dared toward our own lines, there was only a split second between the overhead *"whoosh"* of the shells and the fiery explosions among the trees up ahead.

Then there was a great commotion as two of the rounds fell short within the Company A lines. We heard cries of "Medic," and the word was passed around that two men from Lieutenant Harry Gullborg's 2d Platoon had been hit by shrapnel. They were Privates Sarkis Karibian, who came from a large Armenian family on Manhattan's west side, and Brewster Schoch, a serious-faced young BAR man from Syracuse, NY, where I was born.

"Let's go, men!" Captain Young bellowed. "Keep your skirmish line straight and shoot at everything that isn't growing!"

As we moved forward, I passed within a few yards of Sarkis lying against a tree. He had been bandaged by the medics but looked terrible. His face was greenish or purple. He had always been very generous on the USAT *McAndrews* about sharing his Baby Ruth bars with the other men. It took only a few hours before my fears for his life were confirmed.[20]

We advanced the first one hundred yards back to our old positions without difficulty. Then we continued on until we came upon a German sitting against a tree. He was a big man with a tremendous curly beard, brownish-gold in color. He looked as though he were taking a siesta but he was dead. He was in the approximate place where our first Jerry, the Stroller, had done all the walking back and forth.

"Think it's him?" I asked Herbie Rice.

"I guess so," Rice said. Since Rice, Gardner, Parenteau, and I had all been firing at him, I mentally credited myself with one quarter of a notch on my rifle stock.

Fifty yards or so past the corpse of the Stroller, the 1st and 2d Platoons were pinned down by machine gun fire from the front and right flank. Apparently the Cannon Company 105s had been less successful than we had hoped. On our right, Private George Klein of Harry Gullborg's platoon was hit in the side by a machine gun bullet that ricocheted along the ground from his right and embedded itself between two ribs. Klein, an ASTP boy from Baltimore whose round face reminded me of Babe Ruth, raised his head as though looking for his coach's signal on what to do next.

---

[20]Private Sarkis Karibian succumbed to his wounds not long thereafter.

However, the signal must have been intercepted because the second machine gun directly in front proceeded to knock off George's helmet.

Lieutenant Mueller and Lieutenant Gullborg conferred and agreed that our platoon would go after the gun out front while Gullborg's boys took the one firing from the right flank. Lennie Hershberg took over the BAR from the foot-sore Bob Hogberg and moved forward seeking a field of fire against the machine-gun emplacement that was our objective. The machine gun on the right flank opened fire as Hershberg crossed a small clearing.

"Down here!" Lieutenant Gullborg shouted. Hershberg dived behind a tree stump where Gullborg was crouched.

"Gee thanks," Hershberg said. "You saved my life."

"Don't mention it," Lieutenant Gullborg said.

From behind us, Chester Fraley came running forward with a bazooka.

"Hey! Let me fire that thing!" Lieutenant Mueller cried.

"No, sir!" Chester Fraley replied. "First shot is mine."

When Lennie Hershberg saw what was happening, he sprang to his feet and rushed forward, leveling his BAR in the direction of the machine-gun emplacement. He seemed determined not to let Lieutenant Mueller and Chester Fraley get there first. What followed was a duet of bazooka explosions and loud BAR chattering, followed by loud appreciative shouts as though it were an Italian opera house. I saw four or five German soldiers come out of the dugout with their hands on their heads. One German machine gunner lay dead.

"I got him with the bazooka!" Lieutenant Mueller announced.

"Like fun you did!" Hershberg replied angrily. "I saw him go down when I fired at him."

The machine-gun emplacement was a long narrow rectangular sort of "roofless garage" about three feet high, made of logs, and camouflaged so that it could only be seen by someone looking directly into the "garage door" from which the gun was firing. I was surprised to learn that the German gun could fire only into the narrow sector straight out ahead of the "garage door." When we had first heard the machine guns cut loose earlier, we had imagined they were covering the whole wood. Around us in the woods we could see several other enemy machine-gun emplacements, all exactly like the one Hershberg, Fraley, and Lieutenant Mueller had eliminated. The only differences were that each emplacement faced at a different angle, and some of the fields of fire were planned so that two guns would converge upon the same point. These were some of the fortifications of the German Vosges Winter Line that had been built by forced labor, largely French locals.

"Get moving, men! Keep that skirmish line straight!" Captain Young shouted.

Lieutenant Gullborg's men had taken care of the gun emplacement on the right flank. The skirmish line surged forward again like a slow tidal wave moving through the trees of a coastal forest. For Herbie Rice and me, it was almost like a paid vacation to find ourselves no longer on the point and exposed to all manner of dangers, but in the middle of a long line of diligent, alert skirmishers. I could understand how a wave of strike pickets or singing revolutionaries must feel, or a lynch mob, or vigilantes searching a swamp for some dangerous criminal. We were the forces of law and order, and our collective might would make right prevail today.

Our skirmish line generated a considerable amount of fire power as the men fired into dark dugouts and foxholes in case any Jerries were still lurking inside. L. C. Talley, a broad-shouldered Texan in my squad, ran from tree to tree pointing his rifle in the general direction of the enemy, but never seemed to fire. Later Scotty Kyle told me Talley was always that way, afraid to fire his rifle but very good at digging foxholes. "Good dig, no hit," was how Scotty Kyle summed up Talley's talents as an infantry soldier.

Ten yards ahead of me in the misty forest, I saw what looked like a Crusader in full regalia rushing toward me, arms raised, and a large red cross sewn on the front of his uniform. Then I realized it was a German medic coming into our line as a prisoner. Beyond where I had first spotted him, we came to one of those "roofless garage" log emplacements. This one contained no machine gun, but four or five wounded and bandaged German soldiers on stretchers. Their medic had apparently tended to them until the very last moment when our skirmish line was about to engulf their dugout.

Captain Young kept up a steady uproar behind us, shouting at laggards who drifted four or five yards back of the skirmish line. Herbie Rice kept getting out ahead of the skirmish line until Sergeant Parenteau called him back where he belonged in the line. Rice was a natural born scrapper. A group of about fifteen Jerries came stumbling out of underground dugouts in front of our skirmish line and went running off toward the left flank where Charlie Company's skirmish line took them into custody.

Sam D'Arpino said we should be on the lookout for German *SS* troops who had been spotted giving orders to the regular troops. I hoped I wouldn't run into any of those babies.

We reached a road cutting directly across our front and took up firing positions behind a little embankment covered with snow.

"Open up on the woods across the road with everything you've got," Captain Young shouted, "in case they're dug in back there." Our skirmish line fired everything we had from rifles and BARs to anti-tank grenades and machine guns. Our feeler fire drew a response from the dark reaches of the opposite wood, as enemy machine guns zipped and bullets ripped over our heads.

"Keep them engaged until I give the order to cross the road!" Captain Young said.

Our M-1 rifles were "clip fed, gas operated, and semi-automatic." At least that's what the Army manual said they were. This meant that by pulling open the bolt, inserting a "clip" of eight bullets, and closing the bolt, a cartridge would be introduced into the firing chamber. When you fired, a tiny fraction of the gaseous propellant that drove the bullet out of the barrel was cycled back through a steel tube under the barrel to open the bolt, extract the spent cartridge and feed the next cartridge into the firing chamber, all in a split second. These principles working together gave the M-1 its "semi-automatic" quality in that you could fire all eight cartridges as fast as you could pull the trigger, which was as fast as two or three seconds.

For some unknown reason, however, at this very moment, my M-1's bolt stopped cycling. I got it open once or twice by hand, and then it refused to open for anything less powerful than foot action. So I ended up having to pull the rifle back along my body to where my foot was and "kick" open the bolt to expel the old cartridge and introduce the new one. This ended up costing me eight "kicks" for each clip of bullets I fired into the woods across the road.

The other problem was reloading. I could get a new clip out of my bandolier all right, but how to get it into the chamber? It was snowing again and my hands were red with cold. I pushed the clip with my fingers and nothing happened except that my fingers bent back and ached a little more. Then I swore and pushed the clip with the heel of my hand and sometimes got it in.

Lying behind the snowy embankment, I heard a bullet whine in and whack into the berm directly in front of me. After that I really kept my head down. Finally regaining sufficient courage to look up, I saw Sergeant Jim Amoroso standing beside me, leaning against a tree and holding his pipe calmly with one hand.

"Hey, Ammo," I said. "They're firing at us."

"Oh yeah?" said Ammo, as if I had told him the Giants had split with the Dodgers. Another *"brrrrrrrr"* of German machine gun fire crackled and whined past, and a little branch next to Ammo's head went *snap!* Instead of hitting the dirt, Ammo proceeded to knock the ash from his bowl and put his pipe in his inner field jacket pocket. Finally he knelt down just before I had a heart attack.

Ammo hailed from Cliffside Park, New Jersey (which he, of course, called "Joisey") where before being drafted, he had been employed in the juke box installation and servicing business. Since the Mafia was reputedly also engaged in the same business., it was often necessary for Ammo's company to move its machines around at night in trucks under canvas, and to do some of the installations at odd hours of the day or night.

Who knew? Perhaps Ammo regarded combat as a soft touch after playing cat and mouse with the Mafia in the juke box business. Or maybe he was too lethargic to know what was happening. Whatever the cause of his *sang froid*, I was afraid his hours were limited the way he was exposing himself in the face of the enemy.

After half an hour's pause along the embankment, we received the order to jump off on the final phase of the attack. Our objective was the high ground overlooking a key crossroad near the village of Neufmaisons, some seven to eight hundred yards ahead through the woods. Where were the enemy riflemen and machine gunners who had been firing from these woods toward our embankment only a little while before? The trees stood clustered conspiratorially, refusing to divulge their secrets. Or perhaps they were muttering incantations in nature's universal tongue which men had long since discarded as useless and impractical in our modern world, like all ancient languages.

We passed huge craters from which white smoke still seeped. American artillery had apparently plastered the enemy's rear area, spattering dirt for fifty yards around the points of explosion. When we reached the end of the woods, the ground dropped precipitously in front of us. We saw a Jerry take off down the slope through some baby fir trees scarcely thirty yards in front of us. Everybody and his brother let go with grenades and rifles. I began sliding and sloshing down the grade, figuring we had Jerry on the run and might as well keep chasing him. But Captain Young called me back and told us to dig in. We had reached our final objective.

We were elated and excited after the long day's chase and spent a few minutes exchanging gossip before getting down digging in. But then some sixth sense caused Herbie Rice and me to tackle the foxhole with more promptness and energy than we usually displayed. We both pitched in to penetrate the snow-topped crust and soon had a hole three feet in depth. While Herbie was applying the finishing touches, I went down the line to where there were some wood piles. I made two trips and brought back enough logs to cover the foxhole. We piled dirt, leaves, and pine branches on top of the logs and then snow on top to camouflage it just as it had been.

A few seconds after completing our new home and hanging our equipment on small Christmas trees near our foxhole, we heard a distant whistle. The sound gradually became louder and soon whined out of nowhere until a shattering explosion rent the frosty air.

"*Whistling Annies!*" someone shouted. No one needed to be told to take refuge in their foxholes. In exactly three seconds, everybody was in the bottom of the foxhole trying to make it deeper than it already was.

One after another, the shells came whistling in like a cheery military band, shaking the ground all around. The Germans didn't even need to adjust their fire. The first round had been right on the money and the succeeding explosions were also squarely on target.

We, who an hour before had wanted to chase the Jerries all the way to Neufmaisons, now felt as helpless as flies under a powerful flyswatter. One thing that kept my mind off the deadly whistles was trying to keep Herbie Rice down into the foxhole. He insisted on standing up to see what was going on and I had to haul him back down to the bottom of the hole and practically rub his nose in the dirt to keep him inside.

As one particularly insistent whistle intensified in the sky overhead, I started to shout "Sonofabitch." I had just reached "bi-" when the shell hit so close that Herbie Rice and I were bounced up and down by the concussion. My cussing trailed off into a stammering "bi-i-i-i-i-i-tch." Things had gotten so bad that the German projectiles wouldn't even let you finish your cuss words any more.

After a while, the artillery storm died down and the enemy contented himself with throwing in a "Whistling Annie" every five or ten minutes to keep us awake.[21] We had carried K ration boxes in raincoat pockets and tucked under field jackets that day, but most had fallen out or been discarded in the heat of battle. As a result we went to bed hungry, without bedrolls or field packs, but grateful to have eluded the artillery fire. Herbie Rice and I took turns standing guard and sleeping in our thoroughly soaked clothes with raincoats as our only bedding.

In the morning, we crawled out of our foxhole to find a fresh coat of snow two or three inches deep covering the ground and decorating the Christmas trees around our foxhole. Although we had awakened to a similar snow scene yesterday, the thickness of this morning's blanket made it our first authentic winter's day. One small tree had been destroyed by the artillery shell which had caught me in the middle of a cussword last night. The shell crater was less than six feet from our foxhole, although the

---

[21]We called them "Whistling Annies," but they were really probably German 105mm howitzer rounds, their most common field artillery projectile.

previous evening I would have estimated the distance at six inches. The little crater was now covered with snow and barely perceptible if you didn't have an idea what it was. Perhaps the passage of time would similarly blot out what we were going through here in northeastern France. People back home had probably never heard of the Vosges Mountains or Baccarat or St. Remy and probably never would hear of them.

As soon as it was fully light, we began paying "social calls" on our neighbors, to make sure everyone was still aboard. We swapped yarns on how close the shells had come. The boys held up splintered rifle stocks, canteens with holes in them, and other souvenirs of the barrage. It was good to see the other guys; the fewer there were, the more we appreciated those who were still there.

The company had suffered a number of casualties during the night, including Lieutenant Harry Gullborg, the 2d Platoon Leader, who had been wounded by shell fragments while trying to rescue Private Joseph Manieri, who had also been hit by flying shrapnel. Neither man's wounds were believed to be too serious. Back at Battalion Aid, Chaplain Koszarek had given both men a strong shot of whiskey.

"That guy Harry Gullborg let me share his tree stump with him yesterday," Lennie Hershberg said by way of a personal eulogy. "Why is it the *good* officers have to get it first?" Hersh's Washington Heights humor was not wasted, since we all knew his verbal shrapnel was directed toward our own beloved platoon leader.

"You know what Joe Manieri told me yesterday?" someone said. "Joe started praying for a million-dollar wound after seeing what happened to Sarkis Karibian, Bernie Schoch, and George Klein yesterday. It took less than twenty-four hours for him to get his wish."

Lieutenant Gullborg was the first casualty among our company officers. Sergeant Walter Bull took over as Acting Platoon Leader of the 2d Platoon.

We were accumulating fresh proof every day that the Jerries were not the pushovers they had been advertised to be in August and September when General Patton's and General Patch's spearheads had first linked up near Dijon. Backed up against their own borders, the Jerries were digging in their heels. We could hit them with infantry as we had yesterday outside St. Remy, and they would riddle us with machine guns. When we blasted the machine guns with artillery and bazookas, they would pull back, but in an orderly fashion, leaving few prisoners and little equipment behind. Then, when we reached our objectives they would throw pre-registered, precise, lethal artillery at us.

Probably the only thing that saved us last night was that the German infantry whom we had chased back to Neufmaisons probably took a little while to report their withdrawal to higher headquarters, and to call for artillery fire on their previous positions. By a matter of a few seconds or minutes, we had been able to carve out our refuges in the earth before the shells arrived.

While waiting for food and new orders, we pooled our canteen water and the Nescafé and sugar packets some of us had squirreled away in our shirt pockets. Sergeant Amoroso lit first his pipe and then his little one-pound Turner portable stove. He knelt in the snow beside his foxhole and began making coffee for the platoon.

Off to the right flank, where our visibility wasn't over one hundred yards, we heard a faint sound of gunfire, and assumed that some rival patrols were having a minor dispute of some sort. But soon chattering noises started clipping off branches around us, and Ammo yelled for everybody to get down in their holes. Ammo explained that yesterday in cleaning out the Baccarat woods, our company had pushed our lines straight out and there were still enemy on both flanks as well as to the front. After several minutes of listening to the enemy machine guns chattering like teeth on a frosty morning like this one, I summoned up a drop or two of courage and raised my head to see what was cooking. The Turner stove beside Ammo's hole was emitting steam and there was Ammo amid the machine-gun bullets, still heating our Nescafé.

What a man.

The machine-gun fire finally stopped. Ammo started serving, one canteen cup full of hot Nescafé for every two men. Nescafé wasn't coffee by any means, and I normally didn't make a habit of drinking even coffee, but that stuff of Ammo's tasted better than anything imaginable. On this morning in the bloody, snow-bound Vosges Mountains, I wouldn't have traded Ammo's concoction for gold, silver, or anything else . . . except possibly that white slip of paper discharging me from Uncle Sam's Army.

They brought up mail and a few K rations, explaining that they had to last today and tomorrow. We ate them in a single sitting. The mail brought a birthday package from my folks that had been mailed only ten days before, on 3 November. It contained handkerchiefs, shoe laces, a copy of the news weekly *This Week*, and a birthday card. The Army's mail service was superb, but there was simply no way we could eat those handkerchiefs and shoe laces. I told the boys how sorry I was that there was no food in the package.

Later we were relieved by Company E of the 2d Battalion and went back a few hundred yards to a dark gloomy pine wood where we were to have a "hot meal." The meal consisted of a slice of cooked Spam, some funny-looking beans, and coffee that tasted as though it had some foreign substance in it (unlike the golden Nescafé brewed by Ammo in the morning). At least our kitchen crew was trying.

Captain Young's Executive Officer, Lieutenant Raymond "Mamma" Landis, had come up with the chow jeep and I was able to chat with him for a minute or two. Lieutenant Landis headed up the Rear CP Group consisting of the field kitchen, First Sergeant, Supply, and Administration, while Captain Young ran the Forward CP and directed the company in battle. One thing I had never understood was why Lieutenant White had joined the company shortly before our move overseas, with the same "Exec Officer" title as Ray Landis.

"What's Lieutenant White doing these days?" I asked Lieutenant Landis.

Mamma Landis looked at me. "Do you really want to know?" he said.

"Well, I guess so," I said lamely.

"He left the front line yesterday," Mamma Landis said.

"You mean he was hit in Baccarat woods?" I asked.

"No, he faked battle fatigue and was sent to the rear."

"Oh," I said. Then I remembered how Lieutenant White had tried to feign battle fatigue the night Scotty Kyle drove him back to St. Remy. "He tried that before," I said.

"I know," Lieutenant Landis said. "This time he went to another battalion aid station and the medical officer fell for his swooning act."

"But that's like desertion," I said.

"It *is* desertion," Lieutenant Landis said. "Captain Young told Colonel Zehner and Major Lentz that if he ever lays eyes on Lieutenant White again, he'll kill him."

I was surprised to note that Lieutenant Landis looked a bit depressed, which couldn't be due to the strain of combat—as our officer-in-the-rear he had probably not been closer than two miles to the nearest German.

"How are you fellows all doing?" Lieutenant Landis asked me in his best "Mamma" form. Unlike some officers, he really cared about his men, especially those in our platoon whom he had once commanded.

"Not too bad," I replied. "We lost Jimmy Adair and had a few men wounded, about like the other platoons."

"Don't mention James Adair," Lieutenant Landis said. "I was responsible for sending his personal effects to his parents. One item was a letter in which he proposed early marriage to his fiancée. I don't think I've recovered yet from that."

We lined up ready to march and then were told to take a break dispersed on the sides of a dirt road. An enemy spotter plane circled lazily overhead, probably counting us and writing down our organization numbers and grid coordinates.

Chapter Seventeen
Breaking Through the Winter Line

Soon Major Lentz appeared to guide us to our next position. We were told that the 397th on our right had been pushed back by a counterattack today and we would make a secret move tonight "under wraps" to back them up. Tomorrow, if all went well, we would pass through the 397th's positions and attack the enemy's winter line positions that had stopped the 397th. It was hoped that slipping our Regiment forward through the 397th's lines would take the enemy by surprise, since he would presumably be expecting to cope with only the regiment he was already in contact with. Since our "super-secret" river crossing at Baccarat three days earlier, it still was not known whether the enemy had identified our presence this side of the river. Meanwhile, the other sister regiment, the 398th, was making as much noise as possible on the west bank of the river facing Raon l'Etape, firing 57mm antitank guns, 81mm mortars and .30 and .50 caliber machine guns at targets in and around Raon l'Etape as well as in the steep hills that rose behind the last houses of the town.

Captain Young assigned Herbie Rice and me to lead the procession behind Major Lentz who was wearing a raincoat and pistol belt and carrying a map. I wondered if Barney Lentz remembered throwing me out of the parade at Bragg or telling me to buckle my chinstrap getting off the ship in Marseilles. He hadn't removed or otherwise obscured his gold leaves from his raincoat, the way many of the officers had camouflaged all external signs of rank by removing or rubbing mud on them. Barney Lentz's gold leaves made him a beautiful target for snipers but also an object of respect by his own men. Our stateside and shipboard talk about summary action against officers or non-coms who didn't shape up and treat the men right overseas had, for the most part, evaporated in the Vosges mists. We all needed one another for survival and could not afford the luxury of minor feuds or petty hatreds, even toward some of the more benighted elements among our superiors. If Barney Lentz's courage seemed to be standing the test of combat all right so far, his sense of direction seemed less free from doubt. The hike started out all right as he led us down a long straight firebreak, which offered a sense of coherence in an otherwise jumbled wilderness of trees and hills. Then, leaving the fire break, he got us lost a few times, an unwise practice when one is in the front lines. Up snowy rutted paths and through unbroken forest, Barney Lentz led our endless column of slogging, sloshing, grumbling, worrying dogfaces. As we went along we scooped up handfuls of snow and had free drinks without depleting the water supply in our canteens.

Twilight had overtaken the column when Major Lentz halted and placed one hand thoughtfully on his chin the way he used to do on the parade ground at Bragg. He looked down at his map with a kind of puzzlement and muttered something that sound like "Zum." Turning on his heel, he strode off down a new path in almost the opposite direction. I was beginning to worry over whether his inability to follow a map would end up by leading us all into German captivity in these dark, nearly trackless Vosges woods.

Finally, Herbie Rice and I found ourselves on top of a very steep hill with our sometime navigator and Battalion Executive Officer. He pointed down the road which seemed to descend almost vertically into the semi-darkness.

"Lead the company to the bottom," he told us, "and dig in quietly because you may be under enemy observation."

Major Barney Lentz turned and was gone, leaving Herbie Rice and me sweating under our damp uniforms. It was nearly dark when we reached the bottom and started digging in. The soil was soft and foxholes were quickly dug. Just as we completed this digging exercise in a blanket of silence that would have done honor to a band of stealthy commandos, Captain Beaver's Headquarters Company moved in on our left. Jeep wheels churned in the snow, motors flared up, metal clanked against metal, while irritated voices rose and fell.

"Holy Jeez," Herbie Rice said. "It's the 'Eager Beavers' again. Last time we saw them, Lieutenant Loes got blown up on a mine."

Ray Sholes, from Gil Moniz's squad, and I went back up the steep hill we had just descended to the place where the company bedrolls were stacked, about a quarter mile beyond the top of the hill. Finding our own bedrolls in the dark was out of the question so we just grabbed what looked like the driest ones. We each picked up three of the huge rolls. Tripping, sliding, and tilting over at precarious angles in the churned up snow and mud of the forest path, we negotiated the descent. Every fifty or so yards we had to pause, perspiring, exhausted and arms all but falling off. It was one of those Army endurance contests which seem impossible when you are doing it, but you somehow put it behind you and life goes on.

Ray Sholes and I were completely beat when we returned with the bedrolls, but the blankets and shelter halves inside (however wet) made the difference between sleeping and not sleeping. I gave one bedroll to my foxhole mate, Herbie Rice, and the extra one to Scotty Kyle, thus saving him that long climb.

Herbie Rice and I were in no mood to pull guard since we were worn out and needed to be fresh for the next morning's attack. We camouflaged the area around our hole with snow, tied a shelter half over the hole, threw snow over that too and crawled in. The only way a Jerry could have found us in the dark would have been to fall in the hole accidentally.

"Of course," said Herbie Rice, "if we wake up and find everybody wearing gray overcoats and facing the wrong direction, we'd better say '*Gooten Morgen*' quick and run like hell."

We were up before dawn on Tuesday, 14 November. It had continued snowing during the night and the woods resembled an engraving of an ideal early Christmas morning. Captain Beaver's Headquarters Company was quiet on our left (for a change), probably dreaming of Santa Claus and the Sugar Plum Fairies. Herbie Rice and I dragged on our canteens' diminishing water supplies, rolled up our bedrolls and carried them back up the hill to the collection point. We were issued a day's supply of three K rations, but there was no time to eat since we were urgently needed elsewhere.

Our new guide this morning was a red-cheeked Frenchman wearing a beret and carrying an old-fashioned bolt-action carbine over his shoulder. Unlike the Right Honorable Major Barney Lentz of the Philadelphia Bar and U.S. Army who had guided us yesterday, this fellow knew where he was taking us. Herbie Rice and I had to scramble to keep up with our new French friend, who led the company up narrow paths beneath enormous snow-laded evergreens. At one point, the three of us got so far out ahead of the others that Captain Young told us to halt until the others could catch up.

"You're with the FFI?" I said to our guide.

"*C'est juste,*" he replied. "*Forces Françaises de l'Intérieur. Nous avons eu pas mal d'ennuis.*"

"What's he say?" Herbie Rice wanted to know.

"He's with the Free French," I said. Then my conversation with the guide continued in French. "What did you say about *ennuis*?" I asked him.

"In September, two months ago," he said, "Your Army had almost reached Dijon so it was then or never for our organization here in the Vosges to rise and assert itself."

"So what did you do?" I asked.

"We held a big reunion of several hundred men," he replied. "A bit north of Neufmaisons, just outside the forest. Some of the boys decided to roast a pig."

"*Rôtir un porc?*" I asked incredulously.

"*C'est juste,*" he said. "The pig looked very tasty as they roasted it, but the Germans saw the smoke."

"Then what?" I asked.

"Four of them came to investigate in a command car. At that point some other imbeciles of ours opened fire and killed all four Germans. That brought several hundred more of them and we had a real battle. Dozens of our boys were killed and of course lots of Germans, too. I escaped into the woods as did many others. Did you hear about the Mayor of Raon l'Etape?"

"No," I said.

"The same day as the Battle of the Pig, one of the traitors who secretly belonged to the *Milice* went into the town hall and told the Mayor he wanted to join the FFI. The Mayor told him whom to contact, and two minutes after the man left, the Germans came into the Mayor's office. They dragged him downstairs and machine-gunned him in front of the town hall. The bloodstains and bullet gouges on the outside of the building are still fresh."

"You said the traitor belonged to the *Milice*," I said. "What's that?"

"The *Milice* is a pro-German French para-military group," he replied. "They're all *salauds.*" (bastards)

"Where are we now?" I asked our guide.

"In the Forest of the Little Wilderness, just coming to the Forest of the Big Wilderness. We're not far from *le Rouge Vêtu*, where some of your men were ambushed yesterday."

"A lady in St. Remy told me her daughter's husband was caught by the Germans at *Le Rouge Vêtu*," I said.

"I wouldn't be surprised," he said. "That was all part of the September story of the pig."

"Are the German troops facing us good ones?" I asked.

"Not bad," he replied. "But the higher ups are very angry at being pushed out of the Vosges, and one rumor says even the *Führer* is upset. Yesterday they put the torch to St. Dié and other towns in that area. They have also increased the killing of hostages. It's a nasty business around here."

Captain Young came up. "Okay, proceed," he said.

"*Oui, mon capitaine,*" the FFI man said, clutching his carbine sling confidently and striding on into the silent green and white forest.

After a few hundred meters more, our French guide shook hands with Captain Young, tipped his beret, and left us on a forest trail in a narrow draw between two steep hills covered with evergreens. We found ourselves lined up behind Baker and Charlie Companies. That was the order in which the three companies were to jump off, which suited us just fine. On all sides we heard the staccato *"Br-r-r-r-r-p B-r-r-r-r-p"* noises of German automatic weapons sounding off like a flock of short-tempered woodpeckers.

The battalion's objective today was to clear the enemy from a group of hills, centered around Hill 409.9, that dominated the highway leading south from Neufmaisons through heavy forest to Raon l'Etape, the 100th Infantry Division's objective. Baker Company had already tried to break through the previous afternoon, but had met a stone wall of resistance and lost some men killed and wounded by the well-entrenched enemy. The Krauts were said to have barbed wire, deeply entrenched machine-gun emplacements, cleared lanes of fire, and snipers hidden high in the evergreen trees. This was the enemy's Winter Line, planned and designed to block our progress through the Vosges Mountains until at least the following spring.

We heard a lot of small arms fire as Companies B and C attempted to break through the enemy positions around Hill 409.9. The Germans responded with machine-gun and burp-gun fire and soon barrages of artillery came whistling into the battlefield. Our own artillery responded loudly to the Germans', and the small arms fire by both sides dropped off drastically as the opposing infantry forces sought refuge from the shelling. After the artillery had dueled for a while, Captain Young announced that Company A's jump off was being postponed. We withdrew three hundred yards back down the trail and were told to dig in up on the right hand slope.[22]

Under the snow the ground was very soft. After some rapid digging, Herbie and I had a foxhole five feet deep and five feet long inside of an hour. The beautiful soft ground seemed almost too good to be true. Back at Fort Benning, where they are born with an Field Manual 7-10 in their cribs and a gold bar pinned to their diapers, the prescribed dimensions for a foxhole are four to five feet deep and only two feet wide. This was called the "standing," or "fighting," foxhole. But the Benning theoreticians apparently overlooked the fact that Johnny Doughfoot needs to sleep now and then, and needs to do so in a covered and concealed position. Thus,

---

[22]The Germans called this Winter Line their "Vosges Forward Position." Their *main* Vosges position was 10 or 12 kilometers farther east, along the France-Alsace border, which generally ran along the geographical crest of the High Vosges. As matters turned out, once the forward positions were overrun, the Germans never got a chance to occupy their Main Position—our VI Corps pursued the enemy closely, and chased him out of the High Vosges range with virtually no further resistance.

the actual dimensions of our foxholes tended to be less deep than pre-scribed, but considerably longer. If the Benning brains had devised the blueprint for the prescribed "fighting foxhole," Herbie Rice and I should have been granted U.S. patents for developing and perfecting the "sleeping foxhole, non-portable, M-1." In any case, it was another indication that written doctrine could only take you so far, and could only suggest a com-mon basis by which to operate. After that, the lessons learned from hard experience taught techniques to be built upon the principles laid down in the books.

Before roofing our foxhole, we paused to attack our K rations. I took the "orangeade" powder and sugar from my dinner ration and dumped them in a canteen cupful of water I had scooped out of a small moss-cov-ered pool I had discovered nearby. After treating the water with halizone pills, I heated it on Sergeant Parenteau's Turner stove and drank some. Failing to die immediately of polluted water or enemy poisoning, I passed it around for sampling to the boys of the squad who said it tasted good. I took orders and found several takers. Actually "Red Gurley's Hot Orangeade" didn't taste all that great, but the benefits to the consumer were obvious: he didn't have to use his own precious canteen water, and the only required investment was putting up orange powder and sugar. The hot beverage was a good antidote to our cold wet uniforms and leaky fox-holes. The only risk was that the moss-covered stagnant-looking natural reservoir from which I was drawing our water supply would turn out to be lethal, thus saving the enemy eleven or more bullets or shells to get rid of our squad.

After eating, we returned to working on our foxhole. Just as we got it nicely roofed, we were told to get ready to move. Charlie Company was coming back to occupy our foxholes and we would move to new positions, where there were of course no foxholes. We crossed the trail, climbed a rise, and attempted to dig in. Here the ground was hard and full of roots, and the best Herbie Rice and I could do by twilight was to hack out a shal-low slit trench some eighteen inches deep. If our new foxhole would not qualify as the Fort Benning "fighting foxhole" or the Rice-Gurley "sleeping foxhole," perhaps it could qualify as a "suicide slit-trench." We said the hell with it, stopped digging, and scrunched down under our raincoats. But then the rain began a staccato beat on our already drenched equipment, so we added a hurried log roof to our little Dead Man's Depression.

Companies B and C had now pulled back from their positions 600 yards ahead of us to form a line where we were. They had been unable to advance more than 150 to 200 yards against the Germans on Hill 409.9 during the entire day, and had now been withdrawn to enable Corps

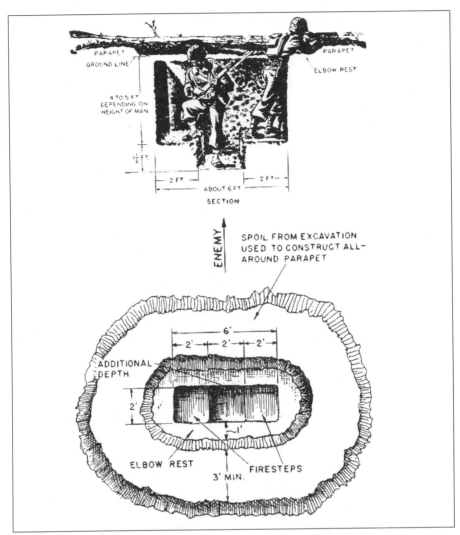

Foxhole schematic, from from Field Manual 7-10, *Rifle Company, Infantry Regiment* (18 March 1944), p. 241.

Artillery to blast the enemy positions during the night. It was so dark when the final elements of our two sister rifle companies of the 1st Battalion came back down to where we were that the men had to hold hands to avoid becoming lost in the dense, craggy Vosges forest. Three Sherman tanks were parked along the trail that ran between our beautiful foxholes of this morning and our miserable slit-trenches of tonight. One of the returning Charlie Company platoon leaders, Lieutenant Jack Jenkins, was so wet and exhausted that he decided to crawl under one of the tanks, despite the obvious danger to life if the tank happened to roar off during the night. He fell asleep immediately and awoke four hours later feeling refreshed.[23]

Baker Company reported that the German defenders had shot down unarmed medics as they tended the wounded. Our medics had large red crosses against a white background on both sides of their helmets. These crosses could not have provided a better target for snipers if they had been designed for that specific purpose. Colonel Tychsen ordered that the Red Cross markings be played down as much as possible through the application of paint or mud.

Herbie Rice and I fell asleep to a lullaby of high-caliber howitzers swooshing in low over our foxholes to blast the enemy positions with a tremendous uproar of sound. The Krauts had stopped our battalion cold two days in a row and our generals were apparently getting fed up. Judging from all the noise, tomorrow was going to be a new ball game.

The morning of 15 November started off with the 3d Battalion, which had been in reserve since Armistice Day, moving up through our lines and attacking the same hills which had stymied the 1st and 2d Battalions for the past thirty-six hours. We heard a lot of friendly artillery pounding the ridges ahead of their advance. As we stood around trying to keep warm, the two Turner stoves in the platoon were in constant operation heating Nescafé and K rations. I shared my fig bar with Eddie Cook, who for once didn't seem to be in a particularly cheerful mood.

"This war is very discouraging," Eddie said in his Missouri twang. "If they keep me in the Army three more years, I'll be twenty-one. Then four years of college and a year or two working before I'll be able to afford getting married. Imagine, waiting till twenty-six or twenty-seven just to get married."

"Yeah, things are tough all over," I said. Eddie Cook certainly had a well thought-out career plan. I had nothing particular in view from a planning standpoint except perhaps tomorrow and the day after.

In mid-morning, Sergeant Chuck Stanley came over to tell Real Parenteau that our squad had been tapped for a special mission providing protection for our Sherman tanks. We would be temporarily detached, reporting directly to battalion headquarters. We hoisted our filthy, soaking bandoleers over our heads and across our chests, hung our grenades on them like Christmas ornaments, shouldered our weapons and were ready to move. The other members of the platoon wished us well, with a few jokes about being a "suicide squad." We filed down off the ridge where we had spent the night and moved back along the trail to the Company CP.

[23]Jenkins memoir.

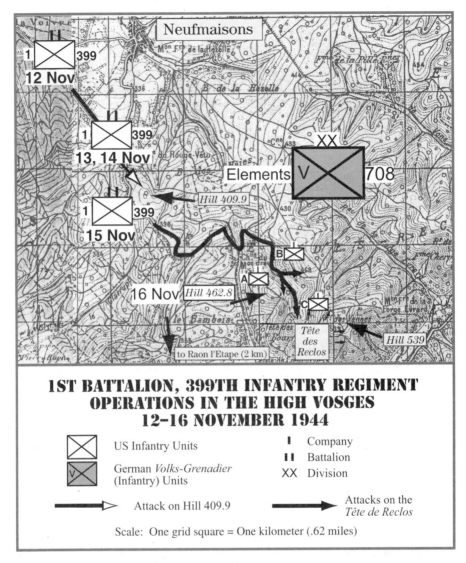

**1ST BATTALION, 399TH INFANTRY REGIMENT
OPERATIONS IN THE HIGH VOSGES
12–16 NOVEMBER 1944**

US Infantry Units

German *Volks-Grenadier*
(Infantry) Units

I   Company
II   Battalion
XX Division

→▷ Attack on Hill 409.9

→ Attacks on the
Tête de Reclos

Scale: One grid square = One kilometer (.62 miles)

A runner from battalion picked us up and led us back. At the intersection of two trails, we found three muddy Sherman tanks, covered with sandbags and wearing bright red air identification panels on their rear decks. The runner said to wait there for Major Lentz. Then he took off.

A few minutes later, Barney Lentz showed up wearing the same raincoat and pistol belt he had worn two evenings ago when he had almost led us into enemy captivity through his eccentric way of reading a map.

"Here's the plan," Major Lentz said. "You will wait here until the signal to go is given. Then ride the tanks as far as the highway where you will see a yellowish painted blockhouse called Rouge Vêtu. Company L just captured the blockhouse with the help of another platoon of tanks, also from the 753d Tank Battalion. You will then dismount and form a protective screen around the front of our tank column. The 325th Engineers will join you and will operate mine-detection equipment in front of the lead tank." Major Lentz looked at Sergeant Parenteau. "Do you have any questions, Sergeant?"

"No, sir," Parenteau said.

Major Lentz went off to confer with a runner from battalion headquarters a short distance away. Parenteau named Herb Rice, Scotty Kyle, L. C. Talley, and me to go with the first tank. Parenteau, Robert E. Jones, Doc Emmons, and Thomas Case would be with the second tank, while Woody Gilbert, Pop Swartz, and Julius DeRubeis would bring up the rear on the third tank. We were awed by our special mission, and plenty scared, too.

We settled down about thirty yards from the tanks. Pop Swartz started heating rations on Parenteau's little Turner stove. Under their mud and sandbags, the tanks were painted green with white stars on the sides. Their 75mm cannons drooped a few degrees below the horizontal, but would (we hoped) elevate before firing at the enemy. The tank crews wore rubber helmets and big athletic jackets like pro football players.

Someone found a five-gallon can full of water, and we refilled our canteens. We sat around munching cheese and cracker sandwiches, drinking orangeade, and bitching. When Parenteau finished eating, he threw half of the cheese away, which I considered a crime against mankind. But what could I do? Parenteau was a temperamental, strong-willed non-conformist of French ancestry, and I was his rankless subordinate. But to waste good food that way while most of us suffered from insatiable hunger was inexcusable in my eyes.

Our old friend, Lieutenant Thomas Plante, rushed up to Major Lentz, waving his long arms and shouting. Tommy Plante, one of the few men in the 399th who offered the enemy a taller target than I did, was a platoon leader in Company L, whence Major Lentz had him transferred from our company before we left the States.

"You sent my patrol into an ambush up there!" Tommy Plante shouted at Major Lentz. "It was suicide! We didn't have a chance!"

I couldn't figure out why Tommy Plante was bitching to Major Lentz since Lentz wasn't in his battalion. If Major Lentz had, in fact, sent him on that patrol as Plante claimed, perhaps it was on some sort of detached basis of the type that now placed our squad on another special mission under Barney Lentz's orders. I hoped the fate of Plante's patrol today wasn't another example of Barney Lentz's tactical talent.

Today's patrol was the second time in two weeks Tommy Plante had been ambushed in these murky Vosges forests. Before being drafted, Tommy Plante's universe had revolved between his residence at 925 Sterling Place in Brooklyn, his Benedict & Benedict insurance office on Pearl Street in Manhattan, and St. John's University, from which he had graduated. To send a man from such a heavily citified environment out to explore the beaches of Long Island was one thing, but to send him into the Vosges forests to locate a cunningly concealed and camouflaged foe was quite another level of challenge. On 3 November, while we were conducting our contact patrol to the 3d Infantry Division in La Bourgonce and eating steaks from the cow killed by errant shrapnel, Tommy Plante led a combat patrol toward St. Remy through the woods west of the town. They ran into an ambush and lost the division's first man to the enemy, Pfc. Estil Crittendon who was wounded by burp-gun fire and captured when the Germans' overwhelming firepower drove back Lieutenant Plante's patrol.

We couldn't hear what Major Lentz responded to Tommy Plante's outburst, but when it was over Tommy stalked off angrily on his long legs. He didn't see us, his old Able Company comrades, sitting nearby.

"All right, let's go!" Major Lentz called to us.

We clambered aboard our iron elephants, feeling like eleven "Bomba, the Jungle Boys." The three Sherman tanks made an incredible amount of noise as they waddled off to war. The ride lasted only about half a mile before Sergeant Parenteau shouted for us to jump down off the tanks. My entrenching shovel betrayed me and got caught on some protuberance on the tank as I clambered down and landed on my hands and knees in the mud. Up ahead through the trees, I could see a shattered, yellowish-colored blockhouse about a hundred yards away. That must be "*Mon Frère du Rouge Vêtu*" about which I had heard so much, beginning with the lady in St. Remy whose son-in-law had been captured here. For 360 degrees around the blockhouse, the woods had been thinned out to provide perfect fields of fire upon any thing that tried to approach it.

Herbie Rice and I led the way through the last trees before the clearing where the blockhouse stood. Double rows of barbed wire ran through the trees. On the ground just outside the first wire, we came upon two very dead young GIs who were still clutching their M-1s. They looked like children asleep and there was no blood or other sign of violence.

"You think it would be all right for me to take one of their shovels?" Herbie Rice asked me. Herbie's regular tool was a small pick, which was vastly inferior to the small folding shovels most of us had drawn.

"Go ahead," I said. I think he'd want you to have it." If the M-1 rifle was the dogface's most prized possession, the small entrenching shovel rated a close second.

The two dead boys belonged to Company G which had tried to take this Winter Line blockhouse two days before. Eight scouts had been sent forward through the trees to search the blockhouse and throw grenades into the cellar. What they didn't realize was that at the far edge of the clearing beyond the blockhouse, a force of Germans was burrowed into the ground at the base of a copse of dark firs, observing their movements like black cats hidden in a shadowed hedge. When the Germans opened fire, only two of the eight scouts escaped. One of the platoon leaders was ordered to take his platoon around the right flank in an effort to relieve the pressure on the main force. He refused to carry out the order. Five officers and twenty-four enlisted men were killed or wounded before George Company finally extricated itself from the carefully crafted ambush. The boy whose shovel Herbie Rice "borrowed" was one of the twenty-nine victims. Company G had already renamed the *Le Rouge Vêtu* area "Purple Heart Lane."

Herbie Rice and I led the tank column forward to the crossroad at *Rouge Vêtu* where the tank platoon leader conferred from his turret with the engineers who would sweep for mines ahead of the tanks. A tall young major who seemed to be the engineers' CO spotted a couple of Krauts in a clump of pines about a hundred yards away. He excused himself, leveled his Thompson submachine gun, started running and yelled, "Why you yella bastards, whatcha running away for?" He let go with a complete clip of ammo toward the place where he last saw them. Returning to the business at hand, he resumed the conversation with the leader of the tank detachment.

The long whine of a passing shell sent the engineers' minesweeping squad diving for the ditches, from which they emerged only when assured it was "friendly freight" steaming past. One of our sources of pride as dogfaces already was that we refused to hit the dirt when an American shell went by. If we called one wrong it might be our last call, yet we would have felt like old ladies to flinch from any shell that wasn't made in Germany and directly intended for us.

Finally the tanks were ready to go. Herb Rice and I moved out fifty yards in front of the first tank and ten to fifteen yards off the road on either side. The other members of our squad were strung out behind us at intervals to protect the flanks and rear of the tank column. A few yards ahead of the first tank, the minesweeping squad waved a mine detector shaped like a pie plate back and forth across the highway as though they were vacuuming a rug. We could hear the methodical "beep" of the minesweeper whenever the roar of the tanks died down enough for normal sounds to be audible. The tanks made a tremendous roar on the asphalt highway and we all wondered how long it would take the enemy to call for and adjust artillery or mortars on us.

There were plenty of trees and rocks for the Jerries to hide behind, but we hadn't met any yet. The tankers acted deathly afraid of hidden enemy soldiers and looked to us for protection the way a schoolgirl crossing the street might clutch the strong arm of the "Man in Blue." They also moaned and groaned about the dangers of firing their main guns in this heavily-wooded terrain, claiming that the shots could ricochet off the trees and destroy the tank. It surprised us that these tank jockeys, so dapper in their football helmets and special jackets and so well protected beneath all that steel plate, could be so skittish and terrified at the thought of the enemy.

Our little caravan passed through several enemy road blocks made of heavy logs and fir branches. The infantry which had preceded us had removed enough of the logwork to permit us to go through. The road's shoulders had now become quite narrow due to rising ground on our left and a sharp drop-off on the right. As a result, Herbie Rice and I were often obliged to remain on the pavement, thereby offering the tanks less protection than we would have liked.

We came to the area where that morning the 3d Battalion had broken through the Winter Line, after Baker and Charlie Companies' failure the previous day. To reach the highway, 3d Battalion had had to descend a wooded slope over on our right, under perfect enemy observation, and then charge up another steep slope protected by barbed wire and honeycombed with enemy dugouts to reach the highway. It was easy to understand how the enemy had stopped Companies B and C cold for two days. General Burress and Colonel Tychsen had finally solved the problem by ordering a rolling artillery barrage to be laid ahead of the assault troops. The barrage moved forward one hundred yards every four minutes and lasted half an hour. Advancing behind the rolling barrage, the men of Companies I, K, and L had cut through several fences of barbed wire with wire cutters and charged up the slope to the highway brandishing bayonets.

When the 3d Battalion had finally reached the highway, one more wooded peak (Hill 431) remained to be seized before the Winter Line could be considered breached. Using the roadway itself as a "parapet," World War I style, they had fired up the slope at the German entrenchments on Hill 431 from the defilade offered by the road. Finally, they stormed across the road and drove the Germans out of their positions. Pfc. Irving Blumenthal started the final assault by standing up behind the road defilade and shouting *"Charge!"* He dashed across the road and on up the slope of Hill 431.

After passing through the 3d Battalion's zone, we began seeing men from our own 1st Battalion. They, too, had passed through the Winter Line to the right of the 3d Battalion's breach and were now moving south along the highway toward Raon l'Etape, the divisional objective, through heavy woods on both sides of the road.

"Boy, am I glad to see you guys!" I heard almost those exact words from a dozen dogfaces from both 1st and 3d Battalions. I felt a tremendous pride to be guiding these huge steel fortresses, symbols of our Army's might. On the other hand, the infantrymen couldn't have been any happier to see us than we were to see them. It meant that our "suicide squad" and our large steel charges were no longer alone in our search for the enemy. One thing was absolutely clear to everyone: the infantry desperately needed the material and moral support of the armor; in these mountains, where their mobility and fields of fire and observation were so limited, the armor reciprocally needed the infantry's protection at least as much as the infantry needed them.

The short late-autumn afternoon was already giving way to twilight and there was no gloomier time in the Vosges. Shades of darkness would soon be drawn over the scene of battle and we knew the tanks couldn't go much farther with such limited visibility. As we passed a dirt road which entered the main road from the left, I thought I heard a feeble voice calling from the roadside ditch near the junction.

"Help!" Had I imagined it? Then again, "Help!"

Real Parenteau behind me also heard it and went over to investigate. It was our 1st Squad Leader, Jim Amoroso, lying in the ditch, badly wounded. He had been lying there for hours and had lost a lot of blood from bullet wounds in the leg and shoulder. He told us briefly what had happened. They had passed through the 397th's line of foxholes and reached the highway one hundred yards beyond without resistance. Charlie Company had crossed the highway and gone on down the dirt road beyond. Everyone *assumed* Company C had also cleared the wood on the right side of the road beyond the junction. The Battalion S-3, Captain Park L. Brown, was there with his maps, telling Able Company to "close it up" and move rapidly through those woods. But Charlie Company had *not* cleared the woods and there were still German defenders there. Amoroso's squad had the point with John Jeske and Garland Cash as scouts. They were following a little path twenty or thirty yards ahead of Ammo and Eddie Cook, who was carrying the walkie-talkie. The Krauts let the scouts go by to get a shot at the squad leader and the radio man, who appeared to be more worthwhile targets. The Germans opened fire and the platoon hit the ground.

Ammo and Cook heard Lieutenant Mueller's voice behind them.

"Cook, call Captain Young and tell him we've hit an ambush in the woods southeast of the road junction.

"All right," Eddie Cook called back from behind a tree. After two or three tries, he reported, "I can't get contact."

"Okay, try again in two minutes," Lieutenant Mueller said.

Eddie Cook looked at his watch. Two minutes to wait. Wondering what the situation was up ahead, he decided to take a peek around the base of his tree. A German sniper was waiting patiently for him to make this fatal mistake.

Seeing that Cook had been shot, Amoroso ran over to try to help. Cook's sniper was waiting and felled Ammo with a bullet in the thigh. The force of the bullet knocked Ammo down, but he continued firing. A short time later, the sniper hit him again in the shoulder. Ammo continued firing until he became too weak from loss of blood to hold the rifle. Lennie Hershberg offered to bring or throw his canteen to Ammo, but Ammo said he had plenty of water. Hershberg said Woody, the medic, had been called and would be along soon.

Colonel Zehner then appeared and ordered that the woods be cleaned out.

"There are no Germans in there now," he announced, incorrectly as it turned out. Able Company formed a skirmish line and advanced down the slope through the trees past Cook and Amoroso and up the opposite slope firing from the hip. Five or six Germans were killed or wounded and a dozen more surrendered.

Meanwhile Woody, our medic, had patched up Ammo and placed him in the ditch for security while waiting for a litter team or jeep to carry him back to the Battalion Aid Station. But hours passed and Ammo became discouraged as darkness came.

Sergeant Walter Bull, acting leader of the 2d Platoon in the wake of Lieutenant Gullborg's evacuation for wounds, led a prisoner back to where Sergeant Stanley and Lennie Hershberg were talking.

"You dirty bastard!" Chuck Stanley said to the prisoner. Stanley was very upset over Eddie Cook's death.

"You heard him," Lennie Hershberg added.

"Ya, ya, me bastard!" the German agreed fervently, hoping he could charm them into not executing him.

"Shall I shoot him?" Hershberg asked Sergeant Stanley.

"No!" Sergeant Bull cried. "I'm standing behind him."

Hershberg's laughter broke the tension and ended their sudden thirst for frontier justice. Several other prisoners came along and Bull's prisoner joined them. They were turned over to the 397th for safekeeping, and Able Company rejoined the battalion advance southward along the highway. What to do about Sergeant Amoroso? Real Parenteau thought fast and told

Thomas Case to help Ammo back to Battalion Aid or at least stay with him. Then we had to start out again with our tanks.

For Herbie Rice, Scotty Kyle, and me, Eddie Cook's death was a tremendous shock since the four of us had been close friends since arriving at Fort Bragg in the spring. Also, Cook was more or less regarded as the unofficial platoon mascot, since he was so youthful in appearance and so pleasant and unwarlike in his behavior toward everyone in the outfit. When Ammo was telling what had happened, he pointed out to Scotty Kyle where Eddie Cook's remains could be found in case Kyle wanted to pay his last respects. Scotty Kyle declined the invitation.

Resuming our advance along the highway, we came across our friend, Raymond Sholes, of Gil Moniz's squad, guarding a horse-drawn "train" of little carts filled with German mortar rounds. The horses had apparently been killed or had been led back in the general German retreat, leaving the ammunition to be captured. Ray Sholes gave me a look that said "You know about Cook?" My answering look said, "Yes." Ray Sholes said Charlie Company had captured the mortars and had then been hit by a counterattack which they repulsed. He said our company had switched to the right side of the road, leaving C on the left and B in reserve.

Ray Sholes told me what had been going on after the company had gone beyond the ambush site where Cook was killed and Ammo was wounded. They had entered a dark forest where the enemy waited like scorpions inside a bottle. Captain Young was moving along with his communications sergeant, Sergeant Joe Nemeseck, and a radio man when a German suddenly emerged from behind a woodpile thirty to forty feet ahead of them, hands on his head in a gesture of surrender. Sergeant Nemeseck whispered to Captain Young that he could see that the Jerry was hiding a hand grenade behind his head. Captain Young, who was holding his carbine in his right hand at waist level, fired his weapon without changing position or any other preliminary movement, killing the surprised German. Not over thirty minutes later, lanky Joe Nemeseck, the "Communications Deity" of Company A, was hit in the heel by a German bullet and put out of action.

The German defenders were as thick as slugs in a lush garden after a heavy rain, clinging everywhere on top of and under things, some visible, others partly visible, still others completely invisible under their camouflage capes and boughs of evergreens.

We continued along the pine-walled road until we came to our Battalion CO, Lieutenant Colonel Zehner, standing in the middle of the road talking to some officers. When you found Colonel Zehner, you found the front lines. The tank column halted. The 325th Engineers' mine-sweeping squad checked with the tank commander and took off post haste for the rear.

Colonel Zehner's party was standing right beside our lead tank. Herbie Rice and I clambered up onto the tank to relax and do a bit of eavesdropping to see what the score was. If we had been watching a war film, we could hardly have asked for more excitement. Colonel Zehner was like a busy executive with everyone trying to talk to him while he studied the situation on his map. He was wearing a red silk scarf and I could just make out the silver oak leaf painted on the front of his helmet in the near darkness. He had decided to call our battalion the "Red Raiders" and his scarf was his way of calling attention to this situation.[24] It was also his equivalent of Julius Caesar's red cape, worn to let his men know exactly where he was . . . which was pretty much always up front, like Colonel Zehner.

Captain Campion of Company C came running up out of the woods on the left side of the road. He leaped around in the road like a wrestler and almost seemed to be pounding Colonel Zehner with his flailing arms.

"We're being cut to ribbons!" he screamed at Colonel Zehner. "We're caught in an ambush situation at the moment and the Krauts have us zeroed in with 88s. We need medics badly. Four of my men took refuge in a ditch and an 88 went right in after them as though it had eyes. The Krauts in front of us are thicker than fleas on a dog."

"Okay." Colonel Zehner said. "Halt your company where they are for the night. We'll get medics to you as fast as we can."

Captain Campion stalked off into the darkness. I didn't know whether he had exaggerated his company's situation or not, but he had obtained what he wanted—authorization to stop advancing farther into the scorpion bottle tonight.

A moment after Captain Campion's departure, Colonel Zehner saw a medic standing in the road and sent him off after Campion.

Captain Campion's onstage leap, tirade, and sudden exit had interrupted Colonel Zehner's map study, which he now resumed while chaos reigned around him. Technical Sergeant Rudolf Steinman of Company D was shouting at his two heavy machine-gun crews to dig faster into the road embankment on the right side and the road shoulder on the left before the enemy started shelling us. Sergeant Steinman, a Swiss-born former Foreign Legionnaire who had fought the Germans in World War I was very savvy about what the Germans might do next in any given tactical situation. The Battalion S-3, Captain Brown, told Sergeant Steinman to tone down the shouting if he didn't want to attract enemy shelling.

---

[24]In US Army infantry regiments during WWII, the radio callsign prefix of any 1st Battalion station was usually "Red," 2d Battalion was usually "White," and the 3d Battalion stations were usually prefixed with "Blue."

Messengers were coming from all directions seeking instructions. Colonel Zehner told the Able Company Runner, George Lorenz, to tell Captain Young to stop advancing and dig in on the hill to the right of the road. Baker Company's runner was told to have the company dig in on the left behind Charlie Company. Dog Company's runner was told where the mortars should be set up. Colonel Zehner instructed an antitank crew to set up their gun beside the embankment next to the second tank.

Through all the interruptions, Colonel Zehner continued to study his situation map, finally being obliged to put his curved nose almost against the map because of the descending darkness.

"Well, what do you know?" he said finally to the half dozen or so staff officers standing around him (and to the two eavesdroppers on the first tank). "We're one thousand yards ahead of the rest of the Seventh Army. We're sort of a Lost Battalion."

None of the other officers spoke. "Of course we're not really lost," Colonel Zehner added. "We know exactly where we are on the map."

I had rarely seen a man enjoying himself as much as our Battalion CO seemed to be today. If Colonel Zehner had been a bit humorless and gloomy back at Bragg, he was now finally emerging in the role nature and West Point had planned for him as a superbly competent and hugely successful combat commander who seemed completely in charge and in his element at last.

"We're going to remain very exposed tonight, so we must be extremely alert." Colonel Zehner went on.

Just then we all heard a faint, distant whine. In a matter of seconds the whine had become a shrieking spasm of air which quickly gave birth to an ugly black explosion halfway between the first and second tanks, which were spaced about eighty yards apart. Other whistles followed, confirming that our position had already been plotted for Jerry's heavy stuff, even though our armored caravan had halted there only fifteen or twenty minutes before.

At the first explosion, we dived off the tank into the ditch. Over a dozen more artillery rounds exploded in the next three or four minutes. To me, German artillery rounds had the smell of death; I knew no other words to describe the "Whistling Annies." Like Old Faithful, they rarely missed the spot for which they were aiming, even with the first round. When they had finished shaking up the landscape and raining debris on our backs and helmets, I peeked up out of the ditch. The area was now devoid of the officer personnel who had been there before with the exception of Colonel Zehner, who was walking off down the road toward the rear with his Prussian gait, probably looking for new fields to conquer or records to break.

The machine-gun crews completed their emplacements beside the road and the tankers prepared for bed inside their mobile metal hotels. We were wet and hungry and in no mood to dig foxholes. I asked the tank commander if it would be all right for us to sleep under the tank.

"A guy got killed under here once," he replied. It wasn't a "Yes," but wasn't a flat "No" either.

"Thanks," I said. "Getting killed by your tank is the least of our worries."

Seven of us opted to sleep under the front tank while Corporal Woody Gilbert and two others went off to negotiate for parking space with the second tank's crew. The tankers loaned us a large wet piece of canvas which we spread out under the tank. There were only three raincoats among the seven of us. Real Parenteau, Herbie Rice, and I shared one of them and used the tank's steel tread for a pillow.

The minute I lay down I started thinking of Ed Cook and started praying. None of us could have slept more than an hour, because anytime anyone said something, the others always answered him.

That night was the low point of the war so far.

Chapter Eighteen
The Battle at the Top of the Wilderness

When we couldn't stand the wet, freezing cold any longer, Herbie Rice and I crawled out from under the tank at about 0500 on 16 November to walk around and try to get up a little circulation going. We looked up at the narrow strip of sky above the road. To our surprise, the sky was clear and all the stars were out. Hooray, we thought, we're in for a clear day at last after the snow, rain, drizzle, fog, mist, and general gloom of the past four days. We were doomed to disappointment, however, for when day broke an hour later the sky had become the same gloomy gray as before.

Everybody was up and pacing around by the time it got light. About one hundred yards ahead, the road curved abruptly left and we didn't know (or care for that matter) what was around the curve. Just then a group of about eight soldiers came strolling out of the woods to the right of the bend and came walking up the road toward the tanks.

I first assumed it was a returning patrol, but then I said to Herbie Rice, "Hey, where did our GIs get those long coats?" We all rushed for our rifles which were back behind the tank where we couldn't get at them quickly.

"Halt!" I called when they were about twenty-five yards away. Then our Assistant Squad Leader, Corporal Woodrow "Woody" Gilbert (who had a German mother), told them *"Hände hoch!"* ("Hands up!"). They dropped their weapons and everything else they were carrying, raised their arms to heaven and shouted *"Polski! Polski!"* and *"Kamerad! Nicht schiessen!"* Herbie Rice left the task of capturing them to the others and made a rush for the stuff they had dropped in the road. He thus pounced upon the only decent weapon in the bunch, a shiny black Luger pistol.

The tankers got out their stove and started cooking ten-in-one rations consisting of fried ham and eggs on cracker sandwiches. They generously invited us eleven starving dogfaces to share their repast. Later, a Company D jeep arrived from the rear bringing K rations and water for Sergeant Steinman's machine-gun crews dug in on both sides of the road ahead of the first tank.

"Hey Real," Pop Swartz said to Sergeant Parenteau. "Who did you say we're attached to on this tank mission?" Swartz called Parenteau by his first name because he was several years older than our squad leader.

"I report to Major Lentz and battalion headquarters" Parenteau replied.

"Then why the heck doesn't he send us up some food and water?"

"Yeah, I never thought of that," Parenteau said, scratching his helmet. Pop Swartz was not hoggish in his food desires (like some unmentioned members of the platoon), but had a strong gourmet's interest in the subject nevertheless. Being located somewhere between a gourmand and a gourmet myself, I wondered what was the matter with Major Lentz, forgetting us in this way. Perhaps Philadelphia lawyers had so many important issues on their minds that they had little time for petty details such as what the 3d Squad would have to eat and drink before today's fighting.

But Sergeant Steinman, too, demonstrated great generosity in passing out some of their K rations to our squad. Sergeant Steinman, who was called "the Unneutral Swiss" and "the Ungentle Swiss," was born in 1898 near Zürich. In 1913, he ran away to join the French Foreign Legion by falsifying his age. A year later, the Great War broke out and he found himself fighting on the side of the French in Belgium. After the war, he emigrated to the mid-West where he worked first in his brother's cheese factory, then as a security guard in Chicago. He joined the U.S. Army and served almost twenty years as a "professional soldier." At age forty-six, he was now an American citizen and old enough to be the father of most of the privates in our outfit.

Sergeant Walter Bull came out of the woods on our right to discuss something with Sergeant Steinman. He reported that our company had spent the night on a high ridge with shells from both sides passing low overhead all night and preventing Captain Young from getting any sleep.

I borrowed Sergeant Parenteau's Turner stove and set it up on the flat surface of the highway. I tore open the K ration packet of Nescafé and soon had a canteen cup of coffee percolating in a normal civilized way. Just then a quartet of urgent whistles sounded and a thick concentration of German artillery shells blasted our position. I was positive the first two rounds had my ASN (Army Serial Number) on them, but all I got was a shower of dirt in the ditch where I had taken refuge and a few splintered twigs and branches raining down on my helmet. Peeking cautiously out of the ditch, I saw the Nescafé still percolating on the deserted road surface where the shells had miraculously failed to riddle it. If, for some, discretion was the better part of valor, for me it was hunger that played discretion's normal role. Crawling up out of the ditch onto the road, I grabbed the Nescafé off the stove and scuttled crab-like back into the depression just as several more shells whistled in. I drank sitting up in the ditch during lulls in the shelling, and when Annie's whistles began again, I simply continued drinking in a prone position.

While drinking Nescafé and listening to the song of shrapnel and the rain of boughs and branches around me, I felt something grate against my heels in the ditch. I had a pretty good idea that the grating sound was being made by the Sergeant's Bull's helmet. I thought I knew what he was agitating about, but pretended not to notice him in the ditch behind me.

"Er, hey Red!"

"Yeah?"

"Er, how about a taste of that stuff?"

"Oh sure, Sergeant Bull." I passed the canteen cup back to our hero who sipped away gratefully. During the next lull, I sat up long enough to make cheese sandwiches which Sergeant Bull and I consumed with our noses against the bottom of the ditch during the next barrage. At least we weren't going to die on empty stomachs. I remembered how Sergeant Bull had figured he'd become a rich man by carrying a small fortune's worth of lighter fluid overseas with him, and carted the stuff three thousand miles from the Camp Kilmer PX right up to the line. Unfortunately for him, it turned out that one creature comfort the U. S. Army in Europe had in plentiful quantities was lighter fluid, and Bull's investment turned out to be a costly waste of time and money.

Finally, the shelling tapered off and Colonel Zehner appeared. He was still wearing his red scarf and moved along the road stolidly and squarely like some kind of human tank. He told the tank commander that the tanks' role today would be changed to an offensive one. They would provide overhead supporting main gun and machine-gun fire for the rifle companies' assault upon Hill 462.8, approximately one kilometer to our front. Our squad's role would remain unchanged—to protect the tanks from enemy efforts to destroy them.

Colonel Zehner said that the Commanding Officer of the 397th Infantry Regiment on our right, Colonel William Ellis, and his driver had been killed yesterday afternoon. He had mistakenly ridden in his jeep straight into German lines in the confused forest fighting. One of the line companies had given an unduly optimistic report of the portion of the forest then under their control, and Colonel Ellis had directed his driver into a sector that was not, in fact, then in their regiment's hands. The poor visibility of the Vosges forest in late afternoon had contributed to the failure of the 397th's leading units to recognize and halt Colonel Ellis' jeep before it went too far. German ambushers riddled the two lost men mercilessly with burp guns at point blank range as they drove along a misty trail under tall evergreens. A 397th patrol sent out at dawn found the disabled jeep and brought back the bodies of the dead colonel and driver.

As we waited around for the tanks to receive the "go" signal, the distant figure of a soldier came reeling around the bend up ahead. We watched him come staggering up the road toward our position. Two of the Company D machine gunners ran out to help him, but he shook them off. He wore the familiar double bar "railroad tracks" insignia of a captain painted on his helmet.

"You told us there were no Jerries out there!" he screamed at Colonel Zehner.

"I said no such thing," Colonel Zehner replied calmly. "Sergeant Steinman," he said, "can you radio back for a jeep to take the Captain to Battalion Aid? He could probably walk back, but he's had enough strain already."

The captain seemed not to hear Colonel Zehner's transportation offer and set off aimlessly back down the road toward the rear.

Moments later, Colonel Zehner turned to our tank commander and said, "Take off, Lieutenant." Take off we did, down the highway to the sharp left-ward bend, then around to the left for a few hundred yards, and finally where the main highway looped back to the right we turned off onto a tiny dirt road on the left. There was a large stone marker, which looked centuries old, at the junction which announced that we were leaving the Department of the Moselle and entering the Department of the Vosges. Funny, we had thought we were in the Vosges for the past two weeks.

The tanks moved slowly along the little road through tall evergreens and past neat stacks of firewood. Soon a platoon of twenty-five or thirty men from Baker Company joined our caravan as additional protection for the precious tanks. The Company B platoon formed a skirmish line of a dozen men on each side of the first tank which now had better protection than a Pinkerton armored truck filled with bank notes. We moved cautiously up a broad draw at the end of which we could see the lower slopes of the Battalion objective, Hill 462.8. Jerry was feeling us out with some desultory artillery, but didn't know exactly where we were. The armor lumbered through a forest of tall trees on the narrow, muddy ribbon of road.

It didn't take long before we came to a marshy, wooded area about two hundred yards from the base of the hill mass that was our objective. Colonel Zehner was there waiting for us. He discussed the situation with the tank commander while our squad and the Baker Company platoon deployed behind the cover of trees. I could hear the tank lieutenant playing his old refrain that a shot fired in woods by a tank might ricochet and destroy tank and crew. Colonel Zehner told him not to worry and climbed up on the tank behind the turret. Under his guidance, the tank roared up to the edge of the marshy area that separated our woods from the base of Hill 462.8. The tank raised its main gun to maximum elevation and let fly four or five rounds up the slopes of the hill. The other two tanks maneuvered into position to the right of the first tank and all three tanks' cannon guns pounded the high, forested slope with direct fire.

Finally, Colonel Zehner gave the cease-fire signal. Then we saw a skirmish line rise up at the far edge of the swamp and start up the lower slope of the mountain, firing as they advanced. We heard some enemy firing in response, but most of the noise seemed to be made by M-1s and BARs. Soon the line had passed out of sight through the trees of Hill 462.8.

For the moment, there was nothing more for our squad to do except to continue guarding the tanks, whose initial firing support mission had been completed. The Baker Company platoon that had joined our tank escort for the final few hundred yards was now relieved of this special guard duty and was sent off on some other mission.

My friend, George Lorenze of Captain Young's CP group, came along carrying a roll of communications wire.

"What's going on, George?" I asked.

"Total confusion as usual," George Lorenze replied. "Some idiot at HQ fixed our Line of Departure at the base of Hill 462.8 over there across the swamp. Would you believe it, the 2d Platoon took seven casualties just getting to the LD? As I understand it, the LD is supposed to be on a piece of ground that's already in our possession, rather than in enemy hands as it was today."

"Who got hit?" I asked.

"I don't know who all of them were, but Peter Siems, Doc Savage, and Arlen Frost were three. They've been patched up in that marshy area, but can't be evacuated yet."

I looked ahead into the marshy area, but could not see any of the wounded waiting there.

"The Jerries threw in artillery even before we reached the point where we are now," George Lorenze said. "That caused some casualties including Lieutenant Henry Majeski of C Company. He went riding out of here on a stretcher and when he passed Captain Young, he said, "Gosh, Dick, you look awful!" When I learned of Lieutenant Majeski's departure on a stretcher, I thought back to St. Remy where he had aimed his carbine at me. Now I had no one to fear except the Jerries.

George Lorenze said, "Our artillery laid a forty-five-minute barrage on the top of Hill 462.8 before we jumped off, but we won't know if it did any good till our boys reach the top, if they can make it that far."

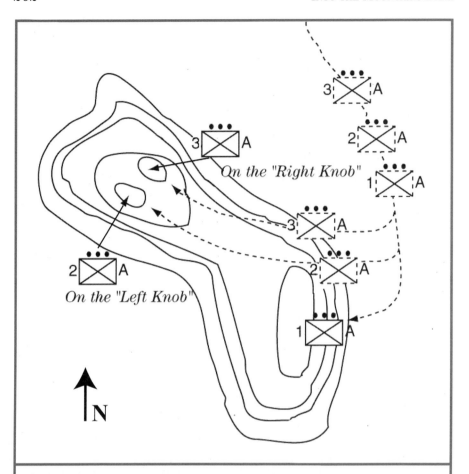

On the "Right Knob"

On the "Left Knob"

N

ATTACK OF COMPANY A, 399TH INFANTRY
ON HILL MASS 462.8
16 NOVEMBER 1944

Examples: 1st Platoon, Co. A, 399th Inf. Regt., enroute to objective

2 2nd Platoon, Co. A, 399th Inf. Regt., final locations
on their objective

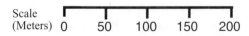

About an hour after we saw the line of skirmishers disappear up the slope of Hill 462.8, we heard what sounded like a lot of crackling popcorn, punctuated by an occasional little "thump." That must be small arms fire and the explosion of hand grenades we were hearing. As we listened, the volume of noise increased and the firing became so heavy and intense that it began to sound like a convention of insane carpenters all hammering at once.

"That's probably our boys on top now," George Lorenze said. "It sounds like a real donnybrook."

Our conversation was interrupted by the sounds of shells crashing in the woods off to the left, unleashing mysterious echoes in a distant glen.

"I got a letter from my aunt," George Lorenze said when the shelling tapered off. "She said she really envies me my unique opportunity to experience French culture first hand. Honest to God, that's what she said."

Colonel Zehner and the tank commander, accompanied by Real Parenteau, crossed the swamp to examine a little road on the other side. The road wound its way up Hill 462.8 in a series of sharp switchbacks, and they were studying the feasibility of sending the tanks up there. The biggest problem seemed to be how to get across or around the swamp to reach the road.

When they returned, Colonel Zehner was told that a German prisoner had been taken on the lower slope of Hill 462.8. Colonel Zehner interrogated him with the help of an interpreter, trying to learn the strength and unit numbers of the enemy forces facing us on the hill. Colonel Zehner told us the prisoner had been quite cooperative about identifying various German units active in the area, including two *Volks-Grenadier* Divisions (infantry divisions with only two regiments, but additional automatic and semiautomatic weapons), some mountain troops, and a regiment of *Panzer Grenadiers* (armored infantrymen, in U.S. Army parlance, or especially heavily-armed infantryman trained to fight from armored half-tracks or dismounted). Colonel Zehner speculated that possibly the reason for the prisoner's naming all those units was to impress us of the futility of trying to break through their Winter Line.[25]

After the interrogation, I was told to guard the prisoner, a clean-shaven Kraut *"Unteroffizier"* (Sergeant). He had very blue eyes and a face that was completely expressionless. He also looked better fed and clothed than any GI I had seen in the last two weeks, no matter what the training films would have us believe. The Krauts wore dark coal scuttle helmets, but they

[25]In fact, we later learned that our enemy all came from the same *Volks-Grenadier Division*, the *708th*, which had one battalion attached from another, the *361st*.

also had ski caps of the type this NCO was wearing. I could feel all sorts of emotions boiling inside. I wanted to give him a piece of my mind, but didn't know more than three words of his language. I certainly couldn't get away with shooting him, with Colonel Zehner within earshot, and I wouldn't have had the stomach for that sort of thing anyway under the circumstances. So I limited myself to feeling very angry at the fact that he looked so well-dressed and well-fed, was on the wrong side in this war, and was now completely out of any danger.[26]

Real Parenteau told us he was awaiting Colonel Zehner's decision on whether our squad would go up the hill to help our company or remain to protect the tanks. Colonel Zehner and the tank commander were still conferring about what the tanks' next mission would be. Sergeant Parenteau asked me to make some Nescafé for the wounded men in the marshy area who were still waiting to be evacuated. I collected six canteens and filled them from the stream in the swamp. After adding halizone tablets, I heated the Nescafé on Parenteau's Turner stove and distributed it among the 2d Platoon's WIAs. I was beginning to feel a little 4-F at not being up with our company in today's tough fight for Hill 462.8.

Of the six wounded men, only Pfc. John W. "Doc" Savage from Tucson, Arizona, wasn't allowed to drink anything, for he had a serious stomach wound from stepping on a "Bouncing Betty" anti-personnel mine. During the past five days, Doc Savage had made major contributions to the company's advance by calling (in fluent German) upon enemy soldiers in their dugouts and hiding places to surrender. But his linguistic talents weren't doing him any good today, due to plain rotten luck in tripping the well-concealed wire of that Bouncing Betty. Doc Savage's face was purple and I was afraid he might not be going to make it. Ultimately, he did not.

Pfc. Arlen Frost from La Crosse, Wisconsin, was another ASTP veteran, who wore glasses and had the intelligent face of a scientist. Frost had spent an idyllic final furlough with his fiancée who worked in Washington, DC. Then in our final "physical" at Camp Kilmer a week before we sailed, the doc said to Frost, "You got it, boy."

"Like hell I have," Arlen Frost replied. "The only contact I've had was with my fiancée, who was certainly a virgin before we got engaged."

The doc said, "I can't help it but facts are facts and clap is clap. And you got it boy." The gonorrhea was quickly cured, but the psychological wound

---

[26]Interestingly, we later found out that the *708th Volks-Grenadier Division* had been formed only two months before from the remnants of the *708th Infantry Division*, and consisted largely of replacements from the Air Force and Navy. . . just as the 100th consisted of many replacements from ASTP and service support units, although we had had much more time together than these Germans had.

remained. Now today, Arlen Frost had a new wound, a bullet in the thigh from a sniper's rifle as he tried to help Pfc. Peter Siems.

Pfc. Peter Siems' dad had been a horse doctor in the smuggler-fighting U.S. Cavalry force along the Mexican border early in the century. On one occasion, the Mexican smugglers kidnapped him and forced him to treat their horses as well. Later, he attended West Point for two years and when war broke out in 1914, he enlisted in the Army. He shipped out to France with the first machine gun company to go over.

Pete Siems' father had always urged him to "Try, Try, Try!" On 16 November 1944, his son got his chance to see what he could do. He was part of the 2d Platoon's skirmish line that crossed the marshy area to reach the Line of Departure at the foot of Hill 462.8. Pete Siems, laden down with a BAR and a few bazooka rounds in addition to other standard equipment, was slightly out ahead of the skirmish line firing his automatic rifle when a German rifleman put a bullet into his shin, straight through his shoepac. When Siems continued to advance and fire his BAR at the German positions, the German sharpshooter put a second bullet in his other leg, at about the same level. Because his boots were tightly laced, the blood circulation was cut off and he was able to continue advancing despite serious wounds in both legs. He was the first man to reach the LD at the foot of the hill and managed to climb fifteen or twenty yards up the slope before his disabled legs finally gave way under him.

Arlen Frost rushed forward to help Peter Siems. Lifting him onto one shoulder, he dragged him back down the slope to the marshy area. Just before they reached the safety of the reeds, a German bullet hit Arlen Frost in the thigh and both men went down. Fortunately the sniper could no longer see them in the swamp. Acting Platoon Leader Walter Bull asked what had happened. Peter Siems replied, "I just couldn't go any more. I'm very sorry about that."

All the wounded men seemed to be suffering from shock. Those who were allowed to take in liquids smiled in appreciation at my home-brewed Nescafé. Finally we saw medics coming from the rear beyond the little stream from which the Nescafé water had come.

A dozen or more litter-bearers from the battalion aid station started across the stream and through the mud to evacuate the wounded on stretchers. Just then some distant German artillery began their death whistle and the litter-bearers dropped everything, turned tail, rushed back through the mud and across the stream and disappeared into the woods from which they had come. As the shells weren't landing in our immediate vicinity, we saw no danger whatever and watched them flee with undiluted disgust. An hour later they summoned up enough nerve to come crawling back and evacuate our boys. An hour could make a lot of difference in battle and I thought again of poor Doc Savage's purpling face and wondered how long he could last.

It was now mid-afternoon and early returns were coming in from the insane cacophony of small arms and grenade explosions we had heard in late morning from Hill 462.8. Like a thunderstorm in the mountains, a certain amount of time had to pass before the first visible effects reached us on the low ground. First came a few walking wounded down the slope, followed a short time later by runners seeking small arms ammunition and reinforcements for the troops on top.

"Do you want us to go up, sir?" Sergeant Parenteau asked Colonel Zehner. Parenteau seemed to be suffering from a guilty conscience like my own at our relative inactivity while our buddies were going through the ringer up on 462.8.

"No, not now," Colonel Zehner replied. "I think we'll take the tanks across that clearing on the right, where they can get a bead on some German troops that have been infiltrating up from that side to Hill 462.8."

While waiting for further assignments, we chatted with some of the messengers and wounded men from Hill 462.8. In stuttering and stammering bits and pieces, they told us about the day's fighting up on top.

Our company had gone up Hill 462.8 first, crossing the LD beyond the swamp after losing Doc Savage, Arlen Frost, Pete Siems, and four others before the main climb began. German resistance was encountered along the lower slopes, where the *Unteroffizier* whom I had been guarding had held out with a platoon-strength force until he saw they would be overrun and raised the white flag at the last moment. From there on up, the main obstacle was sheer steepness, which compelled the men to climb from tree to tree and to rest occasionally against the uphill side of a particularly solid tree. Finally, the steep slope ended and evolved into a gentler grade leading up to the right. Lieutenant Mueller's platoon was the first to reach the top of 462.8, which was free of enemy.

Captain Young ordered Lieutenant Mueller's platoon to dig in on the cone-shaped summit while the other platoons passed through to a saddle some fifty to sixty feet lower than Hill 462.8. The 2d and 3d Platoons descended into the saddle where they took up defensive positions. Beyond them to the northeast, a wooded draw sank into the forest before the ground rose again toward a summit numbered 468 on Captain Young's map. That would be Baker Company's objective later in the day. Across the same draw to the southeast rose an even more formidable projection, Hill 539.

Sergeant Steinman arrived with two heavy machine-gun crews. He discussed with Captain Young the question of where to set up the guns.

Steinman said that in his opinion, their biggest danger lay not in an attack from their front or south, but from their rear or north, from which they had come.

"How do you figure that?" Captain Young asked.

"Because their Winter Line positions run from the north side of the hill around to the west facing Raon l'Etape," Steinman replied. "They were not heavily defending the steep slope at the extreme north side of the hill where we came up because they didn't think we could do it. But if we had tried going up a bit around to the west where it's slightly less steep, we probably would have run into a hornet's nest."

To demonstrate his point, Sergeant Steinman disappeared down the south slope of the draw where the ground dropped off steeply. Ten or fifteen minutes later he returned and told Captain Young there were no Germans down there. "The big threat is from the side we came up," he repeated in a slight Swiss accent.

"Okay," Captain Young said. He then proposed setting up Steinman's guns to cover the saddle's north side in a classic crossfire pattern. The fires of the two guns would intersect in the middle of the saddle about one hundred yards out front of the MLR (main line of resistance).

"Very good," Sergeant Steinman agreed, recognizing that Captain Young knew his stuff when it came to machine guns, on which he had given instruction at Camp Croft before joining the 100th.

As the two men stood talking, Captain Young's attention was distracted by a slight movement in some bushes twenty or thirty feet away, where Sergeant Steinman expected the enemy to come from. Captain Young continued talking without raising his voice. "I'll show you what we do to those fellows," he told Steinman, and suddenly emptied half a magazine into the bushes with his carbine. Something fell over in the brush. Two men from the Company Headquarters Section rushed into the brush and found a seriously wounded German soldier who had been hit in the chest by Captain Young's rapid reflexes and accurate fire.

Just as the machine-gun crews were beginning to dig in, enemy automatic weapons fire was heard coming up the draw from the north side of the hill and also somewhere below the left knob to the left of the saddle. This was exactly what Sergeant Steinman had predicted. Captain Young warned Sergeant Bull on the left to brace his 2d Platoon for a counterattack and, at the same time, told Lieutenant Ballie to work his 3d Platoon across from the right side of the draw to tie in with Sergeant Bull's platoon on the right side of the left knob.

Lieutenant Mueller's 1st Platoon continued to occupy the commanding ground of up to the right of the draw. Lieutenant Ballie's men drew several bursts of machine-gun fire as they scampered across the draw to their new positions. Captain Young was helping Lieutenant Ballie move the men across the exposed draw.

Just then, loud, unnerving bursts of German submachine-gun fire signaled the start of an attack against the left knob. Captain Young remained with Lieutenant Ballie as Ballie's platoon opened fire against the attackers.

A tremendous conflagration of small arms and machine-gun fire from both sides crackled along the slopes of the hill just below the knob, punctuated by grenades, bazookas, *Panzerfausts*, and the sounds of weapons which Captain Young did not even recognize. To the right of the draw, the 1st Platoon had not yet been challenged atop the right knob.

Suddenly, Captain Young saw an unbelievable sight. Most of the 2d Platoon had broken and men were running back down off the left knob. If the Germans came through the hole being created by the retreat of Sergeant Bull's men, they would cut off the 3d Platoon from the rear and overrun the Company CP.

Captain Young sprang to his feet and ran to head off the first three or four fleeing men.

"Hey you guys!" Captain Young screamed. "Cut out that running and follow me." He raised one enormous arm and began running back up the left hand knob. Fifteen or twenty more men paused in their flight, saw the shouting Captain Young running forward toward the enemy, and reversed their direction. Platoon Sergeant Chris Christensen and a few others had remained, pleading vainly for the others not to run. Within a matter of minutes, Captain Young had restored the platoon's line.

A few seconds later, a heavy German counterattack struck the very seam where the 2d and 3d Platoon positions joined. From the 3d Platoon, Squad Leaders Clarence "Pop" Sutton and John Hambric, the Arkansas Indian, led a flying squad toward the endangered sector, joined by Private Roy Lee, who was wielding a BAR. The 2d Platoon did not run this time, but dug in their heels and exchanged fire with the German attackers at close range. A wild melee followed of men firing at one another at ranges as close as fifteen or twenty feet. One of the 2d Platoon's Squad Leaders, Lucien Zarlenga, was killed by submachine-gun fire and his two BAR men, Joseph Hoffman and Tex Ludlow (who was carrying Peter Siems' old weapon), were killed by rifle bullets. In the 3d Platoon, Pop Sutton continued firing his M-1 from a prone position until he was killed by three attackers firing from less than twenty feet. The 3d Platoon Sergeant, Ralph Harrington, fired a bazooka at the attackers, but hit Sergeant John Hambric by mistake. When the two platoons were forced to pull back sixty or seventy feet to escape complete annihilation, Sergeant Hambric lay out in no man's land where he was presumed dead.

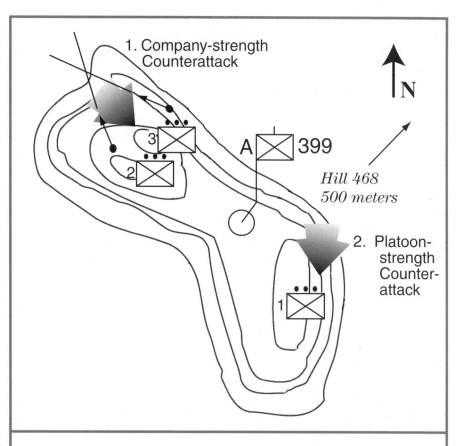

1. Company-strength Counterattack

A ☒ 399

*Hill 468
500 meters*

2. Platoon-strength Counter-attack

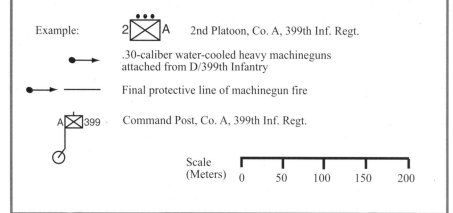

GERMAN COUNTERATTACKS ON HILL MASS 462.8, 16 NOVEMBER 1944

Example: 2 ☒ A   2nd Platoon, Co. A, 399th Inf. Regt.

●→   .30-caliber water-cooled heavy machineguns attached from D/399th Infantry

●→ ——   Final protective line of machinegun fire

A ☒ 399   Command Post, Co. A, 399th Inf. Regt.

Scale (Meters)   0   50   100   150   200

The leftmost of Sergeant Steinman's two machine guns covering the draw was being fired by Sergeant Dick Atkinson and Frank Fischl. Because of the nature of the slope before them, they were unable to see the German attackers in the dead space below until they appeared over the slope's natural crest. To alleviate this problem, Sergeant Atkinson lifted the .30 caliber water-cooled machine gun off its tripod and, cradling the forty-one-pound monster in his arms, fired at the advancing enemy troops from the hip. This offered infinitely better target identification possibilities than firing from the usual sitting position. Atkinson, an experienced weapons instructor, noted that the U.S. Army's machine guns and automatic weapons could not compare with the firepower of the German machine guns and burp guns. He noted several of the enemy in dark colored over-coats who lingered in the German lines, seemingly inspecting their own positions and asking questions or giving advice.[27] Atkinson shook his head at the sight of the piled up American and German dead around the junction of the 2d and 3d Platoons' sectors. He thought there must be between forty and fifty bodies heaped around like a rough log road almost solid enough to drive on. The German dead seemed slightly more numerous than the American.

Lieutenant David Ballie got into an argument with a machine gunner from the Weapons Platoon who said his gun wouldn't fire. Lieutenant Ballie, skeptical at the explanation, drew back his right shoulder and delivered a smashing right fist to the gunner's cheek before stalking off in disgust. Within five minutes, the gunner had the gun operating again. A medic put a bandage on his cheek and someone told him in jest that he should apply for the Purple Heart.

Captain Young told his radio man to give him the handset so that he could try to reach Colonel Zehner and report the tenuous situation. As the man complied, a blast of enemy fire severed his hand and the handset went flying off in splinters. Private George Shapiro, a target of good-natured fun because of his enormous ears, was wounded in both ears during the confused fighting. Later someone told Shapiro the Germans had done him a favor by tailoring his ears to a more attractive size.

The German counterattack finally ended and the enemy troops seemed to evaporate into the cold mountain air down the slope whence they had come. Medics scrambled out to tend the wounded left behind when the 2d and 3d Platoons had been forced to make their limited withdrawals. One

---

[27]Given that the *708th Volks-Grenadier Division* was in its first combat since being reconstituted and refitted, this may well have been commanders and staff from a higher echelon present to determine the situation in a hard-pressed sector.

of the 2d Platoon's wounded men had been shot in the head as he lay there by the withdrawing Germans in a gesture of vindictiveness. The body of Sergeant John Hambric, who had been hit by Sergeant Harrington's misdirected bazooka, was gone. Presumably he had been taken away by the Germans when they withdrew.

Lieutenant Mueller's platoon had watched the violent fighting as spectators from the commanding height of the right knob. They were astonished at all the rushing back and forth, particularly when the 2d Platoon broke and fled before being reassembled by Captain Young and rushed back up to the line. Sergeant Chuck Stanley instructed the platoon to move their positions a few yards farther down the slope to be able to identify any future German counterattack at the earliest possible moment. From where Sergeant Stanley had observed the counterattack, it appeared that if the 2d and 3d Platoons had taken up positions farther down the slope, they would have seen the counterattacking Germans in time to avoid combat at such pointblank range.

Approximately half an hour after the German assault ended, Pfc. Lennie Hershberg saw a column of perhaps twenty soldiers marching up the backslope the way his platoon had come up to the top of Hill 462.8.

"Hey Chuck—" Hershberg called to Sergeant Stanley. "Who are those guys coming up behind us?"

"Charlie Company, I would guess," Sergeant Stanley replied.

"Wearing gray overcoats?" Hershberg asked. This identification of the marching column of Germans was the prelude to the second enemy counterattack, whose objective this time was to drive the 1st Platoon off the hill southeast of the CP. If successful, this would make Captain Young's position in the saddle and the left knob untenable and would force the Americans off Hill 462.8.

Lennie Hershberg was astonished at the way the Germans approached the attack zone in a formal marching formation. But the enemy troops quickly dispersed and demonstrated that they knew more than close order drill. The 1st Platoon defenders had a field of fire of approximately seventy-five yards from the point where the attackers had to expose themselves above the natural defilade of the slope. This was approximately double the field of fire the other two platoons had had in their nearly calamitous encounter with the first counterattacking force.

With our squad absent on our tank-guarding mission, Lieutenant Mueller had only the 1st and 2d Squads at his disposal. The 1st Squad, which had already lost its two non-coms (Amoroso and Daledovich) was being led by Pfc. Lennie Hershberg and Private John Jeske. The 2d Squad was as being led by Sergeant Gil Moniz and "Rye" Rybiski.

The attackers' tactics were to pin down the defenders with automatic weapon and rifle fire while others crept forward to hurl their fragmentation and concussion grenades. Despite the seriousness of the situation, Hershberg could not help noting the resemblance of the exercise to a mechanical game played by children. A *Grenadier* popped up sixty feet away, hurled his grenade, and dived back to the ground. A second later, Gil Moniz leapt to his feet, fired three or four shots from his rifle, and dove for cover. His scout Hugh Price then fired a full clip at the enemy and Gil Moniz shouted "Thanks!"

Since Able Company was now virtually cut off from the rear, there was no way Sergeant Sam D'Arpino could resupply the men with ammunition. He therefore did not feel obliged to stay in his usual position at the rear of the platoon and moved up among the foremost elements when the German attack began. A German *Grenadier* worked his way to within thirty-five or forty feet of D'Arpino's position and looped a potato masher grenade up the slope, but for some reason, the concussion and shrapnel seemed to go straight *up*, without harming the intended target. Seconds later, a second grenade came hurtling through the air to bounce off D'Arpino's prone body and come to rest within a foot of his head. As he struggled mentally for some appropriate final short prayer, he noted the passage of seconds. Nothing happened; the grenade had been a dud. When a third grenade landed three or four feet away, D'Arpino picked it up and threw it back. He then threw his own three hand grenades down the slope in rapid succession and pulled his grenade launcher and rifle grenades out of his ammo bag. Attaching the launcher and grenade to his rifle, he reached for one of the special .30-caliber blank cartridges required to make the grenade launcher function. To his horror, he realized he had forgotten to replenish his supply. Taking one of the antitank grenades in his hand, he hurled it in desperation as far as he could, but these grenades were not designed to explode if tossed manually and thus, as expected, there was no explosion. Undaunted, he took a second rifle grenade from his ammo bag and hurled it after the first. To his astonishment, it exploded in the area where the *Grenadier* had been, apparently because it squarely struck a boulder being used as cover by the attackers.

Lennie Hershberg had turned his BAR over to Bob Hogberg and now carried a rifle and a grease gun. During the fight, he leapt to his feet several times, remaining upright just long enough to fire bursts of twenty rounds from the M-3 submachine gun.

The Fraley twins, Lester and Chester, installed themselves behind two oak trees, their rifle sights converging on a point some seventy-five yards away where there was a narrow avenue or firebreak ten or fifteen feet wide in the forest. Whenever enemy soldiers crossed that open space, the twins opened up and reported several probable hits.

Finally, the counterattack was over, and the enemy withdrew out of sight down the slope. Reports came to Captain Young that the enemy was trying to outflank his company's positions where the land rose through dark stands of trees to the summit of Hill 468. Displacing the 2d and 3d Platoons as well as the Weapons Platoon's machine guns, he directed the defense against three more counterattacks before nightfall ended the day's fighting. For the first time in combat, Captain Young ordered his men to fix bayonets. Unable to be resupplied, his platoons were nearly out of ammunition.

Sergeant Walter Bull, acting on his own initiative, had dispatched himself back to the base of the hill in search of reinforcements for his seriously depleted platoon. All he could find were George Lorenze and another communications section man whom he brought back up with him.

"I guess I'm screwed," George Lorenze told me with that cynical smile of his. "I always said this company couldn't survive without me." He shouldered his carbine and strode off after Sergeant Bull. When they reached the top, Captain Young was setting up defenses for the night. He told Sergeant Bull to move his platoon up on the right of Sergeant Steinman's machine-gun emplacements. Sergeant Bull, apparently feeling the position was too exposed, refused the order. We never heard of anything further from this encounter, and Sergeant Steinman's machine gunners didn't get the protection they needed either. Maybe Steinman and Bull settled things between themselves. Sergeant Stanley told Lennie Hershberg to accompany him in going out after one of the wounded.

"Don't bring your weapon," Stanley told him. "You'll need two arms to carry him."

After they had gone seventy or eighty yards, Sergeant Stanley noticed a suspicious movement behind a wood pile.

"Get him, Hersh!" he called.

"With what?" Hersh replied. "You told me to leave my weapon."

Chuck Stanley stalked whoever was hiding behind the wood pile. A German soldier emerged with his hands raised.

Of the two other men wounded in the attack, one was Ray Sholes who, since Eddie Cook's death, had been Lieutenant Mueller's runner and radio man. He also shared the lieutenant's foxhole as Cook had. When Sholes returned to the foxhole, Lieutenant Mueller refused to let him in.

"What's wrong, Lieutenant?" Sholes asked. "I'm bandaged up all right, but have to stay overnight before I go down to Battalion Aid."

"I can't direct the platoon with a wounded man in my foxhole," Lieutenant Mueller replied. "Find another place."

When Colonel Zehner learned of the infiltration of German troops up toward Able Company's left flank near Hill 462.8, he sent Baker and Charlie Companies up the road with the hairpin turns in hopes of linking up with the Able Company defenders. He also decided to have his three tanks deliver supporting fire to the right of the area that Baker and Charlie Companies were ascending. To launch the tank attack, it was necessary for the tanks to cross an open area for two or three hundred yards.

The tank platoon leader refused to move. "It's too exposed out in the open there," he told Colonel Zehner.

"What about these infantrymen who will go with you?" Colonel Zehner said. "Don't you think they're taking a risk, too?"

"I'm responsible for these tanks," the lieutenant said. "That's all I know."

Colonel Zehner withdrew his pistol from its holster. "If you refuse this very reasonable order, I'll shoot you."

The lieutenant made no reply, but made no move to comply with the order either. I wondered why Colonel Zehner had threatened violence rather than some lesser punishment such as the disgrace of a court-martial. Perhaps the reason was that in the confusion of war, the chances of the lieutenant getting off would be quite good. In any event, what Colonel Zehner wanted and needed was not punishment later but results now.

"That's the last time I'll ever use tanks," Colonel Zehner said bitterly, holstering his pistol. The tank lieutenant said nothing, but it was evident to everyone that he had won the test of wills.

Colonel Zehner then decided that our squad would go back with the tanks to the rear for the night, to be available tomorrow if needed. The three tanks turned around, we clambered aboard, and the show was finally on the road after many hours at the base of Hill 462.8.

I never felt lower than during that ride back. The doughfeet perform without a murmur when kept busy, but given a spare minute to think of the things that they are witnessing, they suffer shock. I closed my eyes as I leaned my neck against the back of the turret, hoping that when I opened them again the war and the Vosges would be gone like a bad dream. But nothing like this happened, and I realized I would simply have to stop my wishful thinking and grow up.

We traveled back a mile or so to the road junction where we had found Ammo the day before near the spot where Eddie Cook had died. I wondered how the Army could be so cruel as to force our squad to spend the night in this haunted spot.

We had high hopes of food and increasing appetites for supper. But there was no sign of anything to eat, so we crawled under the tank again and turned in. The entire squad slept in comparative luxury, with one wet shelter-half under us and another on top. Nine Joes crowded under the tank that night, more than there really was room for. Former ASTPer Private Thomas Case rolled and turned and delivered a night-long stream of comments as the five guys beside him pressed him a bit too enthusiastically (for Case's taste certainly) into the bogey wheels. Apart from Case's griping, the night passed uneventfully.

In the morning, 17 November, a cold sun appeared in the trees, a most heartening weather improvement after all the Vosges fog we had seen.

The tank lieutenant built a good fire. There were about twenty of us around it, doggies and tankers, stamping our feet, clapping our wool mittens together and making cheerful remarks about Colonel Zehner's unquenchable admiration for the tank lieutenant. A captain came over from battalion headquarters and ordered the fire to be put out because it would draw artillery.

"Captain," the tank lieutenant said, "We were up there and it's awful far from here."

"I said put it out unless you want a court martial." Everyone seemed to be threatening strong measures against the lieutenant these days. Why were these rear-echelon types so nervous and timorous anyway? This "put out the fire" routine was the same one Captain Beaver had given us in those St. Benoît woods where the land mines put Lieutenant Paul Loes out of action.

We took a rapid inventory of our squad's K rations and found out that, as usual, there was about enough to feed a nest of healthy canaries. After pooling the rations, heating them on Parenteau's stove and dispatching them, we went out on the main road to follow the sunshine as it crept through the tree branches. Up above, the Army Air Forces, which had been rained out for so long, finally put it an appearance. We stood in the middle of the road waving and yelling at the planes and telling them to "give 'em hell!" Suddenly two of the circling craft peeled off and let go a strafing burst to our rear, back near Baccarat somewhere.

"Why are they strafing behind our lines?" someone asked incredulously.

"Because those are German planes!" someone replied. "They're trying to knock out our Baccarat bridge and cut us off on this side of the river."

After that we quit waving and stopped standing in the middle of the road. One of the things that kept the infantry going in the rain, mud, and snow was the knowledge that when good weather finally came, the Army Air Forces with their great air superiority would be out searching for Krauts and parting their hair down the middle when they found some. And now, our first good day, we looked up expectantly and what did we find? The *Luftwaffe*.

Doc Emmons found several copies of an Army newspaper somewhere and distributed them to anyone whose hands were not too cold to turn the pages. The newspaper was called *The Lightning News*. We were familiar with the Army daily *Stars and Stripes*, but deliveries were slow and we had seen only one issue since entering combat. This *Lightning News* appeared to be some sort of Seventh Army or VI Corps paper, although there was no specific identification of its source.

"Hey, these guys are really on the ball!" Scotty Kyle said. "Listen to this editorial about the election."

It's a strange coincidence that the two Democratic governments, Wilson's and F. D. Roosevelt's, both promised to keep America out of war; both got her into war, and both were and still are strongly tainted with Jewish influence."

I knew that Scotty Kyle had a strong anti-FDR bias, but I was a bit surprised by the article's anti-Semitic slur. The newspaper wrote rather accurately about our lousy weather,

The winter lasts five months in the Vosges, from November 1st to April 1st. The European winter proves every day more severe than we expected it to be. The sufferings our men are put to are beyond imagination. It often happens that they can't change their wet clothes for several days. Then again they can't get any rest due to the fierce fighting of the Germans, and on top of all this, the cold against which they are not sufficiently protected gives them plenty of trouble. These conditions have considerably slowed down our advance and have made us suffer severe reverses.

Do people at home realize how cruel and pitiless war is, and what it means to fight not only against the stubborn resistance of the Germans but also against the nastiness of a climate which we were not prepared for?

In the same vein, *Lightning News* quoted *Stars and Stripes* as follows,

These Joes have a job. It's a life or death job and they're doing it twenty-four hours a day, seven days a week, every week of the month.

The newspaper warned of the housing accommodations in the Vosges, where simple farmhouses were limited to a wood-burning stove in one room as the sole source of heating. There were articles about the Allies' failed attempt to put an airborne force across the Rhine at Arnhem in September and the U.S. Fifth Army's slow progress in the winter fighting in northern Italy.

Another article described the case of an infantry private who decided to walk out on the Army because he felt he wasn't getting a square deal. The private took advantage of a "Safe Conduct Pass" (of which *Lightning News* reprinted the text) stating that he would be accorded safe passage through the German lines and would be luxuriously installed and generously fed in a Prisoner of War facility operated in full accordance with the Geneva Conventions on the Rules of Land Warfare.

Although I had had occasional daydreams about how nice it would be to find myself in a German POW cage with three meals a day and no more danger of death or maiming, I was nevertheless startled to see an Army newspaper practically advocating that we follow this course if we felt we weren't getting a square deal.

"Hey Scotty," I said to Kyle. "Did you read about this Safe Conduct Pass?"

"I'm just coming to it," Scotty Kyle replied. His face took on an incredulous smile as he read the text of the Safe Conduct Pass.

The stories I had been reading in the newspaper (Such as Arnhem and Italy) seemed factual enough, but why was all the news so essentially negative, even if technically accurate? And how had supplies of the paper found their way to this remote road junction in the middle of what until two days ago had been the Germans' impregnable Winter Line?

"Hey Doc," I said to Doc Emmons. "Where did you find this newspaper?"

"Oh I got it from a ditch right there beside the main road," Doc Emmons replied. "There musta been five hundred copies."

By now everyone in the squad was buried in *Lightning News*. Many got no further than page one where a nude woman raised a glass to some wealthy civilian back home and said "Cheerio! This hits the spot!"

Everyone smiled or chuckled at something they were reading. Pop Swartz said, "Let's get inside one of those 'simple farmhouses with a wood-burning stove' right quick like and heat up a nice stew of C and K rations."

Scotty Kyle roared with laughter as he finished reading the Safe Conduct Pass. He then read it aloud to the entire group.

"Do you know who wrote this damn rag?" Scotty Kyle snorted. "It was old 'GI Joe' Goebbels himself !"

The Germans had evidently expected to spend the five-month long Vosges winter right here along the Neufmaisons-Raon l'Etape highway in relatively comfortable bunkers and with cleared lanes of fire overlooking the barbed wire of their Winter Line. The editors of *Lightning News* certainly knew how to explain the problems the Allies were having here in the Vosges, but they forgot to mention that the *Wehrmacht* was having all the same troubles, only more so. Their basic premise—that they would hold us at bay for five months at their Vosges Winter Line—had been demolished two days ago by our breakthrough and yesterday's broadening of the penetration at Hill 462.8. The Germans' unexpected withdrawal from the Winter Line position had had the ironic side effect of delivering *Lightning News* to its American readers simply by pulling back and letting it be over-run by the advancing Americans. As to the overall effects of *Lightning News* on our morale, there's nothing an American soldier likes better than a little personal attention. The headquarters staff of U.S. Seventh Army had other pressing priorities at the moment, such as breaking through the Vosges Mountains. These were perhaps considered more urgent than com-miserating with the doughboys about the woes of their lives in combat.

So, it took Dr. Goebbels' crew to compose a little "war literature" to pep us up and remind us that somebody knew and appreciated what we were going through. But if Dr. Goebbels had naively assumed the pen to be mightier than the sword, he hadn't counted on the high-quality steel being welded by General Burress, Colonel Tychsen, and their subordinates in the 100th Infantry Division. Just as we finished stuffing copies of *Lightning News* under our shirts for mailing home as souvenirs, the tank crew received the latest *Stars and Stripes* which they shared with us. It was older than the 12 November issue of *Lightning News*.

A short time later, the tankers received word that they were being reat-tached to another unit in another zone. "So long, fellas," the lieutenant told us. "Please take your junk off our vehicles and we'll be shoving off." And so they backed their tanks off the side road onto the highway and were on their way.

Sergeant Parenteau got into communication with our company through battalion headquarters and was told that a jeep would be sent to bring us to Hill 462.8 where the company was still holding firm. While waiting for the promised transportation, we spread our raincoats on the ground and gave our rifles a thorough drying and cleaning.

A column of fresh troops from the 398th Infantry Regiment came marching up the highway from the direction of Baccarat and Neufmaisons. It was evident that the 398th had crossed the Meurthe at Baccarat to help her two sister regiments exploit the Winter Line penetration created two days before. Meanwhile, the Germans sat comfortably in their deep fortifi-cations around Raon l'Etape, waiting for the Americans to try to force the river crossing . . . which the commanders of the Seventh Army had no intention of doing.

The streets and squares of Raon l'Etape near or leading down to the river were choked with German antitank obstacles, barbed wire, and all the other paraphernalia used to rebuff waterborne invasions, whether from the sea or simply from a local river of modest proportions such as the Meurthe. Instead of falling into the steel trap, the 398th had purposely conducted a noisy diversion west of the river while the 397th and 399th sneaked across through the pre-existing bridgehead at Baccarat to the north. Now the 398th was pouring through the same Baccarat gate, leaving the Germans at Raon l'Etape to discover at leisure the magnitude of the deception that had been worked upon them. This morning's *Luftwaffe* strafing of the bridge at Baccarat was a good indication of how upset the German high command must have been at finally realizing that while they had slept at Raon l'Etape, the Americans had broken through their Winter Line's right flank and were now entrenched, three regiments strong, *above* and *behind* Raon l'Etape.

"Where are you going?" we asked the 398th men.

"To the front," was the reply.

They were a beautiful sight to behold as they moved along smoothly in "route step" at the prescribed five-yard interval in columns on either side of the road. They wore clean green helmets and spotless field jackets and carried enormous horseshoe roll packs. Their rifle muzzles wore little glove-like covers to keep moisture out. Printed on each muzzle cover were the letters "U.S." in black. The alignment of their bayonets, canteens, and shovels would have passed any Zehner-Lentz type inspection back in the States. Ammo bags were suspended from some of their field packs, containing in some cases (I suspected) personal effects rather than extra ammunition or pyrotechnics. In the case of smaller men, the ammo bags tended to bump against their butts every few steps. They seemed to be gift-wrapped in the same large cellophane bags in which we had been garbed until that morning outside St. Remy, when we had absorbed our first enemy mortar barrage targeted directly at us, the Untouchable Tourists.

I had a lot of friends in the other regiments, so I searched the faces in the passing columns. Where was Don Squires from Ohio U., and Fox Company, 398th? Where was Jack Ellis, from Brookline, Massachusetts, and Mike Company, 398th? How about Lester Bixby from our own Class of 1943 at Newton High and Commonwealth Avenue, Newton Center, Massachusetts, and Item Company, 397th? Would I see Robert Gifford from my Harvard Class of 1947 and King Company, 398th? I could not find anyone I knew. I hoped my friends were all right.

"What're you, the 325th Engineers?" Scotty Kyle called mischievously.

"Infantry," the man replied with pride.

"If you're infantry, why are you carrying all that goddam junk?" Scotty Kyle asked. "I thought you were going to build a bridge over the Rhine."

"Aw dry up!" one of the marchers told Kyle.

These 398th troops looked as though they had not yet seen action. This struck me as ironic since we were now into our third week in the line and had already lost a tremendous number of men. I wanted to *tell* these boys what lay in store for them up ahead. They would soon throw away all that fancy equipment except for a few essentials; what remained would quickly turn the color of mud. They were going to lose some of their best buddies, and live a lizard's life in wet, underground, foxhole accommodations. But how could I tell them these things? I realized I'd have difficulty putting into words the things I wanted them to know. But even if I jumped out into the road and got their attention, would they understand what I was trying to say or would they simply jeer and hoot? Was there really any way for them to learn about combat except by experiencing it personally? Perhaps it was better to let these guys have their peace for now and find out for themselves when the time came, which would probably be sooner than any of them realized. Why should I be responsible for making them shed their equipment and innocence any sooner than absolutely necessary?

The Able Company jeep arrived, navigated by Pfc. Gerard P. Rocheleau from Lowell, Massachusetts.

"Hey *Douche!*" he called to his pal Real Parenteau.

"Hey *Douche!*" Parenteau called back. Men of French ancestry in the outfit seemed able to get away with slightly eccentric behavior more easily than some of other ancestries (although our sons of Italy, Ireland, and Portugal sometimes displayed certain eccentricities of their own as well). Rocheleau's eccentricity was driving the jeep as though it were a bobsled, or maybe a rocket. In what felt like a minute and a half, he had delivered four of us to the foot of Hill 462.8, turned around in the mud to the sound of squealing wheels, and had gone back for the rest.

I walked over to the stream to fill my canteen. Instead of having to muck through the swamp as I had yesterday, I crossed it on a bridge of birch logs installed within the last twenty-four hours by the engineers. It made one think of a makeshift bridge on the American frontier. There were vehicles and ammunition points and the usual confusion and shouting. Doc Savage, Peter Siems, Arlen Frost, and the other wounded men were gone now and one never would have suspected a battle had begun here in the swamp at the foot of the hill.

I made a canteen cupful of K ration orangeade and passed it to Herbie Rice and a 398th soldier Rice was chatting with. The 398th man said his company had been through a lot. They had outposted a bridge one night and one of the boys had stepped on a Schu-mine and injured his leg. That was his company's only casualty so far.

"Yeah, that tough," Herbie Rice said. The 398th fellow didn't ask about our company's experiences and we didn't volunteer anything.

Gerard Rocheleau's rocket ship arrived carrying Real Parenteau and the remaining squad members. We set out on foot across the engineers' corduroy bridge. The climb up Hill 462.8 seemed to be nearly perpendicular in most places. We could climb no more than twenty or thirty yards at a time before needing to rest. Every ten yards or so was a tree (not evergreens for a change), and soon our ascent resolved itself into a struggle to grab the next higher tree. There we leaned against the uphill side of the trunk until sufficient breath returned to permit us to strike out for the next tree. To see a piece of the sky, we had to look practically straight up. It was almost inconceivable that an infantry battalion could have taken this hill by storm, when even climbing it without having to fight seemed nearly impossible. Finally the steepness tapered off and we found ourselves climbing a more negotiable slope which seemed to be leading us toward the summit. On this gentle slope, we encountered Technical Sergeant Ralph Harrington, Platoon Sergeant of Lieutenant Ballie's 3d Platoon. Sergeant Harrington seemed to be going down the way we had come up.

"What's new, Ralph?" Sergeant Parenteau asked. "How far is it to the CP?" Sergeant Harrington, who had gained notoriety (if not fame) in tripping up Sergeant Bull in that simulated hand-to-hand combat demonstration before Southern cotton bigwigs back at Bragg, and who had later fired twenty rounds from a grease gun through an old farmer's front door in St. Remy, didn't appear to be his usual swashbuckling self today. He stared at Parenteau with a glazed look.

"It was awful rough," Harrington said quietly. "I lost all three squad leaders. One of them, John Hambric, I hit by mistake with a bazooka round. We were then forced back and when we retook the ground Hambric was gone." He looked around the wood in a decidedly distracted fashion.

"Where you bound for?" Parenteau asked.

"I need treatment," Harrington replied. "I don't feel right." He resumed his descent down the hill. We soon reached the crest of Hill 462.8. Company C had relieved our platoon there the previous evening and told us the way to our new positions. Descending into the saddle below the hill, we ran into Sergeant Angelo "Babe" Colone of the 2d Platoon.

"Hi, youse guys," Babe Colone said. "Glad to see youse." Babe was from New York's Chelsea section.

"We just ran into Ralph Harrington," Real Parenteau said.

"Yeah, he told me he was taking two wounded guys and two POWs back to Battalion," Babe Colone said.

"He was alone when we passed him on the trail," Parenteau said.

"You ain't surprising me," Babe Colone said. "Did you hear how the Jerries shot one of our wounded guys in the head? I think it was an *SS* non-com who did it. Anyway, our guy is going to live."[28] Babe Colone pointed the way to Captain Young's CP which was located in a gully under a huge fallen tree trunk. The protection offered by the tree against artillery was probably problematic, but Captain Young apparently felt more secure there than completely out in the open. Also, a gully offered defilade protection from snipers.

"Sergeant Parenteau, I'm glad to see you back," Captain Young growled amiably, extending a long paw. He was wearing a wood-knit cap without helmet and had a red beard well underway. He almost could have been a caveman from about a million years back in time. He looked right at home under that huge fallen tree trunk.

"Thanks, sir," Parenteau said. "How was it?"

"A hell of a lot hotter than Guadalcanal, I'll bet!" Captain Young chuckled, referring to Parenteau's past.

We could hear distant noises from the high, dark forest of Hill 468 like someone tapping a tree gently with an ax. Then a long "*twayannnngggg*" sound arrived where we were and departed into the distance behind us all in about a second. We could also hear more immediate tappings of picks and shovels on rock as our company improved its position on the hill.

"Those are snipers up on 468." Captain Young said. "If they miss B Company, the bullets zing on down here, and if they miss us, they might catch C Company which is dug in where your platoon was yesterday."

"Where's our platoon now?" Parenteau asked.

"Up just past Bloody Knob where the 2d and 3d Platoons had heavy going yesterday," Captain Young replied. "The Jerries still want this hill," the captain added. "Just after dawn and before dusk, they shell hell out of us, and during regular working hours, they snipe."

Captain Young picked up his situation map. "Here, let me show you where you are. We're on sort of a wedge pointing south into the German lines from the direction of Neufmaisons to the north. From here to Neufmaisons, we have a corridor including the Neufmaisons-Raon l'Etape highway. That's our lifeline to the rear. We're surrounded on over three hundred degrees on my compass."

Sergeant Parenteau whistled.

"Colonel Zehner says the battalion will get a Presidential Unit Citation for this," Captain Young said. "Considering our company's front-line

---

[28]Many of us seemed to blame sinister events like this on the *SS*. While numerous members of the *SS* certainly proved themselves to be fully capable of such atrocities, we subsequently learned that there were no *SS* units anywhere near us at the time.

strength is down to sixty-five men including your squad, I think a medal like that might be an appropriate gesture to the men who took this hill."

"We ran into Ralph Harrington a few minutes ago," Real Parenteau said. "He was going downhill and didn't look too good."

"Harrington is finished," Captain Young said. "He was all right until he saw the Jerries were using live ammo and the targets moved. There's not a thing wrong with him except his lily liver. He's the worst disappointment of my military career. He was absolutely the finest stateside soldier I had, perfect in all departments."

"Who takes his job?" Parenteau asked.

"I think Lieutenant Ballie is going to propose Jake Sortor," Captain Young replied. "Say, did I tell you how I got shot by a sniper?"

"No, sir," Parenteau said.

"It was two days ago, after we moved on from where Sergeant Amoroso and that Cook lad got hit. We were moving and stopping in thick woods and it was all sort of fluid and I was trying to direct things. So it didn't take the Jerries long to figure out who was the company commander. Also, I hadn't yet plastered mud on my helmet insignia. I felt a burning pain and thought a sniper had got me in the back. But when the medic started looking for the bullet, he found it embedded in my tummy."

"You were lucky, sir," Sergeant Parenteau said.

"C Company on our left said they had a prisoner, so I hurried over," Captain Young continued. "The Kraut was only half my size but I was still hot under the collar from getting hit. I wanted him to finger the one who had shot me."

"*Wo ist Kamarad?*" I yelled. No answer, so I slammed a magazine in my pistol and told him I was going to "*schiessen.*"

"*Wo ist Kamarad?*" I asked him again, and he started singing his guts out about what units they had everywhere, including on this hill. Doc Savage was with me interpreting, and we sent the prisoner's information back to battalion."

Captain Young showed us the place where the sniper's bullet had penetrated his pistol ammo clip. I noticed that his combat jacket was thoroughly chewed up from shrapnel and bullets, apart from his "tummy injury."

"You remember all our super security measures?" Captain Young said. "How we kept our weapons away from the train windows when we went from Bragg to Kilmer? How at La Bourgonce and Woods Six we wouldn't even tell the 3d Division guys who we were? You remember our super-secret trip across the river at Baccarat to fool the Jerries and how we floated behind the 397th lines under wraps so the enemy wouldn't even suspect we were within a hundred miles? Well, some of our men who were captured yesterday and escaped back to our lines say the Germans have the names of every officer in the 100th Infantry Division! They even know my middle initial and my home town of Waterbury, Connecticut. They knew I had two Exec Officers, White and Landis, and they knew all the platoon leaders' names, starting with Mueller, Gullborg, and Ballie. Even I didn't know the home towns of some of my officers. Isn't that unbelievable?"

"Yes, sir," Parenteau said.

George Lorenze guided us to our platoon area where Sergeant Parenteau reported to Lieutenant Mueller, who also had the beginnings of a beard. Few words were exchanged, a situation that had existed since their confrontation at Delta Base near Marseilles when Parenteau had gotten pickled. The lieutenant indicated that our squad would dig in about fifty yards uphill from his foxhole. He left us to find the site ourselves since the *"Zinggginggg"* of the sniper bullets apparently gave him no incentive to leave the security of his underground refuge. We said hello to Chuck Stanley and Sam D'Arpino in a foxhole near the lieutenant's before moving up the slope to our new sector. Sam had already developed a dense black beard making him resemble a mad monk or a wild man from Borneo. They were as glad to see us as we were them. We also said hello to Sergeant Gil Moniz of the 2d Squad, who was now wearing his red and white Good Conduct Medal and his blue and silver Expert Infantryman Badge on his filthy field jacket. Either yesterday's battle had unhinged his reason or (as I suspected) he had the best sense of humor in the company.

Herbie Rice and I began digging our new foxhole. Two neighbors, Lennie Hershberg and John Jeske, came over to visit.

"Hey," Hersh said, "getting your squad back is like having a part of our body come back again."

Both Hersh and Jeske were toting M-3 grease guns at a jaunty angle over their right shoulders. Occasionally Jeske would tap open the ejection port cover of the submachine gun with one finger and then slam it shut with a metallic *"whack."* He was really feeling good. They told the story of the fight for Hill 462.8 with great relish, interrupting one another frequently to get the whole story out as though it were the blow-by-blow account of a football classic which our side had won after a thrilling uphill fight.

"The Krauts really hated to lose this hill," Lennie Hershberg said. "I understand it's one of the best natural defensive positions in the entire Vosges."

When Herbie Rice and I had nearly completed digging our foxhole, Real Parenteau came over and asked if he and Robert E. Jones could share our quarters with them. He and Jones had by error picked a rocky spot to dig in and after an hour had only managed to dig down about six inches. We agreed to house them and broadened the base of the foxhole so that three men could stretch out in it at night. The fourth man would be on guard on a rotating basis. We added a roof of logs, pine branches, leaves, dirt, more leaves, and various touches of camouflage. We carved out three steps from the narrow entrance down to the sleeping quarters and sculpted a seat beside the steps for the night guard. The seat was just far enough below ground to avoid exposing the night guard too much to artillery fire, while, at the same time, providing a good vantage point from which to spot any creeping and crawling Krauts out looking for trouble. We dug small shelves into the walls for candles and personal items, and draped two shelter halves over the narrow entrance to prevent the candlelight from showing.

On a dirt parapet above the guard step, we lined up our four rifles, twelve bandoliers of ammo, and a dozen hand grenades. I was first on guard duty and saw Lieutenant Mueller sneaking around from hole to hole. He came up and said we could expect a bayonet charge during the night. I passed the word down to Real Parenteau who was still awake. His only reply was a snort.

Sitting on the firing step in the narrow opening of the foxhole, I had a good view of the woods in front of me. I could hear Parenteau, Jones, and Rice all breathing at different intervals and intensities. With all these weapons, I felt I could hold off a battalion of Krauts. Although it sometimes seemed a tempting bargain to consider trading your life against one or two hundred enemy lives and possibly winning a Distinguished Service Cross or even a Medal of Honor in the process, where did that leave you personally? I decided I didn't want to trade myself for any number of Krauts in the world or for any medal for heroism, however exalted.

Our first night on the hill passed slowly. Every twig that moved and every shadow that wavered in the breeze found a grenade poised in every hand along the line of foxholes. In the morning, the dozens, if not hundreds of Jerries we had detected during the night crawling up the steep back slope turned out to be mere bushes and small trees.

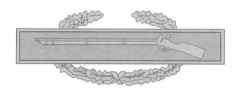

Chapter Nineteen
"Opening the Gateway Through the Vosges Mountains to the Alsatian Plains Beyond"

As soon as it got light on 18 November, the Jerries started shelling us in earnest. Every couple of minutes, they would bring a salvo down through the trees and into the battalion's positions. They knew right where we were and undoubtedly had observation posts in those suspicious-looking dark trees up behind Baker Company on our right. Although Captain Young had mentioned some artillery yesterday, we hadn't noticed much our first afternoon on the hill. But now the Krauts had gotten themselves organized and were making it clear that they regarded our battalion as a thorn in their side which had to be removed. Would they hit us with another counterattack after shelling us for a while? Nobody knew, but we were all braced for the worst and ready to beat them back again if they tried.

I spent about an hour that morning trying to answer nature's call. Every time I clambered out of the foxhole and crept five or ten yards away, I heard those distant whistles starting up again and made an embarrassed tumble into the nearest empty foxhole or depression in the ground. When I finally thought I had won through and found a convenient place, the whistles started up again and I was literally caught with my pants down. Fortunately, the volley landed too far away for the whizzing shrapnel to take advantage of my exposed situation. The Jerries seemed to have a talent for adding insult and indignity to war's normal risks of injury and death.

K rations and one five-gallon can of water per platoon were hand-carried up the steep hill to our little band of besieged defenders by the company's "Kitchen Commandos." They were headed by Mess Sergeant Paul Schmidt, a dapper individual with flaring mustaches whose native language was German. We very much appreciated Smitty's efforts, although the can of water yielded only half a canteen per man after being equitably divided.

After breakfast, Lieutenant Mueller sent me down to Captain Young's CP to get a report on the current situation. Captain Young came out of his cave beneath the fallen tree, looking even wilder than he had the day before.

"Why the hell doesn't the damn fool come down here himself if he wants to be briefed?" Captain Young growled.

"I think he may be allergic to 88s, sir," I opined.

While I was with Captain Young, Lieutenant Raymond Landis and First Sergeant Thomas Mulligan arrived leading a small contingent of fresh-faced replacements. They all looked winded after the long climb up the hill.

Captain Young shook hands with Lieutenant Landis and Sergeant Mulligan and then addressed the half dozen new members of Company A.

"Welcome, men. It gets a bit hot up here at times, but you're joining a seasoned outfit. You can count on everyone here to show you the ropes and to help you to minimize the risks of this kind of life."

The replacements looked wide-eyed at the captain. They looked as though six little eggs had cracked open and out they had stepped, complete with rifles and helmets like Athena the ancient Greek goddess.

"What's your MOS?"[29] Captain Young asked the one standing closest.

"Cook," the man replied.

"You're now Rifleman, 3d Platoon," Captain Young said. "Next man, what's your MOS?"

"Jeep driver."

"Rifleman, 2d Platoon," the Captain said. "Yours?"

"Hospital orderly."

"Rifleman, 3d Platoon. Yours?"

"Special Services Musician."

"Rifleman, 2d Platoon. We get quite a bit of music up here at times. Next?"

"Radio operator."

"I can use you at the CP. My telephone man, er, had a little accident." He was referring to the man who had lost a hand passing him the instrument two days ago. "Next?"

"Clerk."

"Rifleman, 3d Platoon. I'm sure Lieutenant Ballie will be pleased to have someone with your training and background."

---

[29]MOS = Military Occupational Specialty

The six victims were led away to their new assignments. Even after several minutes on the hill, Sergeant Mulligan's eyes were still very wide under his helmet. We had rarely seen him since our arrival in Marseilles and almost expected him to be still wearing the little blue-piped garrison cap he had worn at Fort Bragg. Although Sergeant Mulligan's relatives would perhaps believe he had been through all sorts of dangerous duty here in France, we all regarded his rear responsibilities (First Sergeant, Supply, Kitchen, etc.) as being about as dangerous as being with General Eisenhower back in the Supreme Rear Echelon.

"My God, Captain," Sergeant Mulligan said, "how do you *stand* it?" Their climb had surely taken them past the Able Company dead strewn across Hill 462.8, what we now called "Bloody Knob."

"It's just a question of *go, go, go*," the Captain replied fiercely. "We have to keep pushing the Heinies back and back and back some more, just like in a football game."

"Sergeant Atkinson of D Company told me about six replacements who came up the hill an hour or two ago," Sergeant Mulligan said. "An 88 barrage killed all six."

Lieutenant Landis spoke. "Do you wish me to stay up with your forward CP until the manpower situation improves further?"

"That would be a big help, Ray," Captain Young replied. "I know you have things to do at the Rear CP, but our biggest need of the moment is enough firepower to avoid being overrun."

"Count on me until further notice then," Lieutenant Landis said.

I faded out of their discussion and headed back toward my platoon. Passing within ten or fifteen yards of Bloody Knob, I saw Private David Goland of Bronx, New York, in a foxhole beside his machine gun.

"Hey, Red," Goland said. "How's it going?"

"Good, Dave," I replied.

On the gentle slope in front of his gun lay a tremendous assortment of dead men, both GIs and Germans. This area had apparently been the seam between the 2d and 3d Platoons where the German counterattack had struck hardest. A few feet in front of Dave Goland's foxhole lay Sergeant Clarence L. "Pop" Sutton from Concordia, Kansas, who lay facing downhill, half his head gone, but still clutching his M-1 rifle in a firing position.

"He taught me everything for the Expert Infantryman test," Dave Goland said.

"Same here," I said. Pop Sutton was a baldish man with sandy hair, who knew everything there was to know about bayonet fighting and the other manly arts of the dogface. Without his patient tutelage, I never would have been awarded the Expert Infantryman Badge.

"He taught me well," Dave Goland said, "but the damn monitors flunked me for being too aggressive with my .45 pistol."

"Being aggressive is the best thing to be up here," I said.

"Did you know your dear lieutenant was here yesterday searching the dead?" Dave Goland said.

"Which dead?" I said.

"The Krauts," Goland replied. "It's no crime to search the Krauts and Lennie Hershberg and I were doing it, too. But I saw Hersh search one guy without finding anything. When Hersh moved on to search another corpse, Lieutenant Mueller went over to the first stiff and spent about a quarter of an hour dragging off his outer trousers. In the pocket of the inner pants he found a good watch. I wanted to throw up."

"Maybe he figured with a good German watch he wouldn't be late for the next attack," I said.

"He has no sense of how an officer should behave," Dave Goland said.

I asked Dave Goland why his machine gun was facing downhill on the side of the hill toward our own lines.

"The Krauts came up this way two days ago," Goland said. "While the biggest risk may now be from the south side where your foxholes are, you never know when the Jerries will repeat what they did two days ago. They're tricky guys."

I said goodbye to Dave Goland and walked among the dead, paying my final respects as though I were in a military cemetery. Some were friends, others were casual acquaintances, and still others I barely knew at all. It was difficult to keep track of 190 men, especially with constant personnel turnover both in the States and overseas.

I recognized Sergeant Lucien Zarlenga from St. Louis, a squad leader in the 2d Platoon. Near him were three BAR men, Pfc. Joseph Hofmann, Jr., from Philadelphia; Roy M. Lee from Moorhead, Minnesota; and Pfc. Robert "Tex" Ludlow from Galveston, Texas. The BAR men lay virtually untouched except that each had received a bullet hole in the head. The German attackers had quickly identified the BAR men from their above average size and the large dimensions of their weapons, and had made quick work of them.

I had always had a high regard for Roy Lee, a big bright-looking smiling fellow, but had never had a chance to become well acquainted. With Joe Hofmann, I had forged a bond at Camp Kilmer during a touch football game. Joe and I were on the same team, which was behind and performing in a lackadaisical manner. Although I had never played the passer's position before, I volunteered to throw the pigskin. I tossed a couple of unartful high passes toward a clump of players and Joe Hofmann caught them both, the second one for a touchdown. A few minutes later we clicked again for another TD. I forgot who won the game, but Joe and I became friends that afternoon. It was hard to believe that now, only a month and a half later, young Joe Hofmann had played his last football game.

Tex Ludlow was a tall lanky Texan with an enthusiastic personality and a slightly effeminate way of talking. He was also a natural singer and usually called the numbers during our marches at Bragg. I could still hear some of his lines floating around in my head, even though I couldn't reassemble the complete tune,

> I just called up to tell you that I'm ragged but right
> Just a rovin' beggar woman drunk every night
>
> .
>
> .
>
> .
>
> So if you're like Napoleon, it's your Waterloo.

One of the boys remarked after Ludlow's death that it was a pity no woman was going to enjoy all he had to offer. Still, it took all kinds of people to make a world and Tex Ludlow almost suffered an indignity of an entirely different kind, although he died without knowledge of the incident. Back at Fort Bragg, when everyone was sleeping one night in the barracks, one of the non-coms decided to sexually prey upon Ludlow, who was sleeping on his stomach in the nude in the next cot. But just as the non-com was poised and ready to leap, he heard a voice beside him in the dark, "Do that again and I'll kill you." It was Private Willie Self, a taciturn American Indian of large stature and tremendous physical strength.

Tex Ludlow was now beyond the world of love and lust. If Willie Self had rescued him from an attemped rape, there was no one to save him from the German sharpshooter who had killed him ruthlessly because he was a key player carrying a potent weapon. Tex had been through a lot for a nice eighteen-year-old boy, and now he was dead.

These dead men and boys at Bloody Knob had all been good people, from good families. They all tried to do the right thing, working together to bring the nation out of the Depression, and training for war when the nation's enemies stuck without warning.

But was not something gravely wrong with a nation which educated and trained its youth for rational constructive lives (like Eddie Cook's dream of designing two-family homes with his fiancée, Doris), but in the end sent them off into a nightmarish Vosges wilderness to be shot down impersonally like rabid dogs or foxes? We had been taught that we lived in the American Utopia, with history's adventures and misadventures long behind us. We were told that Europe's problems were not our affair, even when Hitler's forces gobbled up Danzig, Austria, Czechoslovakia, Poland, France, the Low Countries, the Balkans, Greece, and half of Russia and North Africa.

Now we could see with our own eyes and through our own rifle sights that Europe's problems were indeed our concern, since we were the only nation (together with the Russians) with the necessary muscle and resources to stop the aggressors. Why had we been so misled about the true state of the world? Had someone duped us intentionally? In concert with our former allies from the Great War, we apparently had the potential to stop Hitler even back in the 1930s, but did nothing until much later, when the Japanese brought us forcibly out of our reverie one Sunday morning at Pearl Harbor.

We could also now see that world history was not a dried flower pressed between the leaves of a book as we had been taught, but was still very much alive and full of almost too much drama, blood, and violence for rational men to assimilate. Had we been duped or was it simply that the older generation (politicians and diplomats mainly, but also our fathers, uncles, and their friends) wasn't in control of things as much as we had imagined them to be?

We had been taught that the American Utopia resulted from our ancestors' courageous conquest of the frontier against a thousand foes and obstacles. I took a last look at my former friends where they lay. Was Bloody Knob, with dead GIs from two platoons strewn across its slopes, the fabled mountain at the end of the frontier, the Grand Teton, Pike's Peak, Mounts McKinley, Hood, and Rainier of the American Dream? Weren't we, in a way, going backwards, returning to exactly the ancient hills and forests—and conflicts and problems—our ancestors had left, to get away from all this stuff? If so, my fellow pioneers were all much nobler than I had suspected them capable of being, but the end to their quest had proven the world was a far less secure and reasonable place than I had ever imagined it to be. Leaving Company A's newly-made veterans' cemetery, I was moving on toward my platoon's positions when I saw a pair of bright eyes and a chin with bristly stubble pop up out of a foxhole excavated under the roots of a shrapnel-chewed stump. It was Lieutenant David Ballie of the 3d Platoon.

"Hi," he said cheerily, a rather informal greeting, I thought, from an officer with whom I was far from familiar.

"Hello," I said.

He gave me a conspiratorial grin. "What can you steal for me today?" he said with a big wink. Was this the same Lieutenant Ballie who on the *McAndrews* had been so anxious to reach dry land so he could start killing Krauts? Now he had lost several good men, including squad leaders John

Hambric and Pop Sutton. His Platoon Sergeant (and King of the Show-boats), Ralph Harrington, had already said "Uncle" and headed for the "golden rear echelon." If I had to make a guess, based on our limited conversation of this morning, I would have said Lieutenant Ballie's thirst to "kill Krauts" had now been fully sated. I even thought he would now welcome some other activity offering personal and professional growth possibilities in some other phase of the Army's far-flung activities and operations, such as a non-combat assignment far from here. In any event, while I was pretty sure he was not another ghoul like Mueller, I didn't really know what he meant by his "steal for me" remark. Perhaps he was "recruiting" to shore up the depleted ranks of his platoon's leadership.

Leaving Lieutenant Ballie, I soon ran into Lennie Hershberg carrying his "toy" grease gun as though it were a serious weapon.

"Hey, Red," Hershberg said, "Come along to Chuck and Sam's hole. I think Chuck needs cheering up."

"What's the matter?" I asked.

"He's down at the mouth on account of Eddie Cook," Hershberg said. "He says it was his fault"

"How does he figure that?"

"He says he shouldn't have listened to Captain Brown when he told us to close ranks as we advanced into that wood, instead of opening them up as we should have."

"I'll tell him that's all hindsight," I said.

"You know whose fault it really was?" Hershberg said. "It was the lieutenant's."

"How do you figure that?" I asked.

"He put his radio man practically up with the point of the advance. He was with Jim Amoroso and the only thing between them and the Jerries were Jeske and Cash, the scouts. The Jerries see a guy carrying a walkie-talkie and bingo! They pop him off, what else?"

"I see what you mean."

"Moe Moniz, on the other hand, says it was Cook's own fault for peeking his head around the tree. Moniz is telling his squad he'll kick the next guy in the ass who does that."

Sam D'Arpino's mad monk beard greeted us as we reached their foxhole.

"Hey, Uncle Sam," Hershberg said. "Don't throw one of your antitank grenades at me, okay?"

"All right, wise guy," Sam said. Hersh was referring to Sam's improbable feat during yesterday's fight for Hill 462.8.

"Where's Chuck?" Hershberg asked.

"Oh, Mrs. Stanley is downstairs in the foxhole brewing coffee for us. She'll be out of the kitchen in a minute."

Chuck Stanley stood up, his beard a bit less wild-looking than Sam D'Arpino's.

"Here boys, have a swig," he said, passing the canteen cup around. The Nescafé tasted excellent as usual.

"You know what that Amoroso did to us?" Hershberg said. "He went off to the field hospital with the squad's Turner stove! Hoggie Hogberg is fit to be tied."

"How was your duty with the tanks, Red?" Chuck Stanley said.

"It turned out to be an easy detail," I replied. "We were lucky."

"We were lucky, too, compared to the other platoons," Sam D'Arpino said. "After we beat back that attack with the burp guns and potato mashers, the lieutenant wanted to chase the Germans back down the hill. Chuck and I said absolutely not."

"You should have let him ask for volunteers and gone himself," Lennie Hershberg said in a comical voice he sometimes used.

"I'm beginning to think he would have made a great private," Sam D'Arpino said. "He's always firing his weapon and he's not afraid. But the problem I see is he should be standing back and thinking about what to do next, rather than running around shooting like a Pfc. The way it's working out, Chuck and I have to make the decisions for the platoon since he either can't or won't make them himself."

Chuck Stanley grunted as though hinting to Sam D'Arpino that the subject of the lieutenant's idiosyncrasies was perhaps inappropriate for discussion with men below the platoon management level.

"Sam and me figured out a policy on praying," Chuck Stanley said. "We take turns, first it's Sam's turn and then my turn. When things really get hot, like when they was winging those potato mashers at us, then we both pray."

"The next time you're talking to God," Lennie Hershberg said, "please tell him I'd like a thirty-day furlough. And be sure it's a one-way ticket."

We had passed another tense night, waiting for a counterattack that never materialized. We heard that the 398th, which two days ago had marched past us wearing those large cellophane gift wrappers marked "Do not open till Christmas," had gone in to the attack yesterday, the 18th. Our battalion's capture of Hill 462.8 and the 397th's capture of the high ground north of Raon l'Etape had opened the way to the Plaine River valley which ran east from Raon l'Etape toward one of the passes through the High

Vosges. The 398th's mission was to push south across the Plaine River on the east side of the Hill mass of which Hill 462.8 was a part, thus completing the isolation of Raon l'Etape which was already now surrounded on three sides. However, the 398th had run into heavy resistance on the other side of the little river.

Sunday 19 November at about noon, word was received that Baker and Charlie Companies would leave the hill to join the other divisional elements attempting to breach the Plaine River line. Their departure meant we would have two completely exposed flanks.

Up on our right, Baker Company saddled up, moved out of their holes, and started down the gentle slope toward our company in long straggling columns. Just then the familiar whine was heard. A terrific barrage followed and Company B suffered many casualties from tree bursts which hurled shrapnel and tree branches all over the place like an earthquake. When the barrage finally lifted, they patched up the wounded, let the walking wounded go on with the rest, and carried down those who couldn't walk. They were a very professional bunch, Baker Company.

Charlie Company also had its troubles trying to leave the hill, which had exacted its toll upon those who would capture it and was now taking revenge on those who would leave it. One of Charlie Company's casualties from the shelling was Lieutenant Jack Jenkins, who had led the battalion's seven-man combat patrol into St. Remy back on 4 November, which now seemed months ago rather than only fifteen days.

While climbing Hill 462.8 three days ago during the big attack, Lieutenant Jenkins, had discovered a German machine-gun emplacement on the uphill side of the switchback road. Noting an occasional pause in the machine gun's firing which he interpreted as being the reloading phase, Lieutenant Jenkins climbed onto the road surface and crawled over to a point below the enemy emplacement, which was dug into the slope above the road. Hurling his two grenades plus two borrowed from his runner, he silenced the enemy gun for good (his bravery earned him the Silver Star).

Today, when the order came for Charlie Company to leave the hill, Lieutenant Jenkins struck the pup tent he had been using to cover his foxhole. Then word came that Charlie Company's departure would be delayed a day. Lieutenant Jenkins proceeded to re-pitch the pup tent over his foxhole and was pounding a tent peg into the ground when a mortar shell exploded nearby. A shell fragment struck him in the left hip, almost knocking him to the ground. Shortly after that orders changed again and Company C pulled out after all. By the time Lieutenant Jenkins was carried down the hill on a litter, it was dark and the jeep to which they strapped him and another WIA was not allowed to use lights. The jeep fell into the ditch in the blackness and required twelve men to lift it and its strapped-down wounded men back onto the road. Finally Lieutenant Jenkins reached a field hospital where the shell fragment was removed from his hip.

After Company B had gone off down the hill taking their wounded with them, one lost sheep was left behind, a young BAR man from Centralia, Missouri, named Evan Wade. He had been caught out in the open by a barrage and had sweated out burst after burst of German artillery shells all around him. When all the other Baker Company men were gone down the hill, he was still lying there, overlooked, a victim of shell shock. Lieutenant Mueller took him under his fatherly (if adolescent) wing, inviting him to stay with our platoon until we could learn where his outfit had gone. I was the lucky one who drew the honor of entertaining him during his temporary attachment to the company.

Real Parenteau gave me this good news. "Red, you go take over one of the B Company foxholes and stay with the kid."

"Why does it have to be me?" I asked. According to the book I was supposed to be bunking with Herbie Rice, since we were the squad's scouts. Besides, Rice was about the ideal guy to share a foxhole with, being brave as hell, a hard worker, very good humored, and considerate to everyone. Also, Rice and I had let Parenteau and Jones move into the foxhole *we* had dug two nights before, because, like Tenderfoot Boy Scouts, they had dug in a stupid place. Now I was to be kicked out of my own foxhole. Parenteau had his "pets," who seemed to include Herbie Rice and Robert E. Jones, but for reasons unknown to me, I was not among that favored clan. Like every non-com, Parenteau had to assign someone to "shit details" from time to time. I was apparently on the "shit list" rather than on Parenteau's "pet parade."

"You go," Parenteau repeated. He wasn't a big one for discussing the equities of a particular situation. I was already beginning to develop nostalgia for Jim Gardner, our squad leader until a week before. Translated from French into English, the name Réal Parenteau probably originally meant Royal (for Réal) Parent-of-Water (for Parenteau). On the basis of my first week under his leadership, I would have amended the name slightly to Royal Pain-in-the-Behind.

Evan Wade and I moved into the nearest Baker Company foxhole, which he said had been Captain Prince's CP. It was large and even had a stub of candle in a holder dangling from the log roof. I was still angry with Parenteau for getting me involved with this charity case. Evan Wade was a nice kid, but nervous as a cat, which didn't help my own none-too-Gibraltarish emotional equilibrium. Both his helmet and his BAR seemed several sizes too large for him.

I began chatting about some foolishness or other to take his mind off his troubles, but he interrupted with, "I don't mind being here with you, but I'll be listed in the Morning Report as Missing in Action and they'll send my folks a MIA telegram and that'll be very tough for them to take."

"Don't worry," I told him, "my company will contact yours immediately and tell 'em we're taking good care of you. So no MIA report will ever be turned in."

"Man, we took a pounding," he said, "I was lying there between two fox-holes, listening to the 88s falling all around, but I didn't dare to stand up and make a break for either hole. We were all frozen to the ground. My buddies kept screaming they were hit. Then the company went away without seeing me. They'll report me as Missing In Action. I don't mind being here, but it'll be tough on my folks when they're told I'm MIA."

I tried again to explain that there would be no problem, but all I got in return was the same *verbatim* story including the "I don't mind being here but. . . ." You may not mind being here, buddy, I thought, but I sure as hell am not getting all that much out of the relationship. I felt like Sigmund Freud with a prize psycho case.

"What a pounding we took," Evan Wade began again.

"Hey, you got any coffee?" I said, trying to change the record and play something new. Something seemed to click in the kid's brain. His eyes lost their calf-like stare and he said "Sure." We pooled our water, Nescafé packets, and sugar. I explained how we would use one guy's Nescafé that night and the other guy's in the morning. We were very equitable about the whole business, even to pooling our heat tablets, little cubes of some sort of waxy compound from which you ripped off the outside cardboard and set alight. To keep Wade's mind off his recent trauma, I made that the absolute paramount issue in the world—how we were going to divide that Nescafé, sugar, water, and heating tablets fairly and squarely, and how we would enjoy drinking it together.

That afternoon, Sergeant Paul "Smitty" Schmidt's company mess section hauled up our first hot meal, a most welcome event and a further balm to Evan Wade's frazzled nerves.

Our foxhole was on the company's extreme right flank just beyond the last foxhole of Hershberg's and Jeske's squad. Our immediate neighbors were Lester and Chester Fraley who hailed from Tiptonville, Tennessee (and who now had a "winter place" here in France's Vosges Mountains). Just before twilight, the Fraley twins paid us a social call in our spacious foxhole with the candle stub. The four of us discussed the big picture in general and finally reached the consensus that when it became completely dark about 1630, the Fraley boys would move in with us. That would give

us four men to rotate on guard duty rather than only two, and would offer
the Fraleys a good dry foxhole, which their own apparently was not. I was
already getting over the sting of being kicked out of my previous foxhole
by my squad leader.

Lester Fraley rigged a shelter half and some raincoats over the foxhole
entrance, and we were able to light up Captain Prince's candle. I told Evan
Wade about Eddie Cook and he said, yes, he thought he knew some Cooks
in Sedalia. By this time his shell-shocked nerves were much calmer.

It developed during the conversation that I was the oldest man present,
at the ripe age of eighteen. My nineteenth birthday was still one week
away, 26 November. Wade's birth date was 7 December, while the Fraleys
wouldn't be nineteen until January, although Chester was already a married man and father-to-be. Chester had been in the 398th, but just before
coming overseas, had engineered a transfer to our company so they could
be together. This was an exception to the normal rule that brothers were
not allowed to serve in the same combat outfit. We had read articles about
how no soldiers under nineteen would actually be sent into combat and
other such congressional hoop-la. But here we were, very much fighting,
and all still eighteen. I mentioned that Eddie Cook would have turned nineteen today. Actually, the young soldiers seemed just as good as anybody
else and, in some cases, better. The next time someone beat their gums in
the States about not sending youngsters into combat, we four would
remember that when they got a bit short of 88 meat, they didn't yell about
it or argue, but merely sent in the eighteen year olds to fight the battles.

We discussed *ad nauseam* what our first breakfast in the States was
going to consist of: two huge bowls of cereal with cream and fruit; a king-
sized orange juice; six eggs sunnyside-down with crispy, golden strands of
bacon; ten pancakes pinned down by gobs of warm, melted butter and
golden maple syrup; half a dozen pieces of toast; and a full quart of ice-
cold, Grade A milk. Those were no mere flights of fancy, but cold factual
estimates of what we thought our "Grand Canyon" stomachs could accom-
modate when the great day arrived.

Late that afternoon "Smitty," the Mess Sergeant, volunteered to take
three German prisoners down off the hill on his return run after delivering
us that first delicious hot meal. Smitty told the two unwounded POWs,
who understood English, to construct a makeshift litter and carry the third
man, who had a stomach wound. Unknown to the prisoners, Smitty was a
native born German who had gone to the U.S. in 1930 from a town south
of Kaiserslautern. Every seventy-five or one hundred yards, the litter-bear-
ing POWs set down their wounded comrade and complained of sore hands.
But in German, Smitty heard them say they would keep stalling around

until it became completely dark when they would make their escape. Smitty said in a loud voice in English to Carter, the Cook, who was with him, "The next time these prisoners put down the litter, we will shoot them and carry the litter ourselves." After that there was no further stalling by the prisoners who carried their wounded comrade non-stop all the way to the foot of the hill. Next morning, when the wounded man asked for water, his comrades refused to share their supply, so Smitty gave him water and a cigarette. As Smitty and the wounded man jabbered away in German, the other two were wide-eyed as they slowly caught on to the fact Smitty had understood every word of their conversation coming down the slope.

※ ※ ※ ※

We only heard bits and pieces about the big picture at the time, but we later learned that before dawn on 20 November the 3d Infantry Division—veterans of so many combat river crossings in Italy—silently sneaked a battalion of infantry across the Meurthe River between Raon l'Etape and St. Dié without being detected by the enemy. Thus, the main act of the VI Corps attack plan against the enemy's Vosges winter line was off to a favorable start in conformity with the original schedule fixed by VI Corps CO, General Edward Brooks, on 10 November. By daybreak, the 325th Engineers, the 100th's organic Engineer Combat Battalion, had put a bridge across the Meurthe at Raon l'Etape, completing the project in a single night. On VI Corps' left, Seventh Army's XV Corps under Major General Wade Haislip was also making good progress at the western end of the Saverne Gap, in no small part due to our success against the *708th Volks-Grenadiers*, whose defensive sector spanned our respective corps boundaries, and had been unhinged by our progress against their southern flank. Already, the lead elements of XV Corps were through the Winter Line fortifications in their zone, and were within eight or nine kilometers of the major pass at Saverne and the entrance to the Rhine plain on a main road leading to Strasbourg.

On the Seventh Army's right, the French First Army, under General Jean de Lattre de Tassigny, had on 16 November broken through the Belfort Gap separating the Vosges chain from Switzerland's Jura Mountains, as Switzerland's Army Commander General Henry Guisan looked on through high powered binoculars. On 19 November, French tanks reached the Rhine near Mulhouse.

Meanwhile, on the Seventh Army's left, the 8 November offensive by General Patton's Third Army across the Lorraine plain toward the Sarre region and the Rhine 132 miles away had gained less than ten miles in the first twelve days. On 20 November General Patton noted in his diary that the French and General 's Seventh Army were "stealing the show." In a letter to his wife the same day, General Patton wrote, "The Seventh Army and the First French Armored (Division) seem to have made a monkey of me this morning."

———

At dawn we received our usual shelling, which seemed almost as intense as yesterday's barrage, when Baker and Charlie Companies were trying to pull out. Despite the shelling, our house guest, Evan Wade, was much calmer today. I thought the Fraley twins with their Tennessee accents and folksy ways had contributed to his improved morale this morning.

We actually saw the sun come up for a change, and we heard (also for a change) the roar of friendly airplane motors, and the distant firing of aircraft machine guns hammering away like a bank of teletype machines in a busy news room. According to *The Stars and Stripes*, the Army Air Forces had claimed that if ever the Vosges cloud cover would lift for a couple of days, they would show the enemy what they could do. This morning was such a day and the flyboys were apparently trying to make good on their promise.

I finally solved the problem of how to answer nature's call without becoming a statistic by staking out one of Baker Company's many abandoned foxholes and posting a crude "WC keep out" sign above the entrance. Evan Wade and I went scouting with the Fraley twins up through his company's old positions where a tremendous amount of equipment had been dropped or thrown away during Sunday's shelling. We found precious units of K rations; a few pistol belts, which I let the others grab; water in canteens which no one wanted to drink; cleaning kits and cans of oil for our thirsty rifles; rusty tooth brushes and shaving brushes which could also be used to clean our rifles; dry socks which we particularly prized; knives, raincoats; shelter halves; and many heating units to supplement our stringent issue of the one per day. All these bits of salvage or booty would make our life ten times more comfortable on that isolated hill even though it was a piss-poor rate of exchange to be using the possessions of buddies who fell the day before.

Late that afternoon, they shelled us again and L. C. Talley of our squad finally caved in from a combination of shell shock, battle fatigue, and pneumonia. "Good dig, no hit" Talley, as Scotty Kyle called him, had spent his four days on the hill pounding the ground at the bottom of his foxhole as the volleys of German shells shook the earth and rained branches on our foxhole roofs. Lieutenant Mueller was not too tolerant about claims of "battle fatigue," so nothing was done about Talley's case until he developed a certifiable case of pneumonia. Even Lieutenant Mueller couldn't order a man with pneumonia to fight, so Talley was sent to the rear to recuperate.

Another battle fatigue case that day was a handsome, tough-talking former MP in the 2d Platoon whose favorite saying back at Bragg was, "Screw 'em all but six; we'll screw *them* later." Captain Young, who had until then considered battle fatigue "a bunch of bullshit" (as he put it), found himself in the same hole with the ex-MP during a shelling. When the man started beating the ground and whimpering, Captain Young's first inclination had been to "belt the guy," but he quickly became convinced that the man was not shamming. Captain Young sent him off to the rear with L. C. Talley.

Mess Sergeant Paul Schmidt was struck by shrapnel in the back as he doled evening chow from the marmite cans into our mess kits. It was almost as though the enemy was furious at the miracles Smitty's warm food was doing for our stomachs and morale.

Captain Young was so concerned over Smitty's condition that he accompanied Smitty's litter down the hill to where a jeep evacuated him. The first two hospitals to which Smitty was taken were full and it was midnight before he finally reached a hospital which could take him in. Smitty was delirious for several hours, and when he awoke he found himself on the side of the ward with the German prisoners.

"Hey, what's going on? He shouted. "I'm American! Which SOB put me on the German side?"

"But you talked in German all night," the nurse said.

"I was born there," Smitty said. "But I'm in the States since 1930."

"There, there," the nurse said, humoring him.

Smitty's dogtags had been accidentally removed by someone during the long night's confusion, and he had no way of establishing his true identity. A Lieutenant Colonel came into the ward and listened to Smitty's story for quite a long time. Finally he told Smitty, he believed his story and had him moved back to the American side of the ward.

Captain Young called for a reconnaissance patrol down in front of our lines. Sergeant Parenteau was tapped for the assignment and selected Doc Emmons, Scotty Kyle, and me for the job. Real might not have been too enthusiastic about letting me share his foxhole, but I was always popular with him when projects involving scouting and contacting the enemy came along. Doc Emmons told me that of three previous patrols sent by our battalion down this same slope, none had returned.

Our route was carefully marked on Captain Young's map and looked quite long. Parenteau put me out front for the first one hundred yards, after which the four of us went into a skirmish line formation. We turned right up a draw, expecting any minute to run into another defense line. But the only sounds were the drippings and faint rustling of trees. Leaving the draw, we advanced along the steep slope of a hill. If there had been an ambush or machine gun dug in anywhere, we wouldn't have known it until it was too late because keeping our balance on the steep ground occupied all our attention.

Doc Emmons was high up on the slope and I was low man on our four-man totem pole. Suddenly, I heard voices far below at the bottom of the long slope. I couldn't tell whether the voices were speaking German or English.

"What do you think, Real?" I asked.

Sergeant Parenteau cocked his head and we both listened for several minutes.

"Well," he said finally, "from the noise there's plenty more of them than there are of us. I'd say only GIs are dumb enough to jabber that much on the front. But what if they're Jerries talking that way to make us think they're GIs and suck us into an ambush? I think we'll head for home." I doubted that Real had wanted to go down there any more than I did, and I was most appreciative of the way he reasoned the problem through to a "no-go" conclusion. We continued our advance.

Walking just below a white rock cliff which took up the top forty yards of the long slope, Doc Emmons peered into one of the stone fissures and discovered something. When I got up there, they had a young Jerry looking very scared with his hands up. They were giving him a rough and thorough going over. It seemed that he had been left behind when his *Kamaraden* had hauled ass, and not being too anxious to catch up with the others, he had hidden out in the cave. He had ditched his rifle somewhere and seemed more interested in "*nicht schiessen*" than anything else.

Balancing out the good news of capturing a prisoner, I ripped my trousers about ten inches in back on a thorny bush. A few minutes later, my belt broke. After that I had to clutch my trousers with one hand, leaving only one hand free for such mundane tasks as carrying a rifle, handling grenades, and making arm and hand signals to other members of the patrol. By the time I led the patrol up the final slope toward Captain Young's CP, the belt had disappeared completely and was now in the category of battlefield relics.

We must have made a strange procession coming into the CP area. First a tall, filthy-looking character with long, flaring red hair growing out of his neck in back and clutching his OD trousers to keep them from falling down. Behind him in the distance, filtering like shadows through the trees, came three more filthy-looking GIs escorting a sky-grabbing Jerry. If we resembled a band of roving hobos coming in for a long awaited bath, our Jerry was tastefully dressed in blue and gray like a Civil War American who couldn't decide which side he wanted to be on. An immaculate blue overcoat completed his wardrobe.

Captain Young, looking wilder than ever, asked, "Well?" when I came ambling into Able Company Gulch.

"The parade is coming," I replied.

Captain Young was hot under the collar. He said a bunch of enemy soldiers claiming to be Polish conscripts had come walking into the CP a few minutes before to give themselves up. Until then, the he had had peace of mind, thinking the boys in the foxholes were on the alert in front of him.

By the time Parenteau, Emmons, and Kyle arrived with the German, Lieutenant Landis and several others had joined the reception committee.

"Who is this bastard anyway?" Captain Young asked rhetorically.

"He's a prisoner I found, Young," Doc Emmons replied, remembering what Captain Young had told him at St. Remy about not mentioning his rank in public places.

"Do you think it's worth a Bronze Star?" Lieutenant Landis asked.

"Hey, wait a minute," Captain Young interrupted. "Let's not talk about fruit salad when there's work to be done. Emmons, what outfit is this man from?"

"Dunno, none of us speaks Kraut," Doc Emmons replied.

"What outfit are you from?" Captain Young shouted at the young prisoner, who stood seven or eight inches shorter than him.

"*Welche Einheit?*" the youth said.

"Ya, ya, what *Einheit* are you?" Young said.

"*Sieben Hundert Achte Volks-Grenadier Division,*" the prisoner said.

One of the Captain's CP group translated the unit number into English— the *708th Volks-Grenadiers.*

"*Wo bist die Kameraden?*" Captain Young continued in his broken Kraut.

"*Sind weggegangen,*" the prisoner replied, indicating that they had taken off.

"When?" Captain Young asked.

"*Vorgestern.*" The day before yesterday.

Captain Young turned to Sergeant Parenteau. "No need for you and your boys to waste your time here. I'll handle the interrogation. Good work, Emmons."

"Thanks, Young," Doc Emmons squeaked.

We headed back separately to our foxholes. Moving through the CP area, I came upon one of Captain Young's headquarters section men, Pfc.

Ray J. Fields from Long Island, New York. Ray was standing in his foxhole, bending over a little stove on which he was cooking something. Suddenly he looked up and smiled.

"Hey Red, how would you like some lemonade?"

I was parched after the long patrol, which made the thought of ice cold lemonade dizzying to contemplate. But how could Ray Fields afford such generosity when each of us was limited to half a canteen of water per day due to the long dangerous climb to bring it to us? Ray Fields was perhaps attempting to reciprocate for the dangers I had just undergone on patrol.

Ray Fields extended a closed fist in my direction and smiled again. I didn't understand the meaning of the gesture. Where was the promised lemonade? Then the closed fist opened and there was a tiny cellophane envelope of K ration lemon juice powder, but of course no water and no delectable drink. I waved a filthy paw at him to try to express a combat man's impotent rage at rear echelon hoarders and gangsters like this Fields boy. If this was Long Island humor, I resolved never to visit there after the war.

When I returned to our foxhole, Evan Wade was gone. He had gone off down the hill amid many well wishes to rejoin his outfit. I moved in with Private Julius DeRubeis, a tall likeable kid from Chicago. "DeRuby" (as we called him) was one of those quiet riflemen who didn't have a highly visible job such as scout or BAR gunner, but was always there when you needed him. DeRuby was looking for a foxhole mate because of L. C. Talley's departure yesterday.

When the kitchen crew brought up the marmite cans with warm food in the morning and evening, each two-man foxhole sent one representative to the CP area carrying two mess kits and two canteens to pick up "chow for two." The reason for the procedure was to reduce our exposure to shell fire by one-half, and maintain security on the line. Our first evening together, DeRuby and I devised a technique whereby when the first of us returned with "chow for two," the other man went down with two more mess kits and canteens to pick up "chow for two." The extra mess kits and canteens we had salvaged from Baker Company's former bivouac area had made this subterfuge possible. To disguise our trickery, it was necessary for us to vary the routes by which we approached and left the CP area.

My approach the first evening took me past Lieutenant Ballie's 3d Platoon CP, a pile of logs laid in tepee fashion against a shrapnel-chewed tree stump, under whose gnarled roots dwelled the Great Man of Oahu, Hawaii. On the ground near the tree stump, to my astonishment, I spotted a light tan-colored officer's belt with a shiny brass buckle. I had not been having any real problem of holding up my trousers since DeRuby had given me a piece of rope to replace my standard GI belt lost on today's patrol, but the thought of again having a real belt was intoxicating. Within fifteen seconds, I had left Lieutenant Ballie's CP area and had the belt. The last time I had seen him he had asked me, "What can you steal *for* me?" He didn't know it, but I guess he should have phrased it, "What are you going to steal *from* me?"

At the chow line, I ran into Lennie Hershberg who told me Lieutenant Ray "Mamma" Landis was becoming jumpy from the shelling and the loneliness of life on the hill. Lieutenant Landis had told Hershberg such things as, "Take good care of yourself," "Don't walk out on me," and "Be extremely careful." Mamma Landis also expressed concern over what might happen to Lennie Hershberg if the *SS* caught him.

"Don't worry," Hersh told him, "I've got a bullet I'll use on myself if they try to take me alive." I wondered how Hersh, whose arms were of only normal length, expected to be able to fire that long BAR at himself with that silver tracer bullet in it. Varying my route again, I returned to our foxhole via the path leading past Dave Goland's machine gun. He was standing in his hole facing downhill, but when his head turned at my footstep I noticed he had been crying.

"What's wrong, Dave?" I said.

"It's Pop Sutton," he said. "I couldn't stand looking at him with his head shot away so I put a K ration carton over his head. That helped a lot but once in a while I still go through a sad few minutes." It was twilight and I could just make out Pop's K ration carton a few yards down the slope.

"Cheer up," I said. "Got to get this chow up to DeRubeis before it gets cold."

As I reached our platoon area, John Jeske was arriving at Lieutenant Mueller's foxhole carrying two mess kits and two canteens containing chow for two.

"Hey Red, why did you come the long way?" Jeske asked.

"Oh, I wanted to see Dave Goland," I said evasively. "Why are you bringing chow to the lieutenant?"

"I'm his new runner," Jeske said, rolling his eyes so that Lieutenant Mueller in the foxhole would not hear anything slanderous.

As soon as I returned to our foxhole, DeRuby set out to pick up our third and fourth dinners. Before he returned, Chuck Stanley came around. "The lieutenant says everybody should be on the alert for a Jerry bayonet charge tonight," he told me.

"But there are no Jerries around," I said. "That's why we went on patrol this morning, to find out."

"Just doing my job," Chuck Stanley said.

While DeRuby pulled the first guard shift from six to eight, I wrote to my folks for the first time since Armistice Day,

Nov. 21, 1944
Vosges Mts.
7th Army

Dear Folks,

I wrote Nov 11 and just got it mailed today. Pardon scribbling, hands are numb. Don't bother with scarf, it's too good. We make them from blankets. Please send more ink though and self-addressed envelopes, which are convenient in the wilderness.[30]

I don't go around worrying people so I won't cite any battle statistics which are really unbelievable. I will only tell you that Ed Cook went 6 days ago. Two days ago, Sunday the 19th, was to be his 19th birthday and he was already wearing a birthday locket from his girl. As soon as War Dept regulations permit, I think I'll write his mother.

For two days our eight-man squad was chosen by Battalion to ride our General Sherman tanks into battle. It was quite thrilling and since we didn't run into any trouble it was quite an experience.

I haven't spent a penny in ages. At 70 bucks per month, I'll be rich by the time we hit Berlin.[31] Our Battalion is the only one in the Division to receive a citation.[32] We're always in front. Expensive business, though. The Lieutenant Colonel is an ambitious W. Pointer.[33]

It was almost 2000, so I put the letter in a dry place and took over from DeRuby on guard duty. It had turned colder and a freezing rain was falling. As often happened on guard duty, my mind started turning things over. This was our fifth night on the hill. Life here in the wilds had changed me and I didn't intend to return to the way things had been before. For one thing, I no longer felt apologetic for being alive, the way I had most of the time since I was thirteen when we moved from Upper Darby to New England. I now finally realized that what had been troubling me all those years was simply "adolescence," characterized by self-consciousness and feelings of inferiority. Well, I no longer had time for growing pains and was going to leave them all behind right here on Hill 462.8, like a snake shedding his old skin. Our dead here on the hill were all finished with life almost before they had begun. For reasons that would probably forever

---

[30]When I wrote this letter I was unaware that the hill we were holding was called "Top of the Wilderness," but my letter accurately called the place a "wilderness."

[31]A private earned $50 per month, plus $10 Overseas Pay, and $5 each for the "Expert" and "Combat" Infantryman Badges.

[32]The 1st Battalion, 399th Infantry Regiment was awarded a Presidential Unit Citation for capturing the hill on November 16, 1944.

[33]I wonder if my company officers failed to read (and censor) the reference to our battalion commander.

remain obscure, I had been spared their fate and been granted a new lease on life. I intended to exercise my options under the new lease to the fullest.

The romantic idea I had had in the St. Benoît woods about writing a letter "only to be opened in case of my death" was now a dead issue. I no longer felt sorry for myself and no longer thought the world would suffer any appreciable loss if I were to be forcibly removed from the list of players. The men who had died on Hills 372, 409.9, and 462.8 were a grave loss to me, but I would not be to others, except of course my parents, relatives, and a few good friends. Whatever life (or death) had in store for me from now on, I could take it.

From chatting with Lennie Hershberg, I had the sense that he must have felt the way I did. "Things are going to be different," he told me. "The first thing I'm going to do is marry that girl I've been going with. I don't know what I was waiting for."

I also thought about my ambitions to be a Harvard track man and how unlikely that all now seemed, considering our stupefying casualty rates. Captain Young had told us at the beginning of the month that he didn't want to lose a single man, yet he was already down from 190 to 65 (including injured, wounded, battle fatigue, and of course, dead). I vowed that I would gladly trade both legs from the knee down to get out of this in one piece. That wouldn't leave too much to build a track star out of, but I really didn't give a damn.

I was just being realistic.

We had all seen some kind of blinding light here on the hill, a light which would change our lives drastically after we got out of here. Like lightning flashes in a black storm, the dignity of men had been brightly illuminated on this hill during the past week, beginning with those who fell here and ending with us, their successors.

Soon it was 2200 and DeRuby's turn to go on guard.

"Listen, DeRuby," I called down into the foxhole. "The Krauts won't be out in this weather. Let's get some shuteye."

"Amen, brother," DeRuby murmured groggily. "I'll just stay asleep."

Unfortunately, the freezing rain continued all night and caved in the log roof of our hole at least six times. Each time it fell in we got up and repaired it, only to have it fall in again. Finally we gave up and slept through until morning, awakening to find the top half of us dry and the bottom half a family-sized lake.

On 22 November, the freezing rain turned to snow after dawn, depositing a thin white coating on our positions. When I headed down the slope with two of our numerous mess kits and equally numerous canteens to get "breakfast for two," I was surprised to see Lieutenant Mueller ahead of me on the slightly special mission of getting breakfast for himself and a private (Jeske). Later I asked John Jeske what was going on.

"I told him it was his turn," Jeske said, blinking his eyes in that big city way of his.

"Nice going," I said. "Did you get any sleep?"

"Are you kidding?" Jeske said. "Mueller tells you gullible guys to watch out for a bayonet charge so he can get his beauty sleep. Don't let him fool you. We both slept like babies. Probably you did too."

"No comment," I said.

"I think my honeymoon with our Eminent Leader is going to be brief," Jeske said with a wink.

It was so cold that morning that it took me half an hour to unbutton my trousers to answer nature's call and another half hour to rebutton. Some of the boys coped with the problem by simply leaving their trousers unbuttoned.

John Day, the Mail Clerk, arrived with letters, packages, and copies of *Stars and Stripes*. Herbie Rice received eleven packages, an all-time high in the platoon. We ate like kings until the platoon had completely exhausted the tremendous larder that Rice's parents, relatives, and friends around Peoria had sent him. If they knew that those packages were not being used for the luxury needs of one man but for the physical sustenance of an entire (if understrength) starving platoon, I'm sure they would send even *more* parcels of cheer, if it were humanly possible.

Stars and Stripes reported that the November rain and snow we had been experiencing was part of the worst autumn weather in twenty-five years in western Europe. The article also explained the phenomenon we had noticed of occasionally clear Vosges nights, followed by gloomy, misty days. I had tended to become paranoid about the weather and to assume that something or someone was out to make life as miserable as possible for us. It was comforting to realize that we were merely in the grip of meteorological forces for which there were adequate rational explanations. It also offered hope for the sun's reasserted presence in the days and weeks to come.

Hearing that Thomas Case was shacking up with a couple of packages in his foxhole, I rushed down the hill to his hole commanding the draw below. With a hearty "Heigh-ho, Case!" I surveyed his hole with a hungry look.

"Ha, ha, Red, have a nut," generously offered the noted philanthropist, who was something of a "nut" in his own right. He proffered a small bag of walnuts, chestnuts, or some kind of nuts (any squirrel would know what kind) but I had my hopes set upon something more nourishing.

"I heard you got a fruit cake," I said.

"Oh, ha, ha, Red, we just finished it, here's the box."

After demolishing the two remaining crumbs in the bottom of the box, I asked why he had eaten it so quickly and without prior notice to the other squad members.

"Oh, ha, ha, it just seemed to disappear like magic. Won't you have a nut?"

Real Parenteau was assigned to take a patrol to contact a company of the 398th that was protecting our rear at the base of the hill. Real, Rice, Kyle, and I carried grease guns while only Case and Emmons had M-1 rifles. It had snowed a bit in early morning, and we practically skied down the hill, feeling like kids.

As we skidded down the snowy slope, Doc Emmons told me an entire German company had walked into the CP and surrendered as a result of our patrol yesterday and our capture of the young member of their unit. I didn't know whether there was really a causal relationship between the two or whether Lieutenant Landis was trying to develop material for a Bronze Star medal application for someone, possibly Doc Emmons.

At the bottom of the slope, we drank endlessly from a stream while Real was inside the CP. Climbing back up the hill, I found several copies of the 18 November issue of *Lightning News* stashed away in an old German foxhole. The newspaper, the first we had seen since the 12 November issue, reported *Luftwaffe* attacks on the Meurthe bridges at Baccarat on the 17th, which we had observed our last morning with the tanks. *Herr Doktor* Goebbels' writers claimed that the Baccarat bridges had all been destroyed, which struck us as a probable lie, in addition to the fact that the Americans were across the river in overwhelming strength now anyway.

Lightning News also bewailed our dogfaces' fate by pointing out that although the odds of getting killed were not too great, the chances of being wounded were four times as high. We didn't know whether they were assigning all the mental misfits and intellectual imbeciles to their newspaper staff or what, but they were really mixed up. Most of us *wanted* to be wounded (but not too seriously), and those favorable four-to-one odds of being wounded rather than killed in action were what kept us going in hopes of getting a nick instead of a knockout.

We enjoyed the latest episode in the life of *Lightning News'* staff nude. This time she was depicted cavorting in some sunny resort with 4-Fs and fat industrialists. The USO shows never treated us to such refreshing nudity, and Hollywood's Hays Office (the censorship bureau) kept the starlets at least minimally sheathed. Strangely, it took Joe Goebbels to show red-blooded American boys what they really wanted to see, but then again, otherwise, we might not have read the rag at all.

The climb back up the hill was no breeze, but the latest issue of *Lightning News* and the water we had drunk from the stream made the patrol a pleasant adventure all in all.

That evening word spread like wildfire that we should pack up immediately for a move off the hill and a forty-eight-hour rest. It was raining steadily, which complicated our task of assembling our soggy equipment. When we were all set to move, we were told that the move had been postponed at least until morning. Things could not have been rougher in our part of the ETO.

The next day, 23 November, we were again told to saddle up to leave the hill for a forty-eight-hour rest. The nature of the rest was also specified—houses with showers and clean clothes. Let's see. When did we last spend a night in a *house*, with a *roof* on top? Well, the wood barracks at Camp Kilmer certainly had roofs and other conveniences of good housing. After our New York-to-Marseilles two-week sea odyssey, we slept in pup tents from 20 to 29 October, and the same during our move to the front via Valence and Dijon. Starting with our arrival at the front 31 October, it was foxholes every night with rare exceptions for twenty-four straight nights. The only exceptions for our squad were 4 November, when we captured St. Remy, and 7 November (again, St. Remy), when we were being transferred to another sector of the front. The rain continued to fall heavily as we packed, but slackened off as we began our descent from the hill.

"*Rice and Gurley, scouts out!*" Lieutenant Mueller called. We didn't mind being point men for the platoon when there was real danger out front, but it seemed a bit idiotic to use scouts when we were only marching to the rear. Still, we obeyed the command.

We went down the road with the corkscrew curves which wound its way around the far end of the hill. We slipped and sloshed through mud and rivulets down paths that offered short cuts past some of the hairpins. About halfway down, we passed a double column of clean-looking GIs going up, resplendent in green raincoats and full field packs. They made quite a contrast to our columns of bearded brethren.

"Are you from the 1st Battalion?" one guy asked respectfully.

"Yup," I said, recognizing a note of fierce pride in the monosyllable.

A brief month ago, 23 October, our dead were down at the Marseilles Staging Area, still getting back their land legs and looking forward to their first encounter with the backpedaling Germans. Now the war was over for them, a closed book. But at least their brief period of combat would be forever a part of the war's annals, of the war's official history. The 1st Battalion's performance at "Bloody Knob" (twenty-two killed, compared to thirty-five Germans), had earned it the 100th Division's first Distinguished Unit Citation, universally called a "presidential citation" by the GIs. Here is the text of "this heroic Battalion's" award,

BATTLE HONORS/CITATION OF UNIT

By direction of the President, under the provisions of Section IV, Circular Number 333, War Department, 1943, and with the approval of the Army Commander, the following named organization is cited for outstanding performance of duty in action,

THE FIRST BATTALION, 399TH INFANTRY REGIMENT is cited for outstanding performance in combat during the period 16 November 1944 to 17 November 1944, near Raon l'Etape, France. Overlooking the important Muerthe River city of Raon l'Etape, in the thickly forested foothills of the Vosges Mountains, is a hill-mass known as Tete Des Reclos. This high ground, affording perfect enemy observation, barred an assault upon the vital communications city. On the rainy morning of November 16, the First Battalion launched an attack to clear the enemy from these strongly fortified hill positions. Fighting through the dense, pine forest under intense enemy artillery, mortar, machine gun, and automatic weapons fire the First Battalion, after three hours of effort, drove across a trail circling the base of the hill mass. A withering, forty-five minute artillery preparation at this point proved ineffective against the deep, concrete, and log-covered enemy bunkers built into the side of the hills, and it soon became evident that basic infantry assault was the only feasible method for driving the enemy from their positions. In a fierce, close-in, small arms fight, which increased in fury as they climbed the precipitous slopes, the First Battalion wormed their way toward the top of Hill 462.8, key to the enemy's defenses. Battling against fanatical enemy resistance, they finally reached the crest. Bitter, hand-to-hand fighting developed as the enemy hurled repeated counterattacks against the inspired infantrymen. Once the First Battalion was driven from the hill-top, but rapidly regrouping, they regained their positions. At dark, the enemy finally withdrew, leaving the First Battalion in possession of the high ground. Throughout, supplies had to be hand carried up the steep slopes under continuous enemy fire. Only the teamwork, coordination, and determination of all elements in this heroic

Battalion, made the success of this attack possible, opening the gateway through the Vosges Mountains to the Alsatian Plain beyond.

Finally, we reached the bottom of Hill 462.8, which Captain Young and most Able Company men called "Bloody Knob" and which the map readers at battalion called *Tête des Reclos*. Our dead had preceded us down by a couple of days. For once they hadn't had to walk, but were carried down on litters like Indian Rajahs.

About the Author

Franklin L. Gurley, born November 26, 1925 in Syracuse, New York, and graduated from Newton High School, Newton, MA (1943). He entered Harvard College in the summer of 1943, but after enlisting in the U.S. Army, Frank was ordered to Ohio University to study Engineering as an A.S.T.P. student. After the program was disbanded, Frank was sent to the 100th Infantry Division at Fort Bragg, NC. From the time the Division arrived in Marseilles in October 1944 until the end of the war in May 1945, Frank served as a scout in an infantry squad.

For actions in the Maginot Line near Bitche, France, from 23–30 December 1944, Frank was awarded the Bronze Star Medal. He was also awarded the Combat Infantryman Badge, Expert Infantryman Badge, the European African Middle Eastern Campaign Medal with campaign stars for the Rhineland, Ardennes-Alsace, and Central Europe campaigns, Good Conduct Medal, World War II Victory Medal, and the Occupation Medal for his service in World War II.

During the occupation, Frank was assigned to research and write the history of the 399th Infantry Regiment, *399th in Action.* He also served as reporter, then editor-in-chief of the *Beachhead News,* the VI Corps daily newspaper. He later became chief of public relations for the American Military Government in the Stuttgart area until he was redeployed to the United States and discharged in April 1946.

After the war, he received an A.B. from Harvard College in 1949 and J.D. from Harvard Law School in 1952. He was named foreign service staff officer in Washington, Bonn, and Frankfurt (1953–55). From 1955 to 1983, he practiced law with the New York District Attorney (as assistant district attorney); the law firm of Dewey, Ballantine; IBM; and Nestle. He retired from Nestle in 1983 as Senior Vice President and General Counsel.

Frank was named Historian of the 100th Infantry Division Association in 1983. He has conducted numerous "oral histories" with Division members and has published many articles for the Association's quarterly newsletter, as well as articles and reviews for French and English language military periodicals.